Streetwise

TheStreet.co.uk Guide to Beating
the Market and Investing with Confidence

Streetwise

TheStreet.co.uk Guide to Beating
the Market and Investing with Confidence

Edited by Nils Pratley and Lorna Bourke

Hodder & Stoughton

Copyright © 2000 by TheStreet.co.uk

First published in Great Britain in 2000
by Hodder and Stoughton
a division of Hodder Headline

The right of TheStreet.co.uk to be identified as the Authors of
the Work has been asserted by them in accordance with the
Copyright, Designs and Patents Act 1988.

10 9 8 7 6 5 4 3 2 1

A CIP catalogue record for this book is available from the British Library

ISBN 0 340 79257 4

Typeset by Rowland Phototypesetting Ltd.,
Bury St Edmunds, Suffolk
Printed and bound in Great Britain by
Mackays of Chatham plc, Chatham, Kent

Hodder and Stoughton
A division of Hodder Headline
338 Euston Road
London NW1 3BH

contents

Editor Biographies

Nils Pratley – Editor

Nils started his career on *Retail Week* and then moved on to join the *Daily Telegraph* in summer 1993. In 1996 he became editor of Questor, the *Telegraph*'s investment column. He joined *Sunday Business* as City Editor at its successful relaunch in 1998.

Lorna Bourke – Senior Columnist and Personal Finance Editorial Consultant

Lorna is one of the best-known names in personal finance journalism. She has edited the personal finance pages of *The Times*, the *Independent*, and the *Telegraph* and writes a column for the *Sunday Telegraph*.

Contributor Biographies

Sam Barrett – Personal Finance Correspondent

Before joining TheStreet.co.uk, Sam Barrett was editor of *Health Insurance*, the leading monthly publication for advisers in the private healthcare sector. Prior to this, she was features editor on the monthly personal finance magazine *Planned Savings*. She has won two awards for her journalism, Ethical Investment Journalist of the Year and an award for writing on healthcare.

David Burrows – Personal Finance Correspondent

David Burrows was previously deputy editor of *Planned Savings*, the leading monthly magazine for independent financial advisers. Before joining TheStreet.co.uk he was a regular freelance contributor to the *Independent on Sunday*, *The Times* and the *Daily Express International*, covering all aspects of personal finance.

Adam Cathro – Chief Copy Editor

Adam has covered business and finance news in New York, Hong Kong and Sydney, as well as in London. Beginning his career with Australian Associated Press, he moved on to the London bureau of UPI before joining the copy desk of AFX prior to coming to TheStreet.co.uk.

Hilary Clarke – Media Editor

Before joining TheStreet.co.uk Hilary Clarke was City Editor of the *Independent on Sunday*. Before that she spent seven years in Brussels as a correspondent for Bloomberg and before that the *European*.

Jonas Crosland – Markets Reporter

Jonas Crosland worked at the *Financial Times* as foreign exchange and money markets editor for twelve years, prior to moving to FT Cityline as Managing Editor, before leaving to launch Global Newsbrokers, an on-line financial information service.

Guy Dresser – Deputy City Editor

Guy began his journalistic career as a writer for PJB Publications, before moving on to *Leisure Week* as a reporter. He also worked as a reports editor at *Business Intelligence* and as a staff writer at *Accountancy Age*, prior to his most recent post as City Editor at the *Birmingham Post*.

Jeremy Edwards – Associate Editor

Jeremy is a former editor of *Legal Business Magazine*, and Managing Editor at Globe Business Publishing. He began his career news reporting on the *Chicago Tribune* and then worked as a political correspondent in Washington DC for the *Madison Capital Times*. He is also the author of sports travel guide *Live Sport Live*. Jeremy holds a Masters Degree in Journalism from Northwestern University.

Suzanne Kapner – Deputy Business Editor

Suzanne is an award-winning US journalist who was a key player in the success of TheStreet.com in the US.

Annemarie Quill – Telecoms Correspondent

Annemarie was a senior capital markets reporter at *International Financing Review*, covering the credit markets, and high-yield private equity and credit markets. She began her career in the capital markets first in structured media and telecoms finance, and then in syndication sales.

Nigel Spall – Markets Editor

A member of the stock market reporting team at the *Financial Times* before moving to Extel Financial as stock market correspondent, Nigel joined VWD German Economic News in a similar capacity before moving to Global Newsbrokers as managing editor.

Liz Vaughan-Adams – Technology Editor

Liz started her career as a Pearson graduate trainee in journalism. Before joining TheStreet.co.uk she was an equities correspondent at AFX News covering mainly the technology sector but also electronics, food retail, support services and textiles. Liz has also written for the *FT*, *Investor's Week* and regularly appears on the Money Channel.

Oliver Wagg – Associate Editor

Prior to joining TheStreet.co.uk, Oliver was New York Bureau Chief of AFX News. He arrived in New York in 1996 as senior correspondent to cover Wall Street and the banking and brokerage sectors. From 1993 to 1996, Oliver held several posts at AFX and Extel in London, including Economics Editor and Senior Correspondent.

Introduction

'October. This is one of the particularly dangerous months to speculate in shares. The others are: July, January, September, April, November, May, March, June, December, August and February.' So said Mark Twain more than a century ago, and you could be forgiven for sharing this sinking feeling from time to time. Bad days on the stock market, when you watch your greatest investment decisions turn sour, are gut-wrenching.

This book will not guarantee that your guts are never wrenched – no investment book can do that – but it should send you into the stock market with greater confidence. Confidence to weigh up the balance between risk and reward. Confidence to know when it's time to hedge your bets. Confidence to know that you've explored the alternatives before you make your choices.

A casual reader of Mark Twain's quote might wonder why anyone in his or her right mind would want to invest in the stock market. There are lots of reasons but the biggest is that it could be worth your while. Pick any point after the end of World War II and the studies show that over any reasonably lengthy period of time – say four or five years – the returns from investing in the general UK stock market have been substantially greater than from other forms of conventional investment, such as government gilts or cash in the bank or building society.

More and more people are learning this lesson. Once upon a time – actually, it was as recently as the 1980s – individual share ownership in the UK was the domain of the wealthy and privileged few. Stockbrokers were expensive, access to information was limited and the City didn't seem to care about the little guys.

Life is not perfect now, but times have certainly changed. For a start, stockbroking has become a genuinely competitive industry. You can buy and sell shares over the Internet or over the telephone at rates of commission that are a fraction of what they once were. You can still pay your broker to give you advice, but there is a mass of other sources of information. Financial websites, such as TheStreet.co.uk, will give you up-to-date share price information and expert commentary on markets and individual shares. Even specialist television stations, dedicated to covering the markets, have arrived.

The birth of the explosion of interest in the stock market is hard to date precisely, but the wave of flotations in 1997 by ex-building societies, like the Halifax, Alliance & Leicester and Northern Rock, was certainly a major factor. Some £35 billion of shares were released into private hands and, while some sold on day one, the flotations delivered what the Thatcher privatisation programme failed to achieve – something approaching mass share ownership.

The new class of share-owners quickly had a taste of how fickle markets can be. In the autumn of 1997, stock markets around the world slumped in the face of a political crisis in Russia and a currency crisis in Asia. Most did not panic and were rewarded by a rapid bounce-back in valuations, with the best of the new ex-building societies climbing 40 per cent in the space of a few months. It was a pretty vivid demonstration of the speed at which markets can move, even in supposedly dull and boring stocks. To some, it was scary – to others it opened up a whole range of opportunities.

With the growth of the Internet and a new breed of technology companies a couple of years later, something extraordinary happened – the valuation of assets underwent a fundamental shift, and it was the smaller investor who was in the vanguard. Companies such as ARM Holdings climbed tenfold and more during 1999, and their shareholder registers were filled with the smaller investors, who debated the stocks' fortunes on Internet bulletin boards. They spotted the potential in companies such as ARM first – it was possibly the first time in the history of the London Stock Exchange that the outsiders beat the insiders at their own game.

The Internet and technology party came to a painful halt, of course, in the spring of 2000, and some investors were badly burned. But so were the big City institutions who, by that stage, were trying to catch up with the action. In both cultural and stock market terms, it was a landmark period. Share ownership, they said, was the new rock 'n' roll.

It may never quite be that, but a cultural shift has undoubtedly taken place and it is unlikely to be reversed. Few people under forty-five can confidently rely on the state to provide for them adequately in old age, and sensible stock market investment is rightly regarded as both a source of financial security and of excitement.

This book is designed to help investors at all stages of development. We will take you back to first principles and explain the rudiments of company analysis. Our writers will explain what constitutes profit, what is meant by price/earnings ratios and dividend yields and why new valuation techniques are being developed to deal with New Economy companies. We ask whether the mantra of the modern investor – 'the trend is your friend' – is soundly based, or whether investors ought to be trying to spot fundamental value.

We will teach you how to read the financial press with a sceptical eye – how to spot when the writers are offering genuine insight and when they are covering up their own ignorance.

We will also take you into the world of funds and explain the difference between investment trusts and unit trusts and where they should fit into a balanced portfolio. The funds spend small fortunes on advertising their attractions, but we will lift the lid on how they perform in practice. Do they really beat the market consistently?

Modern markets also call for modern skills, and we will give you a guide to hunting down information on the Internet and becoming as well informed as any City or Wall Street professional. We'll tell you where to find annual reports and other important company announcements and how to find out when a company's own directors are buying the shares.

For the uninitiated, we will show you how to buy and sell stocks via the Internet and describe the advantages and disadvantages. And, for those who prefer the old-fashioned approach, we will tell you how to invest via the old reliables – the Royal Mail and the telephone – and how to choose a stockbroker.

At a time when investors are fascinated by new technology, we'll take a tour of the wonderful world of telephony. Just what are WAPs and CLECs? But we haven't forgotten about the old school – the so-called 'smokestacks' – and we offer a guide to spotting value where others may not bother to look.

We will introduce you to TheStreet.co.uk's Golden Money Rules, offering indispensable investment advice for every stage of your life, and guiding you through the minefields of taxation, mortgages and pensions.

And finally we will give you an investor's primer, a glossary of all the financial terms and concepts you are likely to encounter in your investing career. Like all TheStreet.co.uk's journalism, it is designed to be free of jargon and full of common sense. We don't want to add complications to an already complicated area. There are plenty of other people doing that.

By the time you've read the book, we hope you will feel excited about investment and will want to accept the challenge of taking control of your own finances. Markets, they say, hate uncertainty, but it's not true. They need uncertainty just to survive – two views, after all, make a market. Our job is to give you the tools you need to form your own views and, on our website, to give you the facts, information and expert opinions you require on a daily basis. Above all, we want to show you how much fun it can be.

Nils Pratley
Editor
TheStreet.co.uk

Chapter One

| **The City** |

The City is a place where the value of companies and investments is debated and fought over like nowhere else. It is also the place where companies come in search of capital and where corporate reputations can be made and destroyed.

We won't linger on the long and complicated history of the City here, but we will explain some of the basic principles behind how the City thinks and works, and show how they relate to the private investor looking to buy and sell shares.

First, an introduction to some of the key members of the City's cast:

Fund Managers

Fund managers are perhaps the most powerful beasts in the jungle, simply because they are the people with the cash to invest. Most of the big funds manage the pension funds of large companies and may be responsible for tens of billions of pounds. Their aim is to ensure that the fund has sufficient resources to meet the liabilities to the pensioners, and at the same time maximise growth for the long term.

Other funds raise cash from the general public, other institutions and funds, and look to grow the capital. Traditionally, fund managers have been a cautious breed, preferring not to court publicity – but this is changing. Life has become more competitive, and if a fund manager feels that a company's management is underper-

the city

the press

webcraft

the old way

sleuthing

fund managers

short termers

crash!

new economy

telecoms

smokestacks

economics

tax

forming, he or she will sometimes say so. They are also under pressure to meet short-term and long-term performance targets, and generally measure themselves against major indices, such as the FTSE 100 index or the All-Share index (see Glossary). Their job is to pick as many winners, and as few losers, as possible within the investment rules of their particular fund.

Corporate Financiers

These are the glamour boys, the 'rainmakers', the guys who make deals happen. They work for the investment banks and act as advisers to companies on mergers and acquisitions, fund-raising and strategy. At the top of their profession, some will earn millions of pounds a year, much of it in bonuses for successful deals. Increasingly, the advisory work on big deals is becoming dominated by the big US investment houses – such as Goldman Sachs, Morgan Stanley Dean Witter and Merrill Lynch – who can afford to carry greater risk on their balance sheets than anyone else.

Analysts

Analysts spend their days, not surprisingly, analysing company profit and loss accounts, balance sheets and trading numbers. Their job is to decide whether a stock should be bought, sold or held, and to pitch their ideas to the fund managers themselves. Increasingly, the job is becoming comparable to that of a corporate financier – analysts are expected to generate ideas for possible deals. The very best analysts can sometimes move a company's share price with an aggressive 'buy' or 'sell' recommendation on a stock.

Sometimes they get it woefully wrong, but their views are worth hearing. Almost certainly they will have better access to the company's top management than any smaller investor.

Market Makers

As the name suggests, market makers are the people who actually make a market in a share, offering to buy at one price and sell at another (the difference being called 'the spread'), thereby providing liquidity. Again, they generally work for big investment banks and they make their money from the spread. You will often find them abused on Internet bulletin boards – where they are referred to as 'mm's' – on the grounds that they sometimes offer better prices to big City investors than to smaller, private ones.

Takeovers

All of these animals prowl the jungle that is the City, and all can be seen together during takeover battles, the time when the City is at its most raw and exciting. To many people, takeovers are the life-blood of the financial community, and many of the City's top corporate financiers make their reputations in this arena. In the past, takeovers have been a source of controversy – such as the Guinness scandal, which related to the company's bid for Scottish whisky firm Distillers – and the Takeover Panel is there to keep order and ensure that the rules are not broken.

Hostile bids can be enormously satisfying to watch. When two companies collide in a hostile bid, the gloves come off and the superficial politeness that characterises most City debate is forgot-

the city
the press
webcraft
the old way
sleuthing
fund managers
short termers
crash!
new economy
telecoms
smokestacks
economics
tax

the city

the press

webcraft

the old way

sleuthing

fund managers

short termers

crash!

new economy

telecoms

smokestacks

economics

tax

ten. Some of the biggest battles – such as Granada's takeover of Forte in 1995/96 and the fight for NatWest in 1999/2000 – will be remembered for many years. Smaller investors can also learn a lot during hostile bids, partly because they follow a structure and a timetable. The bidding company makes a public offer for all the shares in its prey and invites acceptances. It then lays out its arguments in an offer document, and the defending company responds in its own document.

Usually, each side will publish several documents during the course of the battle. The corporate financiers will attempt to persuade the fund managers of the virtues or flaws of the bid. The analysts will give their views and the market-makers will use their positions to get the best sense of what the general market thinks.

By day 39 – the thirty-ninth day after the initial offer document – the defending company must have published all the new information it plans to announce, such as current trading figures. Day 46 is the last day on which the bidder can raise its bid, and the result is known on day 60, the last day on which the target's shareholders can accept the bidder's terms. Anything representing acceptance of 50 per cent of the target's shares gives the predator control (under UK rules).

The arguments presented by each side give an insight into how the City thinks. Bidders will usually attack the records of the target's senior management, pointing out past investment failings or excessive head office costs. The defending company will plead for another chance to prove itself and, if the bid is in the form of shares for shares, rather than cash for shares, it will attack the value of those shares. In short, the idea is to have an open, honest, frank debate about the value of a company.

Various experts over the years have purported to show that

takeovers end up destroying more shareholder value than they create, largely because the bidding company is tempted to overpay. It is also true that hostile bids are less common than they used to be – agreed mergers are more common – but the old-fashioned hostile bid is likely to be around for a long time. As a way of determining the value of a company, an offer to buy all the shares has the advantages of being direct and easy to understand.

Profit

Profit is what everybody in the City talks about. Companies try to generate it, corporate financiers seek ways for their clients to maximise it, and analysts analyse it. And it is here that we get into the nitty-gritty of investment. It is also where life starts to get complicated. Profit may sound like a simple concept but it is anything but. For a start, do you mean operating profit, pre-tax profit, post-tax profit or retained profit? The difference could be crucial.

Pre-tax profits have traditionally been the main focus of the City's attention. It is the easiest definition to understand. It is the profit earned by a company once almost every cost – such as the cost of goods, sales and administration and the interest bill – has been deducted. The only thing that remains to be deducted is tax, and the bill for paying dividends to shareholders.

On the face of it, pre-tax profits ought to be a good measure by which to compare companies. The companies may be taxed at different rates, depending on where in the world they operate and what capital allowances they may have in a particular year, but they all have to show a pre-tax profit figure. Up to a point, it works well. But only up to a point.

the city
the press
webcraft
the old way
sleuthing
fund managers
short termers
crash!
new economy
telecoms
smokestacks
economics
tax

Take just two areas of controversy and confusion – exceptional items and depreciation. Exceptional items should be items that are one-offs, such as the profit or loss made on selling a business or the cost of implementing a major restructuring programme. Sometimes these one-off costs can be bigger than the profits generated by a company over the whole of the rest of that year. Is it really fair to include such items as part of the profit and loss account?

Most analysts think not. They – and the companies themselves – tend to strip out such items and instead talk about 'underlying' pre-tax profit or 'normalised' profits or 'headline' profits. This is generally considered fair, but problems arise when you have companies that appear to be in a perpetual state of restructuring. Is it really accurate to describe something as 'exceptional' or 'one-off' when it happens every year, such as the cost of laying off surplus staff? At the moment, companies in this position seem to have no hesitation in announcing 'exceptional' items every year. So be watchful.

Then there is depreciation and goodwill. Depreciation, often called amortisation by US investors, is the cost of writing down an asset over its natural lifetime. A company, for example, might expect the fixtures and fittings in its pubs to last for ten years. Rather than charge the whole bill for fitting out a new pub in year one, it will spread the cost over ten years.

That much is common sense. The problem arises with acquisitions. When companies buy other companies they tend to regard their new acquisition as an asset that does not need to be written down. The accountants, however, take a stricter view. They draw a distinction between 'fair value' and goodwill. The former is the price paid for the assets; goodwill is the price paid on top.

So how should goodwill be treated? In the UK in the past, it was allowed to sit on the balance sheet and was kept well away from the profit and loss account. These days, we are moving towards the US system, where a portion of the goodwill has to be charged to the profit and loss account every year. Inevitably, this creates confusion when comparing companies in similar industries that employ different accounting systems. So, again, care is needed. Playing fields that look level are sometimes not.

New Measures of Profitability and Performance

The difficulty in making fair comparisons of pre-tax profit has led to attempts to find new models of comparing company performances. This effort has been encouraged partly by the arrival of New Economy companies whose progress is difficult to measure by conventional yardsticks. A classic example is mobile phone company Orange. It did not make a penny of pre-tax profit before it was sold to German group Mannesmann for almost £20 billion in 1999.

Why would anyone pay £20 billion for a company that had never made a profit? One answer is that Orange was expanding so fast, and so successfully, that the costs of expansion were out-weighing the profits it would otherwise have been making. Think of it like this: if Orange had stopped trying to recruit new customers, and instead just concentrated on serving the old ones, it would have made substantial profits. But such a strategy would have been silly: mobile telephony in the late 1990s was clearly a growth market and Orange had to continue to invest for the future.

But how do you measure the progress of firms such as Orange if

the city
the press
webcraft
the old way
sleuthing
fund managers
short termers
crash!
new economy
telecoms
smokestacks
economics
tax

pre-tax profits cannot be relied upon? One – increasingly popular – answer is EBITDA. This ungainly collection of letters stands for Earnings Before Interest, Tax, Depreciation and Amortisation, and is sometimes thought of as a measure of cash flow. This is not quite accurate, however. It is not, for example, a simple measure of how much cash has flowed into a business and how much cash has flowed out. Rather, it represents operating profits with depreciation and amortisation added back.

When applied to high-growth companies it can work well. In the case of Orange, for example, it would provide a decent measure of profits before the big bill for new infrastructure projects. And, indeed, Orange had grown fast in terms of EBITDA before it was bought by Mannesmann, which was itself gobbled up by Vodafone the following year.

But even EBITDA has its faults. After all, when a company moves into conventional profitability it will have to pay tax and it will have to depreciate the cost of its assets. At some point, as a company matures, old-fashioned techniques of how to value it will have to apply. Let's take a look at some of those techniques.

The Price/Earnings Ratio

The price/earnings ratio, often abbreviated to the p/e ratio, remains a cornerstone of any assessment of a company as an investment. Most lists of share prices in newspapers show the figure for each share, and when you see a phrase such as 'Whitbread is trading below the average rating for the sector' the implicit reference is to the p/e ratio.

It is an easy figure to calculate. It is done by dividing the earnings per share of a company (the amount of profit divided by the number of shares) by its share price. So, if Whitbread's earnings per share are 50p and its share price is 500p, the price/earnings ratio would be 10. Often you will see the concept expressed along the lines of 'Whitbread is trading on 10 times earnings'.

The p/e ratio is most useful in measuring the relative attractions of two or more shares. If, say, one of Whitbread's competitors is trading on 12 times earnings, the competitor is being more highly valued by the market. There may be good reasons for this, and one question for the investor to ask should be: Is the market correct to value the competitor's earnings more highly than Whitbread's? If the general view is 'no', then there may be an investment opportunity.

In any comparison, of course, it is crucial to compare like with like. These days, City analysts use a variety of measures of earnings, which will clearly have an impact on the calculation of the p/e ratio. As we said, analysts will usually exclude exceptional items – such as the costs of restructuring and the profits or losses – from earnings per share. As long as the same rules are applied to each company in the comparison, there should not be a problem.

It is also important to be clear on whether you're talking about an historical p/e ratio or a future one. A company with a p/e of 40, for example, might appear outrageously expensive at first glance. But if earnings doubled, the p/e would drop to 20 and the shares might then seem cheap. Most investors are interested in forward-looking or prospective p/e ratios, but the figures used in newspapers relate to the last reported earnings.

So how useful are p/e ratios? In some cases, they are irrelevant. Property companies, for example, should be judged by the value

the city
the press
webcraft
the old way
sleuthing
fund managers
short termers
crash!
new economy
telecoms
smokestacks
economics
tax

of their assets. In some cases, comparisons are misleading: it is very hard to find two companies (except sometimes utilities) with an identical mix of operations. And in all forward-looking p/e ratios, you are making assumptions about future profitability that could turn out to be wrong.

That said, it is best to have at least an awareness of a company's p/e ratio. Judging a fair price for a company must in some way involve putting a valuation on its earnings and p/e ratios are a vague, if unsophisticated, stab in the right direction.

Dividend Yield

This is usually abbreviated to yield and, like the p/e ratio, is usually printed next to a company's share price in newspaper share price pages. It measures the income you should get from a share. So if a company pays a dividend of 50p per share and has a share price of 500p, the yield would be 10 per cent.

But there is an immediate complication. Companies pay dividends net of basic-rate tax, and dividend yields are usually (but not always) calculated on the gross amount. Assuming a basic rate of tax of 20 per cent, a 50p net dividend would be a 62.5p gross dividend, which gives a yield of 12.5 per cent. But don't forget that higher-rate taxpayers have to pay tax on dividends at the higher rate – so use dividend yield calculations carefully.

Investors looking for 'safe' investments tend to look hard at yield on the principle that, even if the share price goes down, they will still get some income in the form of dividend payments. That's true, but don't forget that even 'safe' companies can't always be relied upon. When ICI – supposedly the bluest of all blue-chip stocks at the time – cut its dividend in the late 1980s, it was regarded as a landmark event.

BTR, one of Britain's most-admired companies in the 1980s, also cut its dividend when it ran out of momentum at the end of the 1990s. There was also an effective dividend cut when Hanson broke itself up, and many of the privatised utilities, especially water companies, have had to cut their dividends to release cash to meet the investment requirements of the regulators. Even Marks & Spencer cut its dividend by 37.5 per cent in May 2000.

But dividend cuts by major companies are still rare, and an investor who is looking for income – as opposed to capital growth – should be examining yields. But be wary of yields that look too good to be true – they usually are. When you see a figure of 20 per cent when the market as a whole is yielding 3 per cent, it is almost a guarantee that a company has announced, or will announce, a dividend cut.

Yields are useful, however, for comparing similar companies, such as utilities. They are also good for identifying potential recovery stocks. If the market expectation that a cut is on the cards turns out to be false, then the share price should, in theory, bounce.

But dividend yields are clearly useless in evaluating companies that don't pay dividends. Small and medium-sized oil exploration companies, for example, have generally not paid dividends (or only small ones) on the grounds that their shareholders would rather they used all available cash to look for more oil.

Nor do many New Economy companies in the Internet and technology fields pay dividends. As with the oil explorers, it is accepted that the best use of their cash lies in investing for the future. But in case the dedicated New Economy investor dismisses

the city
the press
webcraft
the old way
sleuthing
fund managers
short termers
crash!
new economy
telecoms
smokestacks
economics
tax

the whole idea of dividend yields, remember this: investment, ultimately, is about judging the yield of an asset over the lifetime of that asset. Many Internet and technology companies are young, but at some point in their lives they must give something back to their shareholders.

Investment Strategy

There is a mountain of literature on the psychology of investment and most of it goes unread by investors themselves. Few ever stop to examine their own prejudices and preconceptions. As a result, they form bad habits and end up repeating the same mistakes over and over. Some never realise that they get the best results when they look at shares and markets from a particular direction.

Personal investment style is a matter for the individual, but a little honest self-analysis from time to time never hurt anyone. Whether they realise it or not, most people follow a strategy when they buy or sell shares. They may look for shares that have underperformed and which they think have reached their bottom. They may look for undervalued shares in new areas of industry, such as the Internet or mobile telephony. Or shares in sectors undergoing consolidation and where merger and takeover activity is expected. Studying which technique achieves the best results for you personally is part of the skill.

One important piece of self-analysis is to decide whether you're a momentum investor or a fundamentalist. Most people will not fall neatly into either camp and will instead mix and match, but everyone should have an understanding of the philosophies and principles behind the two styles.

Fundamental Investing: You Can't Beat Quality

the city
the press
webcraft
the old way
sleuthing
fund managers
short termers
crash!
new economy
telecoms
smokestacks
economics
tax

If you're a fundamentalist, you're looking for companies you consider to be undervalued. These can be in any industry – the only common thread that binds them is your conviction that you have a better appreciation of the value of each company than the rest of the market.

Put like that, this might sound like an arrogant approach, but the reality is that you *can* sometimes know better than the market. Private investors were the first to spot the potential in technology stocks partly because they could see the way the Internet was changing their own lives – they were using it every day.

Fundamental investing is a close cousin of long-term investing, the idea being that the odds always favour well-run quality companies over the long run – whatever the current investment fashion and gyrations of the market. Two of the most famous investments by Warren Buffett – the sage of Omaha and one of the most successful postwar investors – were effectively simple decisions to buy quality brands run by quality managers. Coca-Cola and Gillette were the companies and Buffett held them for years.

Fundamental investing has also been the guiding tradition of professional fund management in the UK. That's hardly surprising. Fund managers would effectively be talking themselves out of a job if they didn't think that they could beat the market by picking the right stocks.

To critics of professional fund managers – and there are lots of them – the numbers do not support fund managers' confidence in their own abilities. Several comprehensive surveys in recent years have shown that most fund managers actually fail to beat major

benchmark indices, such as the FTSE 100. As a result, one of the fast-growing areas of fund management has been index-tracking funds. These are simply funds that aim to replicate the performance of an index by buying all the stocks that make up the index.

Momentum Investing: The Trend Is Your Friend

The investment idea that 'the trend is your friend' has gained huge popularity in recent years, particularly among private investors. It might sound a simplistic idea but it can work well, and there are periods when the best investment returns are achieved by those who merely follow momentum. Like a surfer, the momentum investor looks to pick the biggest wave and ride it to its conclusion.

At its most simple, momentum investors look to buy shares that have gone up and sell shares that have gone down. To many people, this sounds counter-intuitive. A natural response when a share price has gone from, say, 500p to 600p in a short space of time is to think 'I wish I'd bought it at 500p; I'm too late now'. The momentum investor, however, thinks: 'If it can go from 500p to 600p so quickly, perhaps it will go to 700p.'

Neither point of view will ever be right all of the time. There will always be some shares that stop at 600p and then retreat back to 500p and maybe go even lower. In those cases, the momentum investor will have bought at the top, which is a move that everybody aims to avoid.

But there will be cases where a share price doesn't stop at 600p, but goes though 700p, then 800p, and keeps on climbing. Among investors the 'ten-bagger' – a share that rises tenfold – has gained legendary status, and momentum investors would reckon to have a better chance of identifying these than investors using fundamental analysis. They would also argue that a few ten-baggers make up for an awful lot of losers. After all, the maximum amount that a share price can fall is 100 per cent, whereas the most it can rise is theoretically infinite.

The purest momentum investors will not bother to look at a company's accounts, its price/earnings ratio, its yield or any other yardstick. They may not even know what the company does. All they care about is the share price chart and identifying trends.

What counts as a trend is the big debate among chartists, or technical analysts as they prefer to be known. This is a whole debating area in its own right, but the most common measures usually involve assessing performances against the market, such as three-month and twelve-month relative highs and lows. Their rule of thumb is that unless there is clear evidence that a trend has been broken, assume it is intact.

the city
the press
webcraft
the old way
sleuthing
fund managers
short termers
crash!
new economy
telecoms
smokestacks
economics
tax

Stop Losses

Read interviews with the world's top traders and almost all will say there is a golden rule that must always be obeyed – 'Don't chase your losses'. It could also be worded as 'Don't throw good money after bad'. It means that when you have a poorly performing share, there is usually little point in doubling up investment in the hope that it will all come good in the end.

It is easy to see how investors can fall into the trap. Take Marks & Spencer, a share that used to be a core holding in thousands of small investors' portfolios for obvious reasons – it is a world-famous company and it had a reputation for excellent management. In

October 1997, the share price hit 667p and all seemed to be well at M&S.

From that point, however, life became tricky for M&S for various reasons, mainly related to fundamental changes in shopping habits in the UK that only became obvious in retrospect. By August 1998, the share price had hit 500p, and anybody who bought at over 600p could have been tempted into thinking that the shares were now a bargain. After all, hadn't people been willing to pay 667p for the shares less than a year ago?

Unfortunately, the situation at M&S became considerably worse, and the problems in the industry deepened. By early 2000, the share price had hit 230p. At that point, those who had bought at 500p on the principle that 'M&S must now be a bargain' were kicking themselves. The share price had more than halved even from the point where it had looked too cheap to resist.

Anybody using a stop-loss rule would have avoided the error. The rule dictates that when you make an investment, set a price at which you tell yourself you will cut your losses – and stick to it. Playing catch-up is probably the most common way in which new investors are wiped out.

Sometimes, of course, poorly performing shares do come good. Unfortunately, you can never know for certain at the time. But what you can know if you use a proper system of stop losses is that you will at least live to fight another day.

Spread Betting

Playing the market through spread betting has seen explosive growth in the last few years. Originally it was a preserve of City traders, but it is now attracting large sums of money from retail investors. It is a complex world, but the underlying principle of all spread bets, whether on sports events or financial markets and shares, remains the same – the more right you are, the more you win; the less right you are, the more you lose.

It works like this. If you think Vodafone's shares are set to rise in the short term you might take out a 'buy' bet at £10 a penny movement. For every penny the share price rises, you would win £10, so a 100p climb in Vodafone's share price would be worth £1,000. Alternatively, if the shares fall 100p below your 'buy' point, you would lose £1,000.

With almost all spread betting firms you will not pay dealing costs, but you should be aware of the spread. If Vodafone's shares in the market stand at 300p, the spread might be set at 310–314, meaning that 'buy' bets are calculated from 314p and 'sell' bets are calculated from 310p.

The finishing points for the bets mirror those in the futures markets and are predetermined dates in March, June, September and December. If you want to take profits or losses before then, it is usually possible to close the bet by making an equivalent bet in the opposite direction to your original bet.

The majority of spread betting firms offer a stop-loss facility (at least on FTSE 100 shares), but you will effectively pay for it because the spread will be wider. Most firms offer spreads in individual FTSE 100 and FTSE 250 shares, major indices such as the Dow Jones and Nasdaq, and major currencies.

A couple of advantages of spread betting are that all profits are free of capital gains tax (under UK tax laws at the time of writing), and that investors can go short of a share if they wish – in other words effectively 'selling' a share they do not own. Short selling, however, carries risks – if the share rises, your losses can quickly get out of control.

Some people use spread betting as an insurance policy. If, for example, you have a portfolio of large company shares that you want to hold for the long term but are worried about a short-term fall in the market, one option is to take out a 'sell' position on the FTSE 100. If the market doesn't in fact fall, then you lose on the bet but your shares should rise in value.

Of course, the risk/reward ratio in spread betting is magnified. If you take out a 'buy' bet on Vodafone, rather than buying the shares themselves, all you are effectively doing is adding gearing, or leverage. And leverage works in both directions – when you lose, you can lose heavily.

Spreading Risk – or the Difference between Investment and Speculation – and Other Trading Tips

It ought to be common sense, but it probably needs to be spelled out: putting all your eggs in one basket is asking for trouble. Over-exposure to a single sector of the stock market – including Internet and technology companies – can seriously damage your wealth. No share price – even of some of the world's most successful companies, such as Microsoft – has ever gone up in a straight line. There is no such thing as a one-way bet.

That said, it is true that there are periods in which individuals have become very rich by concentrating on one sector. The boom in technology stocks in the final quarter of 1999 and the beginning of 2000 was one of them, and many people piled in without a second thought. For a while, they were lucky – the boom continued longer than most people thought possible. But it could not last for ever, and inevitably some people were badly burned when the sector turned south in mid-March 2000.

The most badly burned were those who were overexposed to technology and Internet stocks – and there were lots of them. They paid the price for ignoring the most basic rules of investment – spread your risks. Arguably, they were not investing at all, but were actually speculators. There is nothing inherently wrong with speculation (even if the word has got a dirty reputation) but it carries risks of which speculators should be aware.

An investor – as opposed to a speculator – will try to spread risk. A rule used by many of the world's top traders is never to put more than 5 per cent of one's capital into any single investment. It might sound boring, but it does at least ensure that you stay in the game.

Other widely adhered-to golden rules of trading are:

☐ **Be disciplined.** If you are operating a system of investing in stocks, do not undermine the system by ignoring your own rules. Thus, if you have set a stop loss at 10 per cent below your entry point, do not panic if the stock drops 5 per cent immediately.
☐ **Be patient.** Just because a share doesn't start to climb soon after you've bought it doesn't mean that it was a bad trade. It can take weeks or months before results come through.
☐ **Let your winners run.** This one is more debatable. There is often virtue in taking profits from time to time, but it is also true

the city
the press
webcraft
the old way
sleuthing
fund managers
short termers
crash!
new economy
telecoms
smokestacks
economics
tax

that some of the great traders, including Jesse Livermore, the famous US trader from the 1920s, believed in letting winning trades run. A better rule might be: if you wouldn't buy the share at the current price, ask yourself why you are still holding it.

☐ **Play for singles.** There is no point in trying to smash the ball out of the ground every time; you'll never keep it up. Build up slowly, like an accomplished batsman.

☐ **Take a few days off after a losing streak.** A very popular piece of advice. If you find everything you touch turns out badly, why trade? It's not compulsory.

Nils Pratley

Chapter Two

How to Read the
Financial Press

the city

the press

webcraft

the old way

sleuthing

fund managers

short termers

crash!

new economy

telecoms

smokestacks

economics

tax

Information is power, or so they say, and for us investors at least, power is money. You may have the cleverest trading strategies and a determination to profit from trading in the stock market, but it matters little if you know nothing of the companies and markets in which you are investing.

And while information is often abundant, you will need to read between the lines, to sift through the news, the gossip and the tips – and make your own decisions on what to believe and what to disregard.

For most of us, the financial press, in all its various guises, will be the primary source of financial information. But when you read the financial press, be aware of what the publication is, or who the journalist is writing for.

Traditional financial news heavyweights, such as the *Financial Times* and the national dailies, try to be all things to all people, and are aimed both at financial professionals and private investors like you. But because the editors and journalists are, in part, trying to please the professionals, they often use complicated financial terms and language which might seem foreign to the rest of us.

Of course, professionals like to use jargon because they often like to feel there is a mystery and a level of complexity to the financial world in which they move – a complexity which only the most sophisticated professional can understand. This is complete rubbish as, by and large, the City and its rival financial centres across the globe work on a set of fairly basic principles. However,

the city
the press
webcraft
the old way
sleuthing
fund managers
short termers
crash!
new economy
telecoms
smokestacks
economics
tax

professionals tend to prefer those journalists who use their own language, and flatter their egos – so sometimes it's hard for journalists to resist using terms like 'CLEC' (Competitive Local Exchange Carrier) when writing about telecom companies, or 'premium put convertibles' when talking about options.

Using the language of the profession can seem even more intimidating and impenetrable when combined with journalistic jargon. Such jargon can take the form of words which either disguise the fact that a journalist doesn't know what he or she is talking about (describing a stock price as 'fairly valued', when a journalist has no idea at all if a price is too high or too low), or disguise the journalist's real opinions (describing a financier as 'controversial', when he or she really means 'criminal').

Now, of course, the world of the financial press is changing with the advent of the Internet and ever more sophisticated technology. These days, speed is everything – not least in the financial media.

The multimedia revolution can seem frightening to many individual investors because of the ever-accelerating speed at which information is delivered. The global communication era, which has both led and followed the development of the worldwide marketplace, is upon us and the financial press is now a twenty-four-hour-a-day phenomenon.

The speed of the information flow has not just changed the way financial information is delivered, but also the financial media themselves. Understanding how speed has forced changes throughout the financial press is essential if you are going to use the flood of fast and cheap information as the key tool in your investing strategy.

Speed has introduced new forms and forums for financial news and views, such as the Internet and around-the-clock cable television. Stories on twenty-four-hour cable television stations and Internet websites are rolling, not fixed. The advantage of speed enables players in these new media to pull off the Houdini act of never seeming to be wrong. What one organisation said a few minutes ago may not have been completely accurate, but because the story has moved on and the organisation is now reporting on the next chapter, few ever register that the original report was incorrect. The print media have no such luxury. Print stories are fixed in black and white and, if they are wrong, everyone knows it and it will take twenty-four hours to correct the error. The traditional media, such as newspapers and magazines, have had to adapt to the new world order in order to compete. They are being forced to change their focus.

Until a few years ago, the *Economist* devoted pages and pages to domestic stock market reports and share prices. Today, the former emperor of the financial press hardly includes any such coverage, and is instead dominated by lengthy features on international business and economics.

Why? Because the speed with which the Internet, television and their ilk can report basic news and statistics means that share prices in print are, literally, history. Those at the helm of the *Economist* know that the future of print magazines lies in deep detailed analysis, and thoughtful and thought-provoking features. They know they can't compete for news, and have instead decided to concentrate on views.

While daily and monthly magazines have by and large already accepted that their role has changed, the daily newspaper barons are still struggling to accept these new realities. The mixed strategy

the city

the press

webcraft

the old way

sleuthing

fund managers

short termers

crash!

new economy

telecoms

smokestacks

economics

tax

Pearson has adopted for its flagship financial paper, the *Financial Times*, and its new Internet sister publication, FT.com, is a perfect vignette of the issues facing the newspaper industry.

The *Financial Times* remains the City of London's bible, and Europe's leading financial news source. It still breaks more business stories than any other UK business publication, and it remains the undisputed market leader. But it continues to devote several full-length pages to tombstone-style lists of stock market prices. These prices, last night's closing figures, have already changed significantly by the time most of the newspaper's morning readership has had a chance to look at them, and so are practically useless. Furthermore, up-to-the-second prices can be found for free on any number of Internet websites, including FT.com itself. And therein lies the problem. FT.com competes with the *Financial Times* and has many advantages as a delivery platform. The Pearson brains realise that the Internet and television will dominate the future delivery of pure breaking news and share prices. And yet some editors might be tempted to hold back stories for the morning newspaper rather than break them on the website. They are aware that commiting themselves fully to the Internet medium may mean damaging their long-time market-leading newspaper product. This dilemma opens up a gap in the market for numerous new financial news providers in the market, both Internet- and television-based, to beat the *FT* to the news.

The situation is mirrored in New York, where the *Wall Street Journal* and its website Wall Street Journal Interactive share a similar relationship and face a similar problem. Several news players have tried to make the most of this opportunity. Indeed, it is in the United States that most of the models for these new kids on the

Internet block have been developed. Organisations such as our sister website TheStreet.com have pushed back the boundaries and revolutionised old notions of the financial press.

The advent of these new media means you must now learn where to look for different types of information, as well as how to interpret what this information actually means.

Reading between the Lines

Reading between the lines is not simple for the investor. It takes experience. It has traditionally been an exercise involving knowledge both of the media organisation and the journalist. Investors must build up a picture over time before acting, rather than just acting on the back of one story in a seldom-read paper.

Given that it is a relationship-driven skill, albeit a one-way relationship with the reader doing all the work, it is hard to give tips which will lead to immediate rewards. However, in general we would recommend caution. It is a cliché, but don't believe everything you read in the papers. Or, for that matter, don't believe everything you hear on the radio or television, or see on the Internet.

☐ Be wary, because both media organisations and journalists often have their own hidden agenda. Media barons are businessmen who must often be tempted to use their papers to further their own ends and fight their own battles – Rupert Murdoch is constantly accused of using *The Times*, the *Sun* and BSkyB in this way.

☐ Be wary of world exclusives more than widely reported news

stories. Many investors think that once they get a sniff of an exclusive they should act upon it. But, so often, under huge competitive pressure, and despite strict libel laws, the media publish exclusive stories which are not always accurate.

☐ Be wary of opinions more than news. News is usually based on 'investable fact'. Opinion, on the other hand, can be wise and forward thinking, but it can also be bullshit.

Many of the new Internet-based financial news organisations, like TheStreet.co.uk, have tried to change the way people read the business media by focusing exclusively on investors like you rather than on the professional. They have tried to decode all the professional mumbo-jumbo, to provide individuals with the kind of news, information and tools that professionals in the City have had at their exclusive disposal for years. Not only do they take advantage of the speed of the Internet to break news stories, but they also provide detailed analysis, expert opinion, and access to live or slightly delayed price information, charts and other tools, as well as quick links to on-line traders. Reading these new financial sites is a very different proposition from reading their printed forebears.

Many Internet sites have taken it upon themselves to try to address the individual investor by jettisoning the financial jargon, and employing simple, plain language to explain simple, plain events and theories. However, while these new media outlets claim to tell it how it is, many have, unfortunately, developed a new jargon all of their own – the jargon of the Internet. This is a language that is just as impenetrable as that used by the financial professional. So the individual now has to learn new financial slang such as B2B and B2C (business-to-business, and business-to-consumer), as well as Internet abbreviations which litter websites and bulletin boards, such as DYOR (Do Your Own Research), NM (No Message), IMHO (In My Humble Opinion) and NAI (No Advice Intended). For more on bulletin boards, see Chapter Three.

Also, it is worth bearing in mind that many of the new financial publications on the Internet are prepared to be more opinionated than their predecessors, and adopt a more direct editorial approach to that which dominated more traditional financial news. This means a clear division is developing between old and new media publications. But be aware that while many members of the new media claim not to pull any punches, they, like their more established counterparts, also have vested interests and their own agendas. They tend to be more positive about new technology companies, and more critical of traditional industries – the so-called smokestacks. They too depend on alliances with other companies and have their own relationships to promote. In the new media, as well as the old, politics can play a role in the business of financial news.

What to Find Where

One important thing to bear in mind when sifting through the financial press, especially the print press, is 'What day of the week is it?'

This may sound silly, but it will help you work out how important a story is. It is just a rule of thumb, but financial journalists all recognise that Tuesday through to Friday are the peak days for reading the financial press. Saturday papers are now full of analysis and features, and are edging towards placing the emphasis – once

the city
the press
webcraft
the old way
sleuthing
fund managers
short termers
crash!
new economy
telecoms
smokestacks
economics
tax

reserved for the Sunday papers – on personal finance and share tipping. Monday stories are usually written on Sundays, a day when almost nothing happens in the financial world.

For more than a century now the obvious starting point for an overview of the financial media in the UK has been the *Financial Times*. Since it was launched in 1888, and marketed as the 'friend of the honest financier and respectable broker', it has been the key financial news source in the country. Its famous pink pages, introduced back in 1893, carried the first share index 'the 30-share', in 1920, and first sported the Lex column (which even today remains the most closely read finance column in the UK) in 1945. The paper, which was bought by media conglomerate Pearson in 1957, is now a global product and is printed round the world. Its website, FT.com, was launched in 1995 and relaunched in 1999, and was followed by a separate German sister paper, *FT-Deutschland*.

While the paper has extended its global outlook and its international coverage of the world's major markets, it still focuses on the UK market. On weekdays it is divided into two sections; the first contains domestic and international economic, political and business news, while the second contains more specialised coverage of companies and markets. In 1997 Pearson launched a revised Saturday edition of the paper which has a strong features and personal finance-based editorial approach.

Unlike its national daily newspaper rivals, and despite its in-depth reporting, its record for breaking news and its much-admired analysis and feature articles, neither the weekday nor weekend edition makes outright share recommendations or tips.

For those who do not have the time or the inclination to wade their way through the depths of the *Financial Times*, or for those who are actually looking for blatant share tips, all the daily national newspapers boast financial news coverage of varying depth. The so-called quality press – *The Times*, the *Daily Telegraph*, the *Guardian* and the *Independent* – all attempt to compete with the *FT* for major stories and scoops. They claim to offer a simpler, more digestible alternative to the specialist heavyweight *FT*. Many argue that there is not that much to choose between them. It is true that they all cover the same general areas – results, prices, news stories, editorial comment and the odd feature. While Tempus (*The Times*), Questor (the *Daily Telegraph*) and the less pretentiously titled Investment Column (the *Independent*) all offer direct share advice, only the *Guardian* seems to shy away from simple tips. Today, most of the rest of the national press, from the *Express* and *Mail* through to the *Sun* and *Mirror*, offer share tips.

Individuals all have their personal favourites, and you will probably develop, or have developed, your own preferred financial coverage in the nationals. Having said that, the *Telegraph* consistently tops popularity polls both inside and outside the financial world for its coverage. Along with the *Guardian*, it has also made a good fist of covering the new, much hyped technology stocks, and, at the time of writing, these two papers lead their rivals in their reporting of the so-called New Economy. The *Mail* remains a great favourite for its market reports and tips, while *The Times* and *Independent* continue to offer solid all-round coverage.

The financial pages of London's *Evening Standard*, which unashamedly ape the pink pages of the *FT*, are probably most vulnerable to the new media outlets on the Internet. The *Standard* was traditionally the first paper out in the City reporting on results, mergers and change of personnel stories within the financial com-

the city
the press
webcraft
the old way
sleuthing
fund managers
short termers
crash!
new economy
telecoms
smokestacks
economics
tax

munity. However, the advantage of speed means that Internet rivals consistently beat the *Standard* to breaking stories throughout the day as the London daily is constrained by the burdens of production and distribution.

Outside London, major regional titles such as the *Birmingham Post*, the *Yorkshire Post* and the *Scotsman* often compete with the nationals and the TV news for breaking business stories within their own areas. Frequently, journalists at these papers have closer working relationships with many of the companies and professional advisers within their locality than do their national counterparts. Using these contacts, regional newspapers often break relevant financial stories before the nationals. We would add that sometimes regional papers have been known to slant stories in favour of the local companies rather than acquisitive predators or financiers from outside the region. However, we would emphasise that the vast majority of major FTSE corporate headquarters remain in London, and this puts the financial arm of the regional press at a serious disadvantage on many occasions.

Over in the magazine world, quality mainstream UK financial publications are thin on the ground. This is, in part, due to the number of national newspapers and their extensive coverage of financial news. The pack is still led, as we mentioned earlier, by the *Economist*, which is now a global business and economics analytical publication, rather than a source of stories or data. The other major player remains the *Investors Chronicle*, which is also owned by the Financial Times Group.

Today's *Chronicle*, which covers both domestic and overseas markets, company details and personal finance, is actually a result of several other magazines merging together. Its earliest guise was the *Money Market Review* (launched in 1860), followed by the *Investors Chronicle* itself in 1890, which in turn formed an alliance and eventually a merger with the *Stock Exchange Gazette* in 1967. The Financial Times Group took control of the publication in the late 1970s, and it is now part of the Financial Times Business Ltd's magazine stable. Today its circulation hovers around the 60,000-a-week mark. Despite the scope of its coverage, the magazine remains best known for its widely quoted share tips, which certainly move stocks – although by the time you get around to reading the magazine most of the money may already have been made.

These two publications aside, most other magazines in the UK are highly specialised. They range from those dedicated to pooled investment coverage, such as *Moneywise* and *Inside Money*, through to personal finance-based magazines, such as *Money Management*, *Planned Savings* and *Personal Finance Magazine*, and product-specific publications such as *What Mortgage?* and *What Investment?*, as well as trade magazines like *Euromoney* and the *Banker*.

The other print source of financial information – on the fringes of the financial media – are the numerous tipsheets which float around the City claiming to be able to make you a millionaire several times over. These vary enormously in quality – some have solid reputations and good records; others are nothing short of scandalous rip-offs. We warn you against relying on such pamphlets unless you have carefully tracked their advice over a long period of time and the quality of their results matches the quality of their ludicrous get-rich-quick claims.

Over the past few years, a plethora of new TV stations – Bloomberg, the Money Channel and CNBC to name just a few –

have appeared. They are different beasts from both print and Internet publishers. Speed of delivery is everything for television. Television reacts to news rather than chews it over. Most of the news is related to the viewer as it happens, and there is no time for analysis and opinion. Television tends to leave that to other media. By the time other forms of financial news organisations are working on analysis, television is on to the next story. Most TV organisations try to spice up pure news with market and professional views. But, largely because they are all reporting events live, there is very little opinion and/or analysis. Most of the information can be taken at face value – the skill in reading between the lines of financial television is trying to pick your way through the corporate rather than the media spin.

New Kids on the Net

Financial information, like many things on the Internet, is like the Wild West. It's a new medium with wide open spaces and few rules, where you can find everything from well-researched, reliable and timely news and analysis, to dodgy back-street sites where the sole purpose is to ramp up the stock price of shares owned by the author, so that he can sell them fast and make a quick buck before they fall back to a sensible level.

Of course, the medium itself has many advantages over traditional financial outlets. At a basic level the Internet is fast, immediate, not restricted by space, and it has a free distribution network (albeit one which in Europe is currently limited by telephone company pricing). But in addition to that, it offers other advantages: it is interactive, it can combine still text with moving images, it can aggregate news, it can link to other relevant information sources, and it can offer those interested in the markets all sorts of bells and whistles from live prices, to portfolio trackers, to up-to-date broker reports and directors' share dealings.

There are more than fifty financial information websites based in the UK alone. The quality, breadth and depth vary enormously, from the serious players, ranging from the on-line arms of established media heavyweights such as FT.com and the bbc.co.uk, to major web-driven newcomers, which in addition to TheStreet. co.uk, include iii.co.uk (Interactive Investor International) and Moneyworld.co.uk, to simple on-line tip sheets like Citywhispers.com.

There are far too many sites to cover them all in detail here, but there will be more to come in the next chapter.

Warning Tip

One final point about reading the financial press – be healthily sceptical of the journalists themselves. Most editors and journalists are honest professionals, but some are not always what they seem. Most have an agenda of some type or other. That agenda can range from the need to fill space and impress editors and readers to more selfish motives, such as journalists seeking to ramp shares they themselves own.

As the advent of new financial media outlets brings competition in the sector to boiling point, everywhere you look publications are trying to capture the attention of the country's rapidly growing army of investors by introducing share tipping. In general, following share tips in newspapers is an investment strategy that should be

the city
the press
webcraft
the old way
sleuthing
fund managers
short termers
crash!
new economy
telecoms
smokestacks
economics
tax

pursued with a certain degree of caution. You may come across some gems, but you may also find that by the time you get round to buying some shares in a widely tipped company you will have missed the initial boost from the tip itself. In exceptional cases, you may even end up being duped by some paper or journalist needlessly ramping a particular stock.

Fifty years ago editors and journalists would tip shares they owned and the public would be none the wiser, but those were the days when only a handful of people in the City loop owned shares anyway. Today, as the number of shareholders rockets, and access to rapidly available information is widely seen as the key to successful trading, a new culture is developing where tips become self-fulfilling in the short term and some of those behind the tips make a quick profit. Remember that shares which rise on hype will fall when the hype dissipates.

And this trend is not just confined to the newspapers. As you will see in the next chapter, ramping – talking up shares to make a personal profit – has become commonplace on bulletin boards across the Internet.

So, read as much as you can, but don't believe everything you read and hear. Remember, a better long-term bet is to invest on fact, not rumour.

Jeremy Edwards

Chapter Three

Webcraft – Trading The Modern Way

the city
the press
webcraft
the old way
sleuthing
fund managers
short termers
crash!
new economy
telecoms
smokestacks
economics
tax

Dial up, download, click and trade – this is the modern way. Cheap, fast and painless – or at least that's the theory.

The amazing expansion of the Internet has revolutionised almost every aspect of private investment. On-line execution has forced dealing costs down and the array of financial tools and information available has levelled the playing field between the professional trader and you. More and more people are trading the modern way. As recently as January 1998 you couldn't find an on-line broker in the UK for love or money. Now you can't move for them.

On-line Broking

In the modern world the simplest, easiest and often cheapest method of trading is also the newest – the Internet. The first step towards modern trading is to find an on-line broker. Today, all broker buying and selling transactions are computerised from their desks directly to the stock exchange computer networks. You will need to adopt similar technology if you are to maximise profits.

Registering with an on-line brokerage is fairly straightforward. Indeed, some on-line firms have even axed the formalities of paper application forms and allow potential clients to open accounts on-line. When choosing an on-line broker and opening an account there are several key issues to consider: What role do you want your broker to play? What type of account do you want to set up? How fast do you want your trades to be executed? What type of

the city

the press

webcraft

the old way

sleuthing

fund managers

short termers

crash!

new economy

telecoms

smokestacks

economics

tax

charging system suits you and your trading habits? While these issues can initially sound complicated, they are, in fact, quite straightforward.

In the early days of on-line broking, e-mail simply replaced the telephone as a means of contact between client and broker. But this basic approach is rapidly disappearing. Today, on-line trading means clients effectively execute their own shares on-line through the Internet by sending the trade to their broker's computer, which then checks its authenticity, verifies the trade and forwards it to the stock exchange's computers.

Not surprisingly, now that there are several on-line brokers in the UK market the competition is becoming increasingly intense. It is now matching the cut-throat levels that have existed in the US in recent years. This competition means that the costs of trading in the UK are tumbling to new lows – albeit not as low as the costs on the other side of Atlantic.

These costs vary quite considerably from broker to broker, and from service to service. Some brokers offer variable commissions and others fixed. Some will charge nothing more than a dealing commission while others will add on additional charges. It can cost as little as £5 per trade plus 1 per cent commission to £25 per trade and 1.5 per cent commission (remember there is also stamp duty levied on stock trading in the UK, unlike in the US). Be aware that – at the time of writing – many brokers offer a commission-free introductory period. The modern trader shops around.

There are so many on-line dealers joining the market that it can be hard to decide which one to use. Our advice is to click around and find the service easiest to use at a competitive price. But there is little to choose between the leading players.

More and more people are opting for the execution-only on-line broker option. Investors are taking total control of their own destiny. They know exactly which stocks they want to trade and at what price they want to trade them. An execution-only broker will do nothing more than receive your instructions and execute the transactions you request. This is not only the simplest form of client-broker relationship, but also the cheapest.

Another new benefit of on-line brokers is that when you're on the Net you tend to have easier access to Initial Public Offerings, or flotations. Getting customers in on the ground floor with a company has traditionally been the province of financial professionals, but now on-line brokers and investment outfits such as Durlacher are beginning to make IPOs available to their on-line account-holders. New specialist IPO websites are also appearing on the Web.

It may be one of the cheapest and fastest ways to interact with your broker, but you will need to invest in the following equipment if you plan to use an Internet broker. You'll need a PC (almost any PC will do), a modem (preferably 58.8k or faster) and a reasonably modern web browser (ideally either Internet Explorer 4 or later, or Navigator/Communicator 4.5 or later, as these browsers will offer you the maximum Web security).

In the US, day trading centres have taken the revolution a step further and allow private investors to cut out the middleman: to eliminate the broker, and trade their own shares. This trend is only just beginning to spread to the UK; at present day trading centres in the UK only allow investors to trade US shares.

the city
the press
webcraft
the old way
sleuthing
fund managers
short termers
crash!
new economy
telecoms
smokestacks
economics
tax

the city
the press
webcraft
the old way
sleuthing
fund managers
short termers
crash!
new economy
telecoms
smokestacks
economics
tax

On-line Tools

Tackling the markets on-line means you'll need as much techno-logical help as you can get. Arming yourself with the right infor-mation is the key to on-line investing. The endless range of financial websites means the private investor can now construct a portfolio on-line, receive share price alerts, obtain real-time price quotes, use bulletin boards to initiate or contribute to discussion on the market, and monitor company news.

Even the more specialised components of this information, such as the real-time price quotes, are free if you know where to look. The sheer volume of these services, however, means that sifting through the numerous sites to obtain the best information and tools has become a major challenge in itself.

Most sites offering the portfolio service offer links to a range of on-line brokers as well as other financial product providers, where the investor can purchase products such as Isas, pensions, unit trusts, investment trusts, insurance and mortgages on-line. A common feature of many sites is the fantasy or virtual portfolio, through which aspiring investors can dabble in the share market without committing money.

Price or stock quote information is generally offered with a fifteen-minute delay. Some sites charge a minimal monthly fee for accessing real-time information, but not all of them do – soon, live quotes will be available free almost everywhere.

The new tools and direct access to prices have done a great deal to boost the confidence of the individual investor.

Net News

On-line investors also benefit from the plethora of new Internet financial news services. Financial news and information, like everything else on the Internet, is generally of variable quality. As with most new platforms, the Internet is a medium with wide-open spaces and a lack of regulations and rules. At first glance it can be hard for the uninitiated to distinguish between well-researched and reliable news, and unreliable ramping tipsheets.

Net news is cheap, because the basic distribution network is by and large free. It can offer other advantages too: interactivity, video and sound, scrolling as well as static text, and links to other relevant information and investing tools.

In 1996 there were only one or two UK-based net financial news sites, but by the turn of the century there were more than fifty. Of course, the reliability and readability of these varies greatly. To get the most out of the sites available, you need to surf about and build up a relationship with the services you like best. Only when a level of trust has been developed can the on-line trader use such sites as an essential tool in their investing strategy.

Bulletin Boards

Most on-line traders, in addition to using web-based news sites and Internet tools, also search for information on message boards. Bulletin boards (or BBs as they are universally referred to on the Net) are forums where on-line traders share information, and disinformation, with each other. In the financial world every rumour, every piece of gossip, every announcement, every news

the city
the press
webcraft
the old way
sleuthing
fund managers
short termers
crash!
new economy
telecoms
smokestacks
economics
tax

story and every opinion is writ large across the bulletin boards.

The bulletin board is the tool which binds individuals on the Net together into a social environment. Not an environment filled with computer geeks, but one in which everyone speaks a language that everyone can understand – a talking shop, a forum in which to swap tips, strategy, gossip, news and advice, and a means of sharing experiences. In the financial world bulletin boards provide the flavour, the atmosphere and the human element of the dealing-room culture.

Financial bulletin boards were originally designed as places for thought-provoking discussions on investing, fuelled by the latest news and commentary. And to a certain extent this is still their primary function. Such discussions range from detailed postings on particular companies to serious suggestions regarding investment strategy. You can spend a great deal of time surfing the Net hunting for stock tips and market clues.

The very best discussions on bulletin boards are very serious. There are even those who argue that in some sectors of the market the most reliable analysts are found on the message boards. Some maintain, for instance, that it was the individual on-line traders who were responsible for much of the healthy rise in technology stocks in 1999 and for the decline of those stocks in 2000, and that these individuals are the real authorities in that market sector, and the only place to find out what these experts really think is to participate in their bulletin board chats.

Others criticise the power of the boards. They argue that the current volatility in the markets owes much to individual investors acting on the basis of a host of disinformation and rumour on the Internet.

Whichever camp you are in, one thing is certain – bulletin boards move stock prices.

But to get the best use out of bulletin boards you need to understand the culture. It takes experience to work out which posts (and, just as importantly, which posters) are reliable. You will need to build up an impression of a particular board and those who post on it over time, and you must get to know who is reliable and who is not. Only then should you consider acting on the back of information you read on a message board. Similarly, if you want anyone to pay attention to your own messages, you will need to build up your own relationship over time through reliable and intelligent posting.

Using message boards successfully is a skill that involves both knowledge of the individual writing the message and the subject of the message. It is a relationship-driven exercise. The good message board reader is cautious. Be wary, because those posting on the boards often have their own hidden agenda.

The sheer number of message boards means that sifting through the numerous sites to obtain the best information is something of a challenge in itself. Ramping, talking up shares in order to make a personal profit, is rife on bulletin boards across the Internet. In the UK the FSA (Financial Services Authority) is seriously concerned about it, and in the US the SEC (Securities & Exchange Commission) has similar worries. Remember, it is a criminal offence in the UK to attempt to move financial markets with false, misleading comments, or to profit from leaking confidential information on a bulletin board or in an on-line chat room, but as yet no one has been brought to court on such charges, nor has anyone been fined by UK regulators.

the city
the press
webcraft
the old way
sleuthing
fund managers
short termers
crash!
new economy
telecoms
smokestacks
economics
tax

The Day Trading Phenomenon

Perhaps because of the negative but high profile given to day trading by the press, some people associate on-line traders with day traders. This could not be more misleading. Day trading is a phenomenon that was once exclusively the province of professional floor traders. But the availability of cheap yet powerful computers, combined with the tumbling commission costs associated with on-line trading, has enabled individuals to employ day trading tactics.

Day trading is basically a strategy revolving around significant intra-day swings in stock prices. The trader identifies these swings and buys stock, holds on to it for a very short period of time, and sells it the same day before the swing is reversed. A day trader, by definition, trades strictly within the time frame of a single day; buying and selling shares but always closing out all trades by the end of the day regardless of whether money has been made or lost.

Now that it has become widespread, many in the profession try to give it a bad name. The truth is that there are many different types of day trading, some good, some bad. There are a great many myths about it: that some methods are always successful, while others are inevitably doomed to failure; that successful day traders are a different breed from position traders; that day trading cannot be learned. What is undeniably true is that day trading can be very dangerous for the uninitiated. There are tales of day traders incurring huge losses, committing suicide and even going out on killing sprees. But who knows the underlying reasons behind such actions? And remember, there are just as many, if not more, stories about day traders who made millions in a single day.

Day trading does clearly lead to some distortion in the markets. But there is only one certainty: no trading method of any kind is without risk.

On-line Problems

It is important to be aware that on-line investing is not the panacea that many would have you believe. Obviously there are no more guarantees of riches for on-line traders than there are for those who trade the traditional way. But, having said that, when you're on-line, with all the information, tools and execution equipment at your fingertips, you have a better chance than ever.

There are, of course, occasional glitches. Clients often complain that they find it hard to access their on-line brokers. The usual culprits are overloaded servers. During the April 2000 tech sector drop, levels of Internet traffic were such that enormous pressure was put on stockbrokers' websites. Many individual on-line traders complained that they were unable to get through to their brokers to sell off the technology and Internet shares they thought would plummet. Charles Schwab, the UK's largest on-line broker, admitted that a technical glitch delayed the processing of orders. The bulletin boards were flooded with complaints. Some argued that the delays caused by overloaded networks led directly to larger losses than would otherwise have been the case.

Nevertheless, net brokers have formed a united front and declined point blank to offer any form of compensation to investors who claim to have lost out through being unable to sell shares.

So while it is true that trading on the Web is easy, quick and practical, we would advise that whatever your primary means of

accessing your broker you have a back-up communication system – usually the telephone – just in case technical problems cause you to suffer unnecessary losses.

Jeremy Edwards

Chapter Four

Doing It the Old-Fashioned Way

the city
the press
webcraft
the old way
sleuthing
fund managers
short termers
crash!
new economy
telecoms
smokestacks
economics
tax

There is more than one way to skin a rabbit. When several major execution-only stockbrokers' systems crashed in early 2000 as a result of the massive surge in tech stock business, full-service private client stockbrokers throughout the City reported a sudden revival of old accounts. Frustrated investors re-established contacts and relationships with brokers they hadn't spoken to for years, in a desperate attempt to get their share deals executed. There is a lot to be said for talking to a real live person rather than communicating by e-mail.

And if you are a techno-Luddite, don't know your Word from your Works, and prefer doing things the old-fashioned way, there are still plenty of brokers who are keen to have your business. It isn't a question of broking on the Internet or nothing.

Stockbrokers realise that financial services are the ideal products to sell on-line because they are just pieces of paper. Many already offer Internet dealing facilities – as well as the personal service of having a real live broker to talk to when you want to buy or sell. In a few years' time, virtually all brokers will offer Internet dealing as part of their overall service along with postal and telephone communications.

But like everything else in life, you get what you pay for. If you want to be able to talk to your broker, discuss share sales and purchases, ask his advice, get him to send you research material, provide you with monthly, quarterly, half-yearly or annual port-folio valuations, manage your Peps and Isas, and keep tabs on the

running Capital Gains Tax situation, you will have to pay for it. The truth of the matter is that it is much cheaper to deliver large amounts of research information via the Internet than it is to have Harry chatting to you on the phone.

As the last chapter has shown, the big cost saving of the Internet is that the client does all the inputting, and accesses the research material without intervention by another, expensively employed, individual. If you punch in your buy and sell orders, that means one less employee at the broker's office, not to mention a big reduction in other overheads like office rental costs and all the ancillary expenses of running a big organisation with hundreds of employees.

But don't feel embarrassed at wanting to have a proper relationship with your broker. Only someone in daily touch with the market will know what is really happening. When share prices go mad it is just as likely to be as a result of thin trading because everyone's at Ascot or Henley as it is to be through a reassessment of fundamentals. There are plenty of investors who are perfectly competent at electronic communications but still prefer to talk to a real person. Quite apart from anything else, in many instances it is quicker. The Internet is still notoriously unreliable if you are accessing it from an ordinary telephone line at home.

Ask any stockbroker and he will sigh with despair at the fact that there are still so many clients who insist on having proper share certificates rather than a simple electronically generated statement of transactions. There is still a strong demand for a totally personalised service – the technophobe is a very common breed. Indeed, private client stockbroker Killik & Co. built a whole new business in the 1980s based on this concept of personal service, at a time when the rest of the market was saying that private client business was dead. So what do you look for in a stockbroker, and how do you find one who suits your needs?

The obvious thing to do is go to a firm that has an on-line dealing service as well as offering the old-fashioned personal touch. You may prefer now to deal on the telephone, or by writing your instructions to your broker, but you could eventually change your mind. The truth is that it is only a matter of time before all stockbrokers offer on-line share dealing as simply another facility.

If you don't have a stockbroker, your first port of call ought to be the Association of Private Client Investment Managers and Stockbrokers (APCIMS – Tel: 020 7247 7080 – *www.apcims.co.uk*) which represents 90 per cent of all private client stockbroking firms.

APCIMS publishes a list of its member firms and the entry for each indicates all the services offered – discretionary, advisory or execution-only services, on-line dealing, whether they welcome smaller investors with only £20,000 or so in their portfolio, whether they offer Pep and Isa management services, and whether they can buy and sell AIM or foreign stocks for you.

What to Look For in a Stockbroker

Choosing a stockbroker is a very personal thing and your eventual decision will depend on what you want from him or her. If you are going to make your own investment decisions, speed of execution and general service is important. Investors who want advice, and those who prefer to leave the management of their money to the discretion of the broker, will want to know whether the firm is any good at picking shares.

the city
the press
webcraft
the old way
sleuthing
fund managers
short termers
crash!
new economy
telecoms
smokestacks
economics
tax

This can be more difficult than it sounds. Although almost all stockbrokers offer discretionary portfolio management services, they do not publish details of performance. They claim this is because every client's needs are different and there is no such thing as an average portfolio. There is an element of truth in this. But since they all have an in-house investment strategy, and block-deal for their discretionary clients, parcelling out the individual shares after purchase, there is clearly a lot that their clients have in common. The obvious area where clients may differ is in their requirement for income, or capital growth, or a bit of both.

With elderly investors, too, the broker has to be very aware of Capital Gains Tax liabilities. If you have a wealthy client in their eighties, you do not want to deal actively, incur CGT and then have the person die within weeks – leaving the beneficiaries with an Inheritance Tax liability on top of the CGT bill.

One indicator of a firm's performance used to be the unit trusts run by some private client stockbrokers. Unfortunately, however, few stockbroking firms run unit trusts themselves any longer.

Moreover, be aware that if you are an advisory client, whereby the broker consults you before buying or selling, individual brokers will differ in their 'sales' ability – some will be able to make a more convincing case to buy or sell than others in the same firm. Whether they are advising the right decision or not, only time will tell. But remember, stockbrokers earn commission. If you do not deal they make no money.

Discretionary, Advisory or Execution-Only?

The first problem you will encounter is that if you want a discretionary service — whereby the broker makes the decisions to buy and sell shares along agreed investment lines and agreed risk levels — many brokers insist that you must have at least £100,000 to invest before they will buy a portfolio of shares. Below this figure, you will probably be offered a selection of unit trusts.

Discretionary fund managers argue that, because of dealing costs, it is uneconomic to deal in share bargains of less than £5,000. To get a reasonable spread of investments you ought to have around twenty stocks, so this necessarily means a portfolio of £100,000 plus. If you want to hold shares directly but have less than £100,000 you may well be forced to have an execution-only account, and to make your own decisions about what to buy and sell.

The same sort of limit often applies to advisory client status, where the broker contacts you before buying or selling a share on your behalf. Few brokers encourage new advisory clients unless you are a really wealthy individual with a portfolio of £1 million plus who will be an active trader. The cost of giving personalised advice is high. Unless they can see substantial commission income, they really don't want you chatting on the telephone for half an hour, only to decide that you don't want to buy after all. Indeed, some brokers charge an 'inactivity' fee if you do not deal at all during the course of a year.

The reality is that you will have to take an interest in your own investments and do your homework. Even if you are wealthy and have a portfolio of £100,000 plus, all too often private clients get a poor deal. It was common practice in the past to use private clients'

discretionary portfolios as 'dustbin' funds. Shares were bought in a block. If they went up, they were parcelled out to a few favoured clients who were active traders. If they went down, they were dumped in the discretionary clients' portfolios in the hope that the clients would not notice, and that in time they would come good. With the implementation of the 1986 Financial Services Act in 1988, tighter regulation, and the requirement to book out block deals to specific clients immediately, this is less prevalent – but it still happens.

Charges

One of the big benefits of the Internet is that it enables individuals to compare prices very easily, and the effect is to drive down dealing charges. In this respect, if you want the old-fashioned personal service of a broker discussing purchases and sales with you, you will pay heavily for the privilege.

Discount brokers offering on-line execution-only services will transact bargains for as little as a flat fee of under £10. A typical London firm may charge £9.95 per on-line transaction, plus a quarterly service charge of £12.50 plus VAT. Full-service private client brokers, on the other hand, frequently have a minimum bargain fee of £40, plus quarterly service fees, and charges for valuations, CGT computations, dividend collection, etc. A typical middle-of-the-road mainline broker charges commission of 1 per cent on the first £4,000 with a minimum of £15 per bargain and 0.1 per cent thereafter. This means that a £5,000 bargain will cost £16.

You don't have to be a genius to work out that you're paying around 3.5 per cent, plus stamp duty of 0.5 per cent on purchases, so in terms of costs you are paying pretty well as much as you would to buy unit trusts. Moreover, as an individual investor you don't get the benefit of being able to negotiate keener prices that the professional fund managers have. Unit trusts have a bid–offer spread between the buying and selling price of around 5 per cent. But there is no stamp duty on purchases, and if you buy through a discount broker you can frequently get the front-end charge reduced to 2 per cent or less.

At the top end of the scale, if you want full personal service a broker may charge you a £200 a year plus VAT service charge – with a concession for small portfolios of £40,000 or less of 0.5 per cent of the value of the portfolio, with a minimum of £50 a year. Dealing with advice, where the broker rings you to discuss all sales and purchases, is expensive at a minimum of £40 per bargain. For deals up to £15,000 you pay standard commission of 1.65 per cent of the deal – the old Stock Exchange recommended rate. This means that if you are dealing in bargains of £5,000 a time, you will be paying 1.65 per cent commission plus 0.5 per cent stamp duty – a total of 2.15 per cent. Clearly at these prices you are paying heavily for the personal service and advice. It could still be cheaper to buy a unit trust from a discount broker.

Crest Nominees or Certificates?

With the introduction of Crest, the electronic settlement system, in 1996, you are now encouraged to settle bargains electronically. You receive a statement much like a bank statement showing what you have bought or sold. You can still have the share certificates

the city
the press
webcraft
the old way
sleuthing
fund managers
short termers
crash!
new economy
telecoms
smokestacks
economics
tax

the city
the press
webcraft
the old way
sleuthing
fund managers
short termers
crash!
new economy
telecoms
smokestacks
economics
tax

sent to you, but this is slow, cumbersome and, if you lose the certificates, it can be a real problem obtaining copies.

If you have to sell in a hurry, paperless transactions are far quicker, and you need have no worries about using the stockbroker's nominee facility. You will receive a statement of what you have bought and sold, but the shares are held in the name of the stockbroker nominee company, which facilitates fast buying and selling. You remain the beneficial owner of the shares even though your name does not appear on the share certificate. If you are concerned by whether your money is safe in a nominee company where you cannot identify your particular shares, remember that the regulators are pretty hot on checking that all is running as it should at nominee companies. In the highly unlikely event that the company gets into difficulties, you are protected under the Financial Services Act Compensation Scheme for up to £48,000 of your first £50,000 of investments. More importantly, most stockbrokers have additional top-up professional indemnity insurance, which can cover you for up to £5 million a trade. Before you sign up with a broker, ask for a written statement of their compensation cover.

Peps and Isas

If you are investing in shares – whether as a short-term punt or as a long-term hold – it makes sense to put the first £7,000 in an Isa (2000/01 – thereafter £5,000 a year up to an overall maximum investment of £50,000). This ensures that any profits are shielded from Capital Gains Tax. Anyone with a portfolio of existing shares should transfer their core holdings into Isas (or earlier Peps) so that over a period of time the maximum amount is tax-sheltered. Had you put the maximum allowed into Peps every year since they were first offered in 1987, you would have shielded nearly £100,000 from CGT, which today would possibly be worth around £200,000 or more. You cannot afford to ignore this big tax break.

With this in mind, it makes sense if your stockbroker runs an in-house self-select Isa into which you can put the investments of your choice. This can be any quoted share, as well as unit trusts and bonds. It makes no sense at all to buy Isas direct from a fund manager, where your choice will be restricted to the funds offered by that particular manager. If you want to hold individual shares, you will need a self-select Isa anyway. For holders of Peps, it could make sense to consolidate them into one self-select Pep operated by your stockbroker. You then have all your investments in one place, which makes them easier to manage, and your stockbroker will also understand your overall CGT position. Some private client stockbrokers offer advice on Peps and Isas but do not offer them in-house. This is not ideal, since you will end up with a string of Isas from different fund managers which will be a bore to administer.

Investment Strategy

Given the high costs of dealing with advice, you will have to work out an investment strategy. – we touched on this in Chapter One – and make sure you are as well informed as possible. For the real technophobe who will only deal on the telephone or by post, it will pay to choose a stockbroker who puts out regular news bulletins in magazine, newspaper or leaflet format. Most private client stock-brokers communicate regularly with clients, with buy and sell recommendations.

the city
the press
webcraft
the old way
sleuthing
fund managers
short termers
crash!
new economy
telecoms
smokestacks
economics
tax

the city
the press
webcraft
the old way
sleuthing
fund managers
short termers
crash!
new economy
telecoms
smokestacks
economics
tax

If you are a novice investor it pays to read up on your areas of interest before making any decisions. The first golden rule of investment is never play with money you cannot afford to lose. That said, you will only learn by experience, and you must develop a grown-up approach to investment. Shares are more risky than collective investments such as unit trusts and investment trusts, and you must expect to make mistakes. The most important lesson to learn is when to cut your losses. Many brokers (but not all) will accept 'stop loss' instructions. For example, you might be well aware that a punt in a volatile techstock could double your money in a few weeks. But it could also halve your investment in even less time. So you buy, at say 100p a share, hoping the stock will rise, but you put a 'stop loss' sell order on the holding at, say, 80p a share, so that you limit your potential losses. If the shares start to fall, your broker sells out at 80p.

The second point to keep in mind is that potential gains are in direct proportion to the risk involved and potential losses. There are occasionally situations where a company has become unfashionable and even has net property assets in excess of its market capitalisation. Indeed, one successful fund manager has built an entire investment philosophy on this approach. But you may have to wait a long time for the assets to be realised – either through the break-up of the company or through a rerating of the share. Generally speaking, the upside potential of a share is in direct proportion to the downside risk.

If you want to play safe with your money, you would be best advised to choose one or more unit or investment trusts for the bulk of your money – say around 70 per cent – and play with the other 30 per cent in individual shares. All stockbrokers will be prepared to recommend a selection of unit or investment trusts that meet your requirements and risk profile, and the prices of these funds are widely published in daily newspapers like the *Financial Times*, the *Daily Telegraph*, *The Times*, the *Independent* and many others. If you finally succumb and decide that electronic trading has something to recommend it, you will be able to access massive amounts of performance data on all unit trusts, investment trusts, individual shares, AIM stocks, new issues, gilts, bonds and much more. Hardly a day goes by without a new financial site appearing on the Web.

You also have to decide whether you are a short-term speculator (see Chapter Seven) or a long-term investor who prefers to take a view on a share and wait for it to come good. For example, the banking sector and financials generally will see considerable consolidation over the coming years. There are some obvious takeover targets, such as the former building society Alliance & Leicester, or NatWest's rejected partner Legal & General, known to be looking for a suitor. These companies are clearly not going to go bust – the regulatory authorities would not let them. But you may have to wait a few years before a takeover or merger happens.

If you are a gambler and speculator by nature you will want to take a close interest in the share price of your chosen stocks. Clearly it is a much slower process to wait until the morning papers arrive, with yesterday's closing prices, compared with looking at live prices on-line on the Internet. If you insist on using old-fashioned information delivery systems, like newspapers, magazines and the like, then as a short-term speculator you will find yourself at a big disadvantage. By the time you have sent off your 'buy' order in the post, the share prices could have moved against you by 10 per cent or more.

A middle road is to invest on your own hunches but back them up with research. Read the City pages of the serious newspapers, become a subscriber to the weekly *Investors Chronicle*, keep up to date with your broker's recommendations and monitor how well they do. Some firms keep a running table in their monthly newsletter which shows exactly how their recommendations have performed, but few brokers are brave enough to do this.

Stockbroker Hargreaves Lansdown understands the psychology of many new investors who are inclined to buy a share because they use the product or retail shop. The firm produces a *Guide to the High Street*, which analyses popular shares like Marks & Spencer, Sainsbury's, Tesco, the utilities, brewers, hotels and holiday operators, and anyone who produces something sold to the general public.

Finally, to do well at investment you have to take a real interest in what is going on – and be lucky. Even the professionals have difficulty calling the top or bottom of a market.

Lorna Bourke

Chapter Five

Sleuthing – Or How to Hunt Down Information

the city
the press
webcraft
the old way
sleuthing
fund managers
short termers
crash!
new economy
telecoms
smokestacks
economics
tax

Imagine this scenario . . .

As I sat at my desk one bleak March afternoon, the phone rang and the words that every private-eye hungers for poured through the receiver into my ear: 'Have I got a story for you,' said a long-time source of mine.

'Shoot,' I replied. I'm American. We're allowed to say things like that.

Shares in a medical supplies company, Stitches–Are–Us, were soaring on news that the sales of their latest product, an amazing medical gizmo, were growing exponentially. This source contended, however, that Stitches' story was coming apart at the seams. He said sales were nowhere near as robust as the company claimed. Moreover, one of their shareholders had a history of stock manipulation. Then there was the chief executive, who had previously been involved with a company that was sued for fraud.

All of this got my attention rather quickly. Yet, with a reporter's studied scepticism, I said: 'Where can I check this stuff out?'

Like a detective, when it comes to buying and selling shares you should take care to check out the information you're fed from brokers and analysts to see if it actually matches up with reality. Both reporters and individual investors can be easily manipulated by the powers that be. These are everyone from analysts to brokers who are both long (a bet the shares will rise) and short (just the opposite) the stock. My particular source was short the stock, so it

was in his interest to tell me a negative story about the company. As a reporter, I don't like being used, and so I take great pains to verify that all the information coming my way is accurate.

This kind of manipulation happens with the little investor all the time, and it can be even more galling when you have paid for the advice you are given. For example, an analyst, whose firm has just secured a big investment banking deal for Company X, publishes a positive report to appease his boss. After all, bonus time is around the corner and everyone benefits when the investment banking till is full. A broker picks up that piece of glowing rubbish, and begins cold-calling down a list of names until you unwittingly pick up the phone. He's got charm and is a smooth salesman and before long you're telling him to load your account with shares of Company X.

Three weeks later, Company X comes out with a profit warning and its shares plummet. The analyst, who's supposed to warn clients of such imminent disaster, issues a report *after the fact* that it's time to sell. Even if he had done the necessary research, he wouldn't be sharing his findings with you. He may phone a few of his large institutional clients and whisper that now is a good time to scale back their positions. That type of service will score points with his bank's big clients and win him a high rating in analyst polls. But there's no money in helping out the little guy. In fact, if the analyst had widely distributed a negative report, his firm's investment banking relationship with Company X might have suffered.

Luckily, today you have tools at your disposal to help level the playing field. Before I left the US to set up shop in Britain, I could easily access piles of information that were previously only available to professionals and are now accessible to everyone. These include quarterly financial results, merger details and other material announcements which are available in the Edgar databases, part of the Securities and Exchange Commission – a watchdog created to protect investors. There are sites that list director dealings, and others that let you search the background of company executives to determine whether they've left a trail of lawsuits or bankruptcies in their wake. Still others let you check whether a company's product is patented, especially useful for so-called one-product companies that derive all their sales and earnings from a single item.

The proliferation of such resources is less developed in Europe, mainly because reporting rules are less stringent than they are in the US. When companies are only required to report earnings twice a year, sites that allow you to access a company's financial statements in the way Edgar does are far less useful. By the time half-year results are published they are already out of date. There are, however, a few sites that offer the UK investor some useful insight on director dealings, company announcements and share ownership. A list of both US and UK sites can be found at the end of this chapter.

To be sure, this so-called democratisation of information isn't flawless. Some information is still only accessible through hard-to-obtain or costly services. Other details are simply not found in the paper trail and require hours of field research – discussions with suppliers and former employees – to uncover. Other problems persist. Databases are relatively new, so obtaining historical information can still be difficult. The SEC's Edgar database, for instance, only goes back to 1994.

TheStreet.co.uk was founded on these level-the-playing-field principles. And reporters have used them to help make their readers

the city
the press
webcraft
the old way
sleuthing
fund managers
short termers
crash!
new economy
telecoms
smokestacks
economics
tax

money. This type of investigative work can seem overwhelming to the uninitiated. But it quickly becomes routine once you learn some tricks of the trade. Depending on what you're looking for, different documents and their respective sections are more relevant than others. Wading through these documents can be time-consuming and dull, so it helps to know what you're looking for.

For instance, if you're following a merger, you want to look at the merger agreement, the merger proxy and the tender-offer documents. These documents will fill you in on the details of financing arrangements, conditions to closing, walk-away rights, collar mechanisms, pricing periods and the background of negotiations. When it came to Stitches–Are–Us, what I was looking for was a picture of how the company's orders for new products and sales progressed from one quarter to the next. This information is typically found in quarterly filings (10-Q) or annual reports (10-K) in the section entitled 'Management's Discussion and Analysis of Financial Condition and Results of Operations'. Other areas to check for differences in tone or wording are 'Legal Proceedings' and 'Risk Factors'.

To take an example, Bebe, a fashionable US speciality store retailer, had added a note of caution to its 10-Q filing. The stock had been surging, thanks to double-digit year-over-year sales growth. Now the company was subtly warning investors sharp enough to read its filings that the growth might not be sustainable. Subsequently, Bebe's year-over-year sales growth began slipping and so did its stock price.

Another area you'd want to focus on is changes in a company's balance sheet. For instance, if inventory is rising faster than sales, this often signals that a company will be stuck with excess merchandise that it will have to dump on the market. Another red flag is when a company's cash flow is negative, but its net income is positive. Negative cash flow and positive net income can arise as the result of various accounting shenanigans. One such trick is when a company lumps regular operating expenses into merger-related charges and writes them off as a one-time occurrence, rather than accounting for them as a continuous cost of doing business. This would have the effect of artificially boosting net income. The problem is that without access to a company's books it's often impossible to know for sure how the firm is recording these expenses. What is certain is that when cash flow and net income start to polarise, professionals will begin to question the quality of a company's earnings. And that scepticism can depress the stock price.

Wireless technology giant Lucent, for instance, used several perfectly legitimate, but aggressive accounting techniques to keep earnings in positive territory even as cash flow turned sharply negative. Among them was a four-year-old reserve fund, which the company used to help pay its bills. It also reconfigured the way it calculated the cost of its pension fund to cut reported expenses. Meanwhile, the negative cash flow was the result of soaring receivables and inventory – a sign the company had overestimated demand. These issues raised questions about the quality of Lucent's earnings – a black cloud that depressed the company's valuation for a time.

Crunching the numbers on Stitches–Are–Us was a bit more difficult, but not impossible for those unafraid of nitty-gritty bean-counting. The company's publicised return rate of its product failed to match up with independent calculations by several money

the city

the press

webcraft

the old way

sleuthing

fund managers

short termers

crash!

new economy

telecoms

smokestacks

economics

tax

managers, who were short the stock. They concluded that Stitches was 'stuffing the channel' – that is, shipping more product to distributors than they could sell. The company denied these allegations, but a month later they were facing a sales shortfall when one of their distributors said it would order from Stitches only as it shipped products to dentists, rather than storing up stock as it had previously done.

There were other signs: one of the shareholders had previously been accused of helping to manipulate the price of shares in a major US company in the early Seventies. The shareholder had pleaded no contest, and had served probation. Then, several years later, he had been a defendant in an SEC civil case charging him with selling unregistered securities to the public. When this shareholder, who had received Stitches shares in a private placement, registered to sell stock, a Form 144 filing popped up in the SEC database and I was able to find it. (A Form 144 is a form that must be filed when someone wants to sell restricted securities, that is, typically, securities received in a private placement.)

Other details were less available to the general public, but such information is likely to become more accessible in the future. For example, Stitches' chief executive had previously been involved with a company that had tried to defraud the US government. And while involvement with a company that is found guilty of fraudulent activity is no indication that an individual is guilty of fraud, this is the kind of information that an alert investor should be aware of if they are to have a comprehensive investment strategy.

You should obviously be aware that just because someone with a chequered past bought shares in a private placement, doesn't mean they were manipulating the stock. And, as I said, the Chief

Executive could've been blind to the goings-on in his previous company. All that this could indicate is they were bad managers, not crooks. Taken separately, none of these issues signify much, but taken together, along with the suspicions the short sellers had about Stitches' sales figures, the red flags began to add up to one giant warning sign.

This information I rooted out would've been difficult for the average investor to obtain, since SEC documents require the professional biographies of company executives to date back only five years, but it wouldn't have been impossible. The chief executive's history was only patchily described in the company's prospectus, but a search on Lexis-Nexis (a massive database useful for researching companies and those who run them) would've turned up the connection.

Ultimately, the short sellers were proven right. Stitches' gizmo never took off in the way management said it would. That year the company recorded a net loss of millions of dollars, on sales that decreased by 68 per cent. Shares that once changed hands at around $30 today trade at around $1.

Stitches–Are–Us is obviously not a real company – although it bears more than a passing resemblance to one – but it does teach a valuable lesson: when issues regarding a company's sales figures, management or major investors don't add up, there's probably a better place to invest your money. And with today's Internet sleuthing tools at the average person's fingertips, there's more opportunity than ever before to make smart investment decisions. Sure, not all the pieces of the Stitches puzzle would've been evident using the Internet alone. But enough questions would've been raised to prevent you from buying into the share.

the city
the press
webcraft
the old way
sleuthing
fund managers
short termers
crash!
new economy
telecoms
smokestacks
economics
tax

Here's a quick due diligence checklist.

1. Identify the Principals
   Find companies with which the principals are involved
2. Who are the Sponsors?
      Review underwriters
      Check for venture capital financing/leveraged buyouts (when a company borrows a large amount of money to buy another company, sometimes a much larger one)
3. History of the Company
      Read news stories related to the company
      Obtain analysis of director buys/sells
4. Review Financials
      Read the latest 10-K and 10-Q
      Analyse EBITDA (see Chapter One) and cash flow
      Review the liquidity section
      Be aware of days inventories and receivables
      Summarise debt obligations
5. Analyse Comparable Companies
      Access relative p/e (See Chapter One)
      Study multiple to EBITDA (similar to a p/e ratio, but comparing a share price to the company's operational earnings, rather than its headline profits)
6. Review Trading Pattern/Charts
7. Compare and Contrast Analyst Research

Where to search

Citywire.co.uk
Offers news on director dealings for UK companies

Sharepages.com
Lists all material announcements for companies trading on the London Stock Exchange

Hemscott.co.uk
Basic information on publicly traded companies in the UK, including historical financial results and analyst research

Google.com
Great search engine to help you find other sites not listed here

Suzanne Kapner

the city
the press
webcraft
the old way
sleuthing
fund managers
short termers
crash!
new economy
telecoms
smokestacks
economics
tax

Chapter Six

What Value a Fund Manager?

the city
the press
webcraft
the old way
sleuthing
fund managers
short termers
crash!
new economy
telecoms
smokestacks
economics
tax

Ever felt that you have been promised the world but you've ended up with something closer to Basingstoke?

In terms of promises on performance, fund providers are legendary for their marketing and advertising. If you were to believe it all, every fund manager in history would have offered the best performing fund at one time or other. It is easy to be persuaded by blanket advertising which tells you that a fund has won the best fund performance award for that year. It's all pictures of rosettes and champagne corks popping as the fund providers pat themselves heartily on the back. And at the bottom of the advertisement there is reference to the fact that the company is regulated by the Personal Investment Authority and IMRO (Investment Managers Regulatory Organisation), so you are reassured that their boastful claims must at least have some credibility.

The problem is that after reading the Sunday financial pages you have already come across at least another dozen fund providers claiming that they are offering the best-performing fund. What starts out as a simple choice soon becomes a real headache.

How can there be so many fund award winners? In an industry that loves self-congratulation more than most, there are a multitude of awards from monthly magazines such as *Money Management*, *Planned Savings*, and the weeklies, such as *Investment Week*, *Money Marketing* and *Financial Adviser*. There are also awards from the major fund statistic providers, such as Standards & Poors Micropal.

the city
the press
webcraft
the old way
sleuthing
fund managers
short termers
crash!
new economy
telecoms
smokestacks
economics
tax

Some of these awards are based purely on performance statistics and others are voted for by independent financial advisers, and take into account service as well as performance.

These awards should be taken into consideration when you are thinking about where to place your investment but they should *never* be the sole reason for any decision. One of the dangers of awards and good performance statistics is that they can be easily manipulated to fit the story the fund provider tells. It is not that you are being told a pack of lies – more that the company in question is being, shall we say, economical with the truth.

For example, even though for over three years from June 1996 to June 1999 a fund may have been the best performer in its sector by a large margin, this in no way takes into account that over the following eight months its performance was appalling. This is not to say past performance is irrelevant – it is a guide of sorts – but, as the cliché goes, it is no guarantee of future performance.

What you must do is look at the most recent statistics then look at past performance – then you will have a more balanced picture.

Avoid the Worry – Go for a Tracker Fund

Index trackers – which, as the name suggests, simply track indices like, say, the FTSE 100 – are seen as an easier low-risk option compared to actively managed funds. They also offer lower charges since the fund is only tracking whatever index it has been linked to. Over the years there have been many grandiose claims from tracker funds to the effect that they will beat the vast majority of actively managed funds, and charge less for doing so. And it is true that in many cases trackers have outperformed managed funds, although there is no guarantee that this will continue to be the case.

Most tracker funds are available in ISA form (see Chapters Four and Thirteen) and there are distinct advantages in the tracking ISA compared to its tracking Pep predecessor. Most notably, ISAs can freely invest worldwide, whereas Peps had to invest primarily in UK stocks. In simple terms, investments within a tracker fund are in companies that make up the index they follow. This could be the FTSE 100, the FTSE All Share index or, more recently, technology index trackers (Investec Guinness Flight's Wired Index fund and the Close Brothers FTSE TechMARK being the first in this new breed).

Traditionally, FTSE 100 tracker funds were seen as low risk with a neat spread across most business sectors. In recent years, the spread among the top twenty companies within the index has become very narrow, with technology, new media and communication companies taking a dominant position. So the danger for FTSE 100 trackers is obvious – if there is a crash in the dominant sector within the index, there is little protection for the investor. The collapse in high-tech stocks seen in the spring of 2000 is a great example of how the FTSE 100 can be left vulnerable if it is too heavily weighted towards New Economy companies. For those looking to spread their risk further but keen to persevere with trackers, the clear solution is to invest in an All Share FTSE tracker, since the fund is free to invest in the 800 or so companies listed.

There are also other variations on this theme if you decide to invest outside the 100 top UK companies. There are funds that invest solely in the 250 companies just failing to get into the FTSE 100 fund. They are seen as a halfway house between the FTSE 100 trackers and those following the All Share index. The argument for

the city

the press

webcraft

the old way

sleuthing

fund managers

short termers

crash!

new economy

telecoms

smokestacks

economics

tax

the city

the press

webcraft

the old way

sleuthing

fund managers

short termers

crash!

new economy

telecoms

smokestacks

economics

tax

going into the Mid 250 tracker funds is not very powerful, however. You are not investing in the best companies, nor do you have the maximum diversification you would enjoy in an All Share fund.

In recent years, we have seen the rise of the 'robomanager'. Also known by its official title of quantitative fund management, thus is a purely mathematical approach to stock selection from the All Share index. Every fund management group will have their own particular formula which will determine whether an investment is made in a company. This could be based on price/earnings ratio, the size of the company, or the sector and analysts' reports. The criteria for selection will be laid down in stone, based on the fact that the mathematical formula will, according to probability, provide above-average returns. In effect the quantitative fund is a tracker that is tweaked to be weighted more heavily in the stocks within the chosen index that its formula has picked out. Robomanaged funds have their detractors, not least because as an investment approach it is seen as excessively rigid.

There are various other tracker hybrids designed to appeal to all tastes. Legal & General has an ethical tracker fund which is based upon the FTSE 350 index but excludes investment in companies that do not meet particular ethical and environmental guidelines. In theory such funds should appeal to those who want the security of investment in leading companies combined with the knowledge that they are not investing in anything disreputable. But interpretations differ as to what is ethical or disreputable. For some investors, a fund that agrees not to invest in arms manufacturers or in companies that have a poor record of polluting the environment is suitable for investment. For others, the criteria may be far stricter, relating to any company with a link, no matter how tenuous, to, say, meat manufacturing or animal testing. For those who are concerned about where their money is invested, there are far more fund options in the actively managed fund sector than among trackers.

With all these conflicting messages, how do you know whether to go for a managed fund or a tracker? There is no obvious answer because there are so many other factors to take into consideration, such as the money at your disposal and your attitude to risk. Last year managed funds fared well. If you look at UK equity ISAs, for instance, there wasn't one tracker fund in the top fifty. As an argument for managed funds, therefore, the year 1999/2000 was good. The main reason for such solid performances was the huge returns seen in the technology sector, and the resurgence of some of the South-East Asian and Japanese funds, which had previously taken a pounding.

But in the early part of 2000 we saw technology stocks take a real hammering, and there are obvious concerns that some actively managed funds may seriously underperform this year. This is nothing new – if you look at past performance statistics over five or ten years you will always see years when performance has either levelled off or shot right down. What you need to know is how this fund has performed compared to the others in its sector over the years. If the whole sector has taken a clobbering but you see that even during good years your fund was still underperforming, you have probably picked a dog.

One popular misconception about tracker funds is that they are a safe investment. Not true. They are probably going to offer a greater degree of security than managed global specialist or emerging market funds – with a larger percentage of holdings in blue

the city
the press
webcraft
the old way
sleuthing
fund managers
short termers
crash!
new economy
telecoms
smokestacks
economics
tax

chip companies, a tracker does provide certain reassurances for the nervous investor. But when you see that FTSE 100 stalwarts such as Marks & Spencer and British Airways have had their share price halved in twelve months, it becomes increasingly evident that there is no safe place to hide in equities. Yes, you can reduce your exposure to volatility, but there will always be a degree of risk.

Low Charges Are Not Everything

No one likes exorbitant annual management charges or the hefty initial charges some funds impose when you start your investment. It goes without saying that tracker funds have lower charges since there is no active management. You will find that most tracker funds will have annual management charges of around 1 per cent, although this has been falling. For actively managed funds you are looking at 1.5–2 per cent management charges and initial charges between 5 and 6 per cent. Tracker funds charge lower initial charges – on average between 4 and 5 per cent.

Anyone who does not look at the charging structure of the fund they are considering deserves a sharp slap. Paying over-the-odds charges for an underperforming fund is unforgivable, though it happens frequently. However, if you are paying more in charges, even if it is significantly more, but the performance is far superior, the charging levels become irrelevant. The performance in itself justifies the higher fees. Do you really care if you are paying a 2 per cent management charge compared to 0.5 per cent for a tracker fund if the performance is superb over three, five and ten years?

Consider Being Your Own Fund Manager

As we have already stated, making the right investment decisions relies on detailed research, in-depth knowledge and understanding of a particular sector, and an element of luck. Most private investors do not have the time to carry out this kind of detailed research. But with access to the Internet, things are changing and individuals now have access to fund performance and individual stock prices and can buy either individual stocks or collective investments (unit trusts/investment trusts, equity ISAs) on-line.

The speed with which an individual can find the information necessary to select their preferred investment and then pay for it with a credit card has had a huge impact on the financial community. Any fund provider that isn't already offering products on-line is about to.

In the past, you would only really have been able to follow fund performance in the monthly financial magazines. Now you can have immediate access to stock prices and fund analysis on our own site, TheStreet.co.uk, and detailed fund performance statistics and graphs from sites such as micropal.com and moneyworld.com. The sites are refreshed constantly, a factor that gives them an enormous advantage over the print media, where publications are traditionally about a week out of date as soon as they go on the shelves. In saying that, monthlies such as *Money Management* do provide annualised fund performance statistics over five and ten years, which not all the dot.com sites do. The other advantage in keeping one of the monthlies in your bag is that you can always do a quick performance check on the train to or from work. Trying to key into your laptop on a busy commuter train is no fun at all.

DIY Research and Selection

If you are keen to do all or some of the research and select a fund manager yourself there are certain steps you should always take. Firstly, phone up the fund provider and check that the fund manager is still there. Find out a bit of background. The fund may have performed exceptionally well over the last ten years, continually up with the top 25 per cent and showing performance of twice the sector average. But how long has the present fund manager and his team been there? If the manager has been there right from the start, then clearly they must take the bulk of the credit. Be wary of funds where the whole management team has left. While the figures may look good, the track record is no longer relevant since those responsible are no longer in charge. That said, with some companies there is an overall investment strategy that all its fund managers have to adhere to, so the departure of one fund manager is not always crucially important if their successor is going to work to the same strict investment strategy.

There are established names in the world of fund management that investors and financial advisers will follow if they move from one investment house to another. Rory Powe at Invesco, Mark Mobius at Templeton and Nicola Horlick at SocGen are good examples of individuals whose profiles rose during the nineties.

As an illustration of how sensitive investors are to changes of personnel at the top, consider the departure of William Littlewood, head of the successful Jupiter European growth fund. He announced he was taking a sabbatical owing to stress (and has since left altogether). This immediately saw a mass exodus from the fund. Something of a knee-jerk reaction, no doubt, but it serves to emphasise just how much reassurance high-profile fund managers provide when they are seen by the investment community as the linchpin in their whole organisation. It is estimated that 57 per cent of funds invested in the UK have experienced a change of manager over the last three years. Fortunately, most literature sent out by fund management groups will give details of the managers currently employed, how long they have been there and where they worked before. If you are able to establish that their track record prior to becoming fund manager at the new company was exemplary, then it is fair to assume that they were headhunted because their ability had caught the eye of their present employers.

the city
the press
webcraft
the old way
sleuthing
fund managers
short termers
crash!
new economy
telecoms
smokestacks
economics
tax

But many advisers and fund providers despair at the level of importance attached to individuals seen as fund gurus. There is a real danger in a volatile climate (where private investors are already wary about their exposure in equities) that advice to leave a particular fund based primarily on a change of personnel could seriously damage, if not finish off, a fund. Assets in the unit trust could be way below market value and could go up enormously, but nervous investors insist on selling anyway. Money pours out of the fund, as it has to make sure the cash is there to pay deserting investors. This is bad news for the investors left in the fund.

How Can You Identify a Company or Fund's Investment Strategy?

Many investment companies have spent a lot of time and money on developing a clearly identifiable image. For example, at the time of writing, Scottish Widows is seen as steady and consistent while Fidelity is seen as a far more volatile risk-taker. Both these

the city
the press
webcraft
the old way
sleuthing
fund managers
short termers
crash!
new economy
telecoms
smokestacks
economics
tax

companies have their fans since investors want different things from their fund providers. But to be able to tell what sort of investment strategy is in place within a particular fund, you will need to look at the short-, medium- and long-term performance. One-year performance is seldom more than a snapshot: a fund manager can be either very lucky or unlucky over a twelve-month period. It is not a timescale that investors should pay much serious attention to when making an investment decision. You may see a steady but undramatic growth in fund performance over one, three, five and ten years. This would tend to indicate that the investment strategy errs on the side of caution. Probably with a portfolio heavily weighted in established blue chip companies. Alternatively, if you see the performance over one, three, five and ten years varying hugely, going from huge highs to dramatic lows, you can be pretty certain that the fund is in the higher risk category.

Most fund statistics providers will actually give you a figure on volatility, which you can use to compare funds. Many fund managers make it clear from the outset that the fund is geared towards steady, long-term growth. By checking past performance you can see whether their claim is accurate. If fund managers are taking a longer-term view on the companies they invest in, and are trying to buy companies when they are small and therefore good value, it is logical that returns on investment may take time to materialise.

Valuing Individual Stock

While the Internet has provided the private investor with far easier access to buying and selling shares at affordable prices, there is no on-line solution to choosing where your money is to go. Private investors are at a disadvantage here in comparison to the fund manager, since they have neither the time nor the access that institutional investors enjoy. Most successful fund managers will visit the companies they invest in. They will meet the top management and question them on business strategy and cost-effectiveness, and may discover far more than they would if they just had access to the companies' annual reports. You, as an individual investor, will need to make the most of these annual reports – which include a company's balance sheet – if you plan to do your own research. In particular, if you are going to go it alone, then it is worth spending some time looking closely at the company's balance sheet. What you should concentrate on is takeover value, investment value, market value, net asset value and liquidation value.

Given the crashes in technology stocks we saw in the spring of 2000, investors are inevitably reminded of the benefits of realistic valuations. How do you value a technology company that has virtually no assets to speak of and no track record to look at in terms of earnings or long-term comparisons with competitors? The answer is not very easily. (For more on this subject, see Chapter Nine.) With many New Age companies, the attraction is to invest in the 'intellectual assets'. This means the innovative concepts, which could be worth a fortune farther down the road or could be completely worthless. There is little concrete to sell if everything goes pear-shaped.

In recent times we have seen companies develop flat hi-fi speakers that can be hidden in pictures or mirrors and computerised navigational systems that can be built into your car windscreen. There are some great innovations out there, but some of them will leave the public completely cold and will never see the light of

the city
the press
webcraft
the old way
sleuthing
fund managers
short termers
crash!
new economy
telecoms
smokestacks
economics
tax

the city
the press
webcraft
the old way
sleuthing
fund managers
short termers
crash!
new economy
telecoms
smokestacks
economics
tax

day. If the companies do go belly up, there will be little or no compensation for their investors. This is where the liquidation value of the company comes in. This is the value of the company if it has to cease trading and its assets are liquidated. In many cases, with traditional smokestack companies, there is much that can be broken up and sold off – property, goods already manufactured and expensive machinery. The sale of all these assets goes some way towards repaying those who have invested in the failed company. Because these traditional companies have these assets to fall back on, they are often a safer investment (see Chapter Eleven).

A Strategy for Volatile Markets

As we have demonstrated in earlier chapters, if you are going it alone without a fund manager, or even an adviser to choose investments on your behalf, you must have a strategy. There are periods of volatility when markets experience sharp swings over short time periods. In this type of environment, it is always tempting to try to avoid exposure by selling out of the market, then buying back at a later, more settled stage – often termed market timing. But this can do more harm to long-term investment returns than good.

History shows that equity market returns tend to be concentrated in a relatively small number of strong trading days. Some of the biggest rises come immediately after sharp market declines, a time when many market timers may still be out of the market. As a result, it is very easy to miss some of the strongest recoveries in the market.

Market timing is certainly tempting, and the returns can be

impressive. But unless you are extremely lucky, it is almost imposs- ible to time the market accurately and consistently. For starters, markets are impossible to predict even on a day-to-day basis. It's something that people have been trying to do since the early days of stock market trading with little or no success.

Take, for example, the US market during the late 1990s. US market analysts predicted that the remarkable bull run of the 1990s would come to an end at the start of 1994 – they came out with the same story year on year until 1998. These predictions were wrong every time. Whether the market's rise was justified by the underlying economic fundamentals, or valuations were pushed well beyond what would normally be regarded as realistic, is academic – the point is that even the experts cannot call the market accurately and consistently.

But so long as you are aware of the trends usually seen in the market, you will have some idea of how to react if it starts to misbehave. For example, black or grey days in the market often arrive very shortly before or after the best. This can be explained by basic economics. When markets fall sharply there is often a short-term bounce. By the same token, after a rapid rise many investors choose to cash in and take quick profits. For market timers, the fact that the best and worst days often come in quick succession only adds to the chances of getting it wrong.

Investors can minimise the risks associated with moving in and out of markets by staying fully invested for the long term.

the city
the press
webcraft
the old way
sleuthing
fund managers
short termers
crash!
new economy
telecoms
smokestacks
economics
tax

the city

the press

webcraft

the old way

sleuthing

fund managers

short termers

crash!

new economy

telecoms

smokestacks

economics

tax

Keep Your Head – Don't Panic

When the markets are in turmoil, the temptation may be to get the hell out, but this is precisely when you must keep your nerve. If share prices have taken a real hammering, the only sure thing about throwing in the towel is that you will take a loss. It may not be an option for some who cannot afford to lose what could be their retirement savings, but for those who have other income or assets to fall back on, the best course of action could be to wait for the bounce back. In the longer term, if your stock selection is not in fly-by-night operations, you should see a recovery.

Despite all the sound advice given when markets are stable, as we shall explain in Chapter Seven, everything goes out of the window when share prices start to plummet. With private investors now able to use direct and on-line share dealing services, there is a temptation to repeatedly jump in and out of the equity markets as part of a damage limitation exercise. When this happens the investor may be paying out large transaction fees to brokers and forking out multiple stamp duty fees as they continue to move money around. Also there are the Capital Gains Tax implications to worry about if you sell the bulk of your portfolio. The best course of action in such circumstances is to act quickly if you are certain that you must get out, but do not get involved in frenzied and uninformed trading at the eleventh hour when you are not thinking straight.

Diversification May Save Your Skin

Whether you choose active or passively managed tracker funds, or even build you own portfolio of shares, diversification should rank pretty high on your list of priorities.

With actively managed funds, or at least those with a cautious or balanced approach, the fund manager will look to spread risk by varying the weighting in stocks from different sectors and geographical locations. For example, the fund may have a hefty exposure in high tech companies but will try to balance the volatility associated with companies in this sector by investing in low-risk and well-established industries. Electricity and gas companies and retail manufacturers in food and beer are often thrown into the fund mix to introduce a level of stability. In the most recent market slide of spring 2000, on the morning when it seemed all major stocks were going through the floor, the brewer Whitbread and National Power were both notable by their absence from the long list of casualties. Both saw a modest rise in share prices as investors switched from New Economy stocks to the greater protection of the old favourites. It is amazing how quickly a much-ridiculed smokestacks stock can suddenly be hailed as a saviour when the market nosedives.

With tracker funds there is also the question of diversification. Now that the FTSE 100 is dominated by only five sectors – technology, media, telecommunications, oils and pharmaceuticals – there is little in the way of diversification. For most investors looking for a greater spread on risk, the FTSE All Share tracker has far more appeal.

When it comes to the individual spreading risk on individual

the city
the press
webcraft
the old way
sleuthing
fund managers
short termers
crash!
new economy
telecoms
smokestacks
economics
tax

shares that are not part of a fund, things become a bit trickier. What you must ask yourself is do you have enough capital to hold sufficient quantities of stock individually to spread risk? If you consider technology stocks, for example, it makes far more sense to go into a technology fund where there is the opportunity for investment in twenty companies. Otherwise you are relying on picking winners from your own very limited pool of investments.

There's no such thing as free advice, so ignore the ramblings of those active on Internet message boards, and stick to the principles of your own research and trust your own judgment based on the time and effort you have put in. It is not uncommon for investors to throw money into companies they know absolutely nothing about. You hear good things about an unheard-of Taiwanese hi-fi manufacturer which claims to have developed a system that can be built into your bath and shaving mirror. Even if this is true, do you really want to risk your money on a gimmick that could find itself on the scrapheap after a few must-have gadget nutcases have made their purchase?

Don't follow fashion trends; look for value and shelf life. There are enough good companies and good ideas out there without resorting to these sorts of sideshows. If you are looking to make a fast buck, then sure, invest in the Rubik's cube developers of tomorrow, but make sure you are prepared to lose money as well when these fads disappear from the face of the earth.

It is almost impossible to give sound advice that will apply to everybody since so many investors want different things. But here is a final checklist that should apply to most:

☐ Whether you are in an actively managed fund, a tracker or are investing off your own back, you should do as much of your own research as possible. If you have some idea of what your fund manager is up to in terms of asset allocation or any wholesale change in investment strategy, then you will be in a position to switch elsewhere if you don't like what you see.

☐ Look at *all* performance statistics – especially look at quartile ranking and volatility over the longer term. Be wary of buying into a brand – many fund management groups have a few real dog funds among their star performers. They are hardly going to tell you if you make an impulse buy and choose the wrong one. Check the small print and see exactly what they mean by their proclamations of 'award-winning expertise'.

☐ Have a working knowledge of the companies you are investing in. It never hurts to know that the company that was a start-up two years ago is a prime target for a takeover by Sony or Sky.

☐ Don't gamble with money you can't afford to lose.

If you follow these basic rules, you should be able to keep your blood pressure low and actually enjoy the thrill of investing in the markets.

David Burrows

the city
the press
webcraft
the old way
sleuthing
fund managers
short termers
crash!
new economy
telecoms
smokestacks
economics
tax

Chapter Seven

Where Have All the Traders Gone? The World of the Short-Term Speculator

the city

the press

webcraft

the old way

sleuthing

fund managers

short termers

crash!

new economy

telecoms

smokestacks

economics

tax

Benjamin Franklin once said: 'In this world nothing can be said to be certain, except death and taxes.' We can't add to that but we can introduce you to something that could include both at the same time. Welcome to the world of the stock market, the casino in which anyone can take part. For every winner, there is a loser. The name of the game is to ensure that the loser is not you.

Before we start, let's explain the endgame. The best way to make a small fortune in the stock market is to start with a large one. Turning a small sum into a large one, however, is a completely different ball-game, because unfortunately the old adage holds true – money goes to money.

Now that you have been introduced to the delights of buying and selling in the previous chapters, let's go and take a look at the London Stock Exchange on Old Broad Street to see where it all happens. But where has everyone gone?

In the good old days, when hacks grappled with typewriters and the only kind of net was one used by fishermen, today's market makers were known as stockjobbers, while the men that acted as the intermediary between the stockjobber and the investor were known as stockbrokers.

Business was transacted on a rather cosy, face-to-face basis on the London Stock Exchange floor. Pieces of paper, the nod and

the city

the press

webcraft

the old way

sleuthing

fund managers

short termers

crash!

new economy

telecoms

smokestacks

economics

tax

'my word is my bond', the London Stock Exchange motto, were sufficient to run an entire stock market trading system. Then someone invented the screen and the techno-nerds finally emerged. The electronic dealing system was created. It was much talked about in the wine bars scattered around the Square Mile, and developed into everyone's worst nightmare.

Look at it this way. If you are short of money and need a loan until your ship comes in next month, what would you prefer? A conversation over a glass of claret with your friendly bank manager, or a one-to-one with a Dalek? This is how the stock market is now, with the ability to press a button becoming more important than the ability to press a shirt.

Now you can trade from anywhere, including the comfortable safety of your front room. The professionals rely on an expensive trading screen to help make decisions on whether to buy or sell a share, while you will probably have to rely on a TV set, or subscribe to one of the now numerous Internet sites that will quote a price, albeit on a fifteen-minute time delay. (Chapter Three examines how to trade on the Internet.)

Although you may not own a trading screen, it is good to know how the professionals go about their business. It is also good to understand the risks involved in buying and selling shares. Then, if you ever decide to pack in your day job and devote yourself to a life of short-term speculating (not to mention a life of ulcers and hair loss), you'll know how to go about it. Firstly, let's imagine you've decided to fork out £200 a week for a trading screen. Turn it on and what do you see? Well, assuming you've taken a weekend to read the instruction manual, you suddenly find a stock quotation on the screen. Now, it's not difficult. The market maker quoting the prices is making a bid and an offer, which, of course, for you, the investor, is an offer and a bid.

Still there? A market maker will make a bid to buy your shares, in which case you are offering to sell them. And the same applies for a market maker's offer and your bid. The point to remember here is that you can tell which way round the bid and offer is because you have to pay more to buy a stock than you will receive to sell it. Just like a car, the minute you drive it out of the showroom it's worth less than you paid for it.

But unlike most cars, shares can improve in value. Next on the screen is the list of market makers making a price. These differ. You may see three quotes at 500–510, one at 495–505 and two at 500–515. For the investor, the spread available in this case will be 500–505. This represents the highest price at which you can sell the stock (the first of the two numbers), and the cheapest at which you can buy it.

Why the difference in quotations and why is there a difference in prices? The price difference is the market maker's way of making money on the deal. It's as simple as that. As for the different quotations, some market makers are long – that is they own many of the shares – of the stock already and are trying to dissuade investors from selling any more. Hence the unattractive price. Others may have a buyer, or they may know something about the company and are anxious to take on as much stock as they can get. These guys fight each other as well as the punters. There are very few prisoners taken when money is involved.

Against each quotation, you will see a number like 1x1 or 5x5 LxL (LxL means the market maker is willing to deal in at least 100,000 shares). This represents the maximum number of shares

the city
the press
webcraft
the old way
sleuthing
fund managers
short termers
crash!
new economy
telecoms
smokestacks
economics
tax

the city
the press
webcraft
the old way
sleuthing
fund managers
short termers
crash!
new economy
telecoms
smokestacks
economics
tax

that the market maker is obliged to deal at this price. If you want to buy more shares than the amount quoted on the screen with any one particular trader, it starts to get tricky. The market maker will take your bid for, say, 5,000 shares, or on request make you a price in a larger size. This will be more expensive. Unlike the discount centre, where you get a reduction for bulk, the opposite applies here. The logic is simple. If you want to 'fill your boots' in a particular share, the market maker will make you pay up.

There is the physical question as well. He may not have those shares to hand. And if he sells them to you and then has to go into the market to actually cover his position, he is going to drive the price higher and could end up paying more for the stock than the price at which he sold them to you. So you have to pay up.

When it comes to selling stock, the situation is reversed. Selling your 5,000 shares will be relatively simple because with shares of this size, the market maker will trade at the price he is quoting. For a larger number of shares, say 10,000, as with buying, he will present you with two options. The first is to take 5,000 shares from you and then quote you a price for the remaining 5,000, which will be a lower price, or he will simply make a price for the 10,000 shares that you want to sell. And of course, this will again be a lower price.

To be able to see competing quotes between market makers, you have to be trading in a stock that is not dealt through the SETS system, the Stock Exchange's widely disliked electronic trading system. In the case of a stock traded through SETS, the screen will give you no list of competing quotes and no list of market makers. There's just one bid and offer price, and you try to make the best guess.

Now you might be wondering how the average punter can afford to buy 10,000 shares at 500p per share, a total of £50,000. Well, you don't have to buy them, really. It all depends on what sort of relationship you have with your broker. And now we come on to the method in which shares can be acquired. It's a matter of Ts – T2, T5, T10, T20 or T whatever you can get away with. The T stands for trading days, with T10 meaning ten days. This means that you can buy shares and will not need to cover the cost of that purchase until the end of the trading period known as 'the account', under which the transaction was enacted. It's not quite that simple, but we get on to that later.

In short, if you are trading in the account, you can buy shares on a T10 basis and sell them three days later without having to put up the money to cover the deal. If your shares rise sufficiently, this means that the bottom line is a credit to your account from the sale of stock at a much higher price than that which you paid.

This is the sharp end of the market. Most trades can be transacted at the screen price (in the right size) at T10 or less. Anything more than this is usually subject to a premium. The market makers know exactly what you're doing. They know you want the best part of four weeks, twenty trading days, before your position is in profit. They see you coming and they make you pay up. This usually means that a price on the screen of 87p–90p will see you paying 91p or 92p for a T20 position.

In reality, you cannot run a T20 position or any other position for the full term. In the case of T20, your broker will want you to settle the position after eighteen days, as this allows him to settle your position by enacting a counter-trade with someone else on a T2 basis.

Nothing is set in stone, however. You can run the stock right

the city
the press
webcraft
the old way
sleuthing
fund managers
short termers
crash!
new economy
telecoms
smokestacks
economics
tax

up to the wire, and some, but not all, brokers will charge you a nominal amount to run the position for an extra day. After that, you have a choice. Of course, if you have made a profit, you can just sell the stock. If you have not made a profit, you can cut your losses and sell the stock at any time. Or you may feel that the share is still a good bet, and in this case you can ask your broker to 'cash and new' the position.

To explain 'cash and new', let's say you are buying stock at 50p, the spread being 48p–50p. After the allotted trading period, the stock is quoted at 45p–47p. You can sell the shares at 45p and take a 5p loss. Or, if you think that the stock will rise very soon, but after the expiry of your current trading period, you instruct your broker to sell the stock at 45p and buy it back immediately at 47p – cash and new it.

We are now getting into last chance saloon territory. You have already sustained a five-point loss, and if the stock revives to be quoted at 50p–55p, you can close your position and come out square, apart from the usual costs. If the stock falls further to 40p–45p, you're stuffed. At this point, you get out your cheque book and decide one of two things. Either sell the stock and pay the broker, or decide that the stock is going to come right at some point. And here is where you put your money where your mouth is, because if you don't sell the stock and take a loss, you have to take shares up, which means buying them.

A loss of 10 points on 10,000 shares is £1,000, £100 a point. Taking up the shares is going to cost you in this case £5,000. This represents the cost if you had bought them in the first place. So you are buying stock for £5,000 which at the point of purchase is now worth £4,000.

The difference is that if you do not take up the stock but simply close the position, you lose £1,000, game over and no going back. If you take up the stock, it costs you real money, but you also buy the ability to recoup your losses. Your downside is £5,000; the upside is early retirement.

So far, we have only mentioned buying shares as a contract. You can also sell them, and the principle is simple enough. When you buy shares, you do so because you think that the price will rise and you can sell the stock at a profit, even though at no time did you actually physically own the stock.

Now all we do is reverse the position. If you think a stock is overvalued and due a fall for whatever reason, you simply instruct the broker to sell stock, hoping that before the end of the trading period the price falls and you can buy back the shares at a lower level.

For example, ZZZ plc is due to release its annual earnings next week. The sector has been performing badly; the exchange rate is adverse, and the interim figures were lacklustre. The stock is quoted at 50p–55p. You 'sell' 10,000 shares at 50p. Next week, the results come out, the chairman resigns, the dividend is cut and the company issues another profits warning. The share price collapses to 35p–40p. At this point, you buy 10,000 shares at 40p. This covers your obligation to come up with 10,000 shares which up until this point you didn't have. The net result is that you make 10 points a share, or in this case £1,000. Thank you very much.

But there is a snag. What happens if the figures are good and the price rises? You are now in a position where you have sold 10,000 shares at 50p, which you do not have, and the price is 55p–60p. At

the city

the press

webcraft

the old way

sleuthing

fund managers

short termers

crash!

new economy

telecoms

smokestacks

economics

tax

this point, or before the end of the trading period, you will have to buy those shares to honour your first bargain. So, you sold shares at 50p which you are now having to buy at 60p. Ouch!

You can, of course, execute a 'cash and new' on your short position. But the situation is slightly different from renewing a long position. The point here is that unlike shares bought on the account and subsequently taken up in the hope that one day the share price rises, you cannot 'take up' a short position. If you're long and wrong, you can live to fight the position another day. If you're short and caught, you are stuffed and have to take the loss on the chin.

Some brokers will allow you to run a short position without a time limit, but this carries a number of provisos. It is usually only possible in a FTSE 100 constituent company, and the broker likes to sleep at night by ensuring that you have a rather large lump sum deposited with him.

Apart from the occasional bout of madness, the broker never loses. He is the broker and nothing more. He executes your orders and you make a profit or a loss. Either way, he makes a commission.

So, your best friend, a man in the pub or your best guess puts you into a stock. It's a tricky one because it's racy, and let's face it, that's where the short-term play pays off. But, oh dear, the stock is suspended. This does not mean that someone is two foot off the ground with a rope round his neck, although to you it may feel like it. Suspension entails a cessation of all transactions in a stock, usually pending an announcement from the company. Now this may mean a restructuring, it may mean there is another company making a bid, or it may mean that the company is about to go bust.

It's a good-news-bad-news ulcer situation because either way you are stuck. The reason you are stuck is that your arrangement with the broker still stands, but no one can trade in the shares. To cut a long story short, your broker will require you to provide the money to take up the position. Sometimes, stocks are suspended for twenty-four hours, sometimes it's twenty-four weeks. If you get lucky, the company makes an announcement before the trading period on your transaction expires. If not, get yourself another mortgage.

What else can go wrong? Sometimes companies catch the market off guard and make a bid for another company. Sometimes, the bid is rather well signposted and the price of the company about to be bid for can move significantly even before any official announcement. If you're quick, you can buy some stock while the price is still rising, and be out again in a few days, having made a nice profit. But sometimes it can go wrong. You switch on your information screen, on Teletext or on the Internet, and the first thing you read at seven in the morning, when official announcements start to be released by the Stock Exchange, is that bid talks are off. Oh dear. The market doesn't open until 8 a.m. and the first price quoted is going to be horrible.

Avoiding the Twenty-Third Floor

The Stock Exchange polices the market. The rules are quite clear and the penalties harsh. Price-sensitive information is always going to be in the hands of a small group of people. Sometimes, however, information has a tendency to leak. A company is in discussion with another with a view to being taken over, which could result in the share price rising sharply. The boards of both companies

the city
the press
webcraft
the old way
sleuthing
fund managers
short termers
crash!
new economy
telecoms
smokestacks
economics
tax

the city
the press
webcraft
the old way
sleuthing
fund managers
short termers
crash!
new economy
telecoms
smokestacks
economics
tax

will be privy to the information, as will the banks and financial organisations advising both companies. So, this very well-kept secret is suddenly common knowledge to a hundred or more people. Most of these people have families. Many of them talk in public places. Careless talk in this case does not cost lives, but it can bring a mixture of disgrace, prosecution and a lot of money. The money comes first, the grief later.

For those who have sailed close to the wind, a visit to the twenty-third floor of the London Stock Exchange will be nothing new. The trouble for the LSE is that proving a case of insider trading is extremely difficult. If you buy a stock the day before a bid comes out, there is a chance that you may receive an invitation to explain your trading performance. The only evidence that the authorities have is the record of the transaction and, of course, the taped message between you and your broker (yes, they're all taped). When the inquiry team asks you why you bought the shares, you will quite rightly plead your innocence and suggest that it was a lucky guess or one based on recent media speculation. The problem for the authorities is that this would also be the stock reply for anyone who had traded in receipt of privileged information. And if your taped conversation with your stockbroker provides nothing to suggest otherwise, there is very little more that can be done. The Stock Exchange can strike a line through the bargain if it so wishes, and there is very little that you can do about it. Afterwards, you will be left under no illusion. Big Brother will be watching you, and the first time you trip up, a ton of bricks duly falls upon your head.

Parlez-Vous Finance?

Market commentators will try to blind you with science, using their own particular phraseology. Most of them are uncomplimentary and brutal. An underperformer is usually referred to as a 'dog', whereas a strong performer will no doubt be described as being 'off to the races'. 'Fill your boots' we have already mentioned, and the explanation is fairly obvious. It is a recommendation to buy as much of any one stock as you can.

Every quality newspaper and financial magazine provides a share information service. Company news is carefully analysed, and while journalists are not really entitled to advise readers to buy a certain stock, these are ways round the rules. The simplest is to say something like, 'If I were licensed to give impartial financial advice, which of course I am not, I would suggest filling your boots in XYZ.'

So, having carefully read four financial reports, you are left with a choice of two 'buy' recommendations, one 'hold' and another saying sell. What do you do? Who do you believe? Our view is that none of them will be exactly right. It can't be an exact science. Take the journalist who says buy. He has no way of knowing whether a major institution of an opposite opinion may have a million shares to sell. The institution cannot sell a million in one hit, but has made its intentions known to the market maker that it wishes to unload the stock. The buy recommendation in the morning paper becomes history the moment the market opens. You buy 5,000 shares first thing and watch the share price sink and you wonder what the hell's happening. Suddenly you're in for the long term. Short-term gain, at least until the stock hangover is cleared, is just not on the cards.

the city
the press
webcraft
the old way
sleuthing
fund managers
short termers
crash!
new economy
telecoms
smokestacks
economics
tax

the city

the press

webcraft

the old way

sleuthing

fund managers

short termers

crash!

new economy

telecoms

smokestacks

economics

tax

RNS – Regulatory News Service. Big bold words. These are official company announcements that are pushed out by the London Stock Exchange from 7 a.m. Sometimes, the announcement from XYZ company is straightforward – financial results, trading statements, and so on. But occasionally you get the sting in the tale. Everything is hunky-dory – this week – but the following week trading has deteriorated to the extent that we are going bust. A company says it has sold its stake in this or that company and realised a profit on disposal. The point is that it's the only thing that is keeping the company solvent. Spot the profits warning – read the statement to its conclusion, even do a bit of number-crunching. Although you must remember that the market makers will have read the same statement, and so have their analysts.

Take the computer game designer Eidos. In 2000, it sold its stake in Opticom, but at the end of the statement it casually mentioned that trading has badly deteriorated across all its divisions. Lara Croft was tired and emotional, and so would you be if you had earlier bought 10,000 shares for a fiver each, and they were suddenly worth £2.50. Glad you played?

Going Long

One of the reasons it looks dangerous and difficult to perform successfully as a short-term player is because it *is* dangerous and difficult. 'Short-term investor' is basically a nicer way of saying punter or speculator. Remember, the whole process of buying shares involves companies issuing pieces of paper that you pay for. The company now has some money to produce things, make a profit – over time – and eventually repay you for your trust and money by giving you a dividend. Hopefully, the share price will also rise as the value of the company increases. Short-term traders don't play by these rules, however. They are the smash-and-grab merchants of the stock market world, who will make a quick buck or get hurt in the attempt. And when their commitment to the shares is confined to a hope that they will rise in the next ten days, it is not surprising that the penalties for failure are as extreme as the potential profits that can be made.

Why does anyone do it, you may ask? Well, as we said, the reason is because you can make a lot of money. But as with everything else, fortune only favours the brave or the lucky.

Overall, our view is to invest, not speculate. That lump sum left to you by your great-auntie doesn't make all that much in a deposit account, or at least not enough to change your lifestyle. Investing in shares for the long term is a sound move. Since the Wall Street crash of 1929, there has been only one five-year period in which shares did not finish higher than when they started.

The tricky thing is that this is true of the market as a whole. It does not mean that any particular blue chip stock will gain in value over a five-year period. Despite recent gains, some leading stocks are currently trading at a ten-year low. So, it's all down to picking the right stock.

Professional gamblers sit at home in front of their personal trading screen with nothing else to do but punt. The rest of us rely on what we read and what we hear down the pub.

But remember, for every tip, there's a tap.

Nigel Spall and Jonas Crosland

Chapter Eight

Crash!
Or How to Know When the Fat Lady's Singing

the city

the press

webcraft

the old way

sleuthing

fund managers

short termers

crash!

new economy

telecoms

smokestacks

economics

tax

Let's take a moment to recall the events of 19 October 1987. Wall Street had already sneezed by the time that trading started in London. In fact, Wall Street had gone down with flu, and pneumonia was about to hit London.

Anything that was traded in the form of an ADR (an American Depository Receipt – a kind of share used by many non-US companies to trade in American stock markets) had already been badly hit on Wall Street, and institutions were staring down the barrel. For the small investor, there was not even the pleasure of a last request before the firing squad let loose. On that first fateful day, there were conversations like this.

From a broker to a market maker, trying to save one of his small clients:

'What price is XYZ?'

'Well it was 90p to 92p had you been quick, but that was half an hour ago.'

'So what is it now?'

'60p to 65p. What do you want to do?'

'I've got a tenner [10,000 shares to sell].'

At this point, the stockjobber, wondering what his senior partner is going to say when he sees his dealing book at the end of the day, says:

'I'll give you 50p for them, but I don't really want them.'

the city
the press
webcraft
the old way
sleuthing
fund managers
short termers
crash!
new economy
telecoms
smokestacks
economics
tax

'Thanks very much,' comes the broker's reply. 'What price are they now?'

'30p–35p.'

Of course, it was not all over in one day. Shares were lower the following day as well, and it was only then that the cherry-pickers came out from the bunkers and started to pick up stock that had become extremely cheap extremely quickly.

For the small investor, the scars took a lot longer to heal, and it was some time before their confidence returned.

Now let's look back at early April 2000, when the technology-laden US Nasdaq index fell 13.5 per cent in four hours. The tin hats came out. Newspaper layouts were thrown away, and contingency plans for covering the Great Crash swung into action. Yet three hours later, the index was down just 2 per cent.

Trying to analyse the reasons for a stock market crash would fill a book in itself, and besides, experts have agreed that predicting a crash and a recession is an inexact science. If we could see a crash coming, it would never happen, or at least we could minimise our exposure to the downturn.

It is also well to remember that a stock market crash and a recession do not go hand in hand. A sharp fall in share prices may lead to a retreat in global output, but the latter does not have to be preceded by a crash in shares. We can define a recession as a time when a country records two successive quarters of negative GDP (see Chapter Twelve), but what is a stock market crash? Perhaps it can be defined as a severe and sustained fall in share prices over a relatively short period. This has some merit, but was there a crash in the mid-1970s, then, when the FTSE 30 index lost 78 per cent of its value but took from May 1973 to January 1975 to do it. Is this a crash or a sustained downturn?

It is fair to say that when economic indicators are expanding too fast – as they were in the 1970s when output was growing by nearly 10 per cent, (it is currently nearer 3 per cent), money supply growth was up 30 per cent (against 6 per cent now), and at the same time unemployment was actually rising – two things will happen. Governments will take steps to slow things down by applying both the monetary handbrake and the fiscal airbrake. The alternative is to allow the economy to accelerate further before finally crashing.

A combination of successful postwar recovery programmes and the social revolution of the 1960s led to politicians in the 1970s desperately trying to balance the books and feed what seemed to be an insatiable demand for better living conditions. This desperation was reflected at the polls – between 1963 and 1974 there were four elections and two political parties in power – until the early 1980s, when Mrs Thatcher's Conservative government received a mandate from the electorate to try a different tack to solve the country's economic problems. Perhaps with hindsight, the electorate would have had second thoughts, because the Conservative's economic reformation took twenty years to mature, helped at the end by some useful fine tuning from the New Labour administration. But in the process, the Conservatives became the least popular government this century. However, the spell was strong enough to see it win four general elections on the trot, probably because we were all brought up to believe that the effects of medicine are only beneficial if it tastes absolutely disgusting.

Looking back thirty years, the pattern of events leading up to the recession, the secondary banking crisis and the collapse in share

the city
the press
webcraft
the old way
sleuthing
fund managers
short termers
crash!
new economy
telecoms
smokestacks
economics
tax

the city
the press
webcraft
the old way
sleuthing
fund managers
short termers
crash!
new economy
telecoms
smokestacks
economics
tax

prices simply looked like an accident waiting to happen. There is no industrialised country now that currently pursues anything remotely resembling the monetary and fiscal policies that were regarded then as the norm.

So what has changed to make stability the byword, low inflation the norm and steady but sustainable growth the rule rather than the exception?

For a start, social liberalisation has slowed down. The differences between 1970 and 2000 are not as great as the differences between 1970 and 1940. And after all, although we elect the politicians to look after the housekeeping, it is the people in a country who dictate the pace. It is we who respond to fiscal stimulus. We are the ones who have to be reminded to save a little money instead of blowing it all on imported electrical equipment. We are the sheep and the government is the shepherd.

How, then, could the crash of 1987 have taken place? The answer lies in the fact that sustained downturns on share prices are an inevitable consequence of the economic cycles between strong growth and weak growth (see Chapter Twelve). But share price crashes are the inevitable consequence of greed, selfishness and panic. It's a bit like the fire alarm in the cinema. It turns out to be a false alarm but nine people die in the stampede for the exit. And like all cattle, they are quite easily led to the slaughter.

Given the fact that there is no rule book on how to anticipate a crash, we have to make do with analysing the circumstances that precede such an event. Without doubt, all previous speculative booms and subsequent crashes have been preceded by a strong rise in credit. To the ordinary hard-working and cautious man on the street, it may seem like madness, but people do borrow money to speculate. It is bad enough losing money that you have saved up to invest in the stock market; it is a positive disaster when the money you lose is not yours in the first place.

Of course, banks do not just lend money to anyone. Well, that's not strictly true. They will lend money to anyone they think will make them some money as well. When you owe the banks £500 they've got you by the balls. When you owe them £50 million, you've got them by the balls. Unsecured loans attract very high rates of interest and are largely confined to short-term overdrafts and credit cards. Secured loans require collateral. Sometimes, instead of property as in bricks and mortar, venture capitalists will take a significant stake in the company as collateral instead. But if the company doesn't prosper, where is the lender left?

Then there are derivatives. There is not enough space here to detail the finer points of all derivatives and the ensuing combinations of futures and options, swaptions, collars and caps. Suffice to say that they represent a myriad of ways in which you can play the investment game which make simple cash transactions look a safe and dependable way of trading. This is because with derivatives the gearing is so much greater while the margin calls are low enough at the start to tempt you in that bit farther. And when you are in far enough, the jaws snap shut and there's no way out. Writing options is actually not as bad as that, as long as the obligation is covered by shares that you actually own. Uncovered options are only for those who find Russian roulette boring.

These factors tend to accumulate without any fanfare, and bubble away under the surface, but they all have to be in place before a crash occurs. The actual catalyst that eventually triggers the run on share prices may appear to have little to do with any of the above.

the city
the press
webcraft
the old way
sleuthing
fund managers
short termers
crash!
new economy
telecoms
smokestacks
economics
tax

When you wake up in the morning and find out that ABC Technologies has issued a severe profits warning, you start to think: I wonder what the other companies in that sector are like. Perhaps I'll close my position and move into cash or a defensive stock for now. But what if a lot of other people are thinking and doing the same? The lucky guy gets his sell order in before anyone else does. And of course, the faster the price falls, the longer the queue of sellers becomes.

Stock markets comprise little more than little bits of paper with writing on. Water, air and food are the only properties on this planet that cannot have their worth devalued. Everything else is merely a physical manifestation of whatever level of trust and confidence we care to attach to it.

So, it's all a matter of confidence, and when that confidence is shattered, then the trouble starts. Assuming that the investor who was desperately trying to sell his shares in the crash of 1987 had hung on, he would have been all right. If you see £9,000 worth of shares reduced to £3,000, it becomes almost academic whether you sell or not. The shares are not going to fall to nothing, and they will recover, but there has been a panic.

And of course, while speculators are more likely than not to have another source of income, the market makers do this sort of thing for a living. So, if investors start to panic, why should market makers want to buy all the stock that everyone is getting rid of? There is no buyer-of-last-resort facility for stocks and shares, although the certificates can make a nice picture when framed.

It is true that many investors have a nose for which way the wind is blowing, but the greed factor makes it that much more easy to throw caution to the wind. There are two maxims which the wise investor would do well to remember. The first is that it is never wrong to take a profit. The second is that it is never wrong to leave something for someone else. Both are all too easily forgotten when a stock market panic sets in.

Of course, we all dream about buying shares at the lowest price in the current cycle and selling them at the peak, but this rarely happens, and attempting to achieve this usually fails.

For the slightly more wary investor, the question must be asked as to whether or not it is wise to chase the game. If a stock has risen from 100p to 140p in three days on, let's say, bid rumours or an upward revised profits forecast, is that enough gain to reflect the better circumstances, or will it run up to 170p? One thing is for sure. There will be people who bought the stock at 100p who will be turning sellers any time now. So there is a good chance that the shares will actually fall from the current level, just as you are thinking of buying some.

These examples provide an idea of how confidence levels can be shattered. And it is a crisis in confidence that can provide the trigger for a crash. When media reports claim that share prices have collapsed, what they mean is that investor confidence has collapsed and prices have fallen as a result.

Fine, but having said that, we have seen this happen quite regularly, and at no time has anyone thought about a crash. A crash is the inevitable consequence of a set of economic factors that are unsustainable. And this perhaps is the key point. The US economy has been in a steady economic upturn for a decade, and there has been only the occasional hiccup in that time because the growth levels and economic pointers are all sustainable. Inflation has been quashed, and money supply has been kept under control. Federal

the city
the press
webcraft
the old way
sleuthing
fund managers
short termers
crash!
new economy
telecoms
smokestacks
economics
tax

the city

the press

webcraft

the old way

sleuthing

fund managers

short termers

crash!

new economy

telecoms

smokestacks

economics

tax

Reserve chairman Alan Greenspan has presided over one of the most successful and sustained periods of economic expansion ever seen.

So much for the cause; let's have some effect. The ingredients for the meltdown minestrone, which the stock market resembles when it all goes wrong, are not brought together overnight, and even though some of the warning signs will be there for all to see, very few people are willing or capable of submitting to the notion that it will all end in tears at some point.

The basic worth of any share is the value of the company it represents divided by the number of shares in issue. And even here the price is not guaranteed. Preference shares in issue have to be accommodated first. As the name suggests, the holders have preference over ordinary shareholders if the pot has to be shared out. The pay-off is usually that preference shareholders are stripped of any voting rights. When an ordinary share price reaches the low we mentioned earlier, the company, of course, is not only on the verge of bankruptcy, but is also extremely vulnerable to a takeover bid. But takeovers are not on anyone's mind when shares are collapsing. Indeed, for a strong company that survives a massive downturn, there is little immediate need to gobble up the opposition because much of it will have gone bust.

This was best seen in the banking sector during the 1970s. The secondary banking crisis occurred because some banks had lent a great deal of money secured against over-inflated property prices. When these prices collapsed, the collateral to cover the loans disappeared, and when banks called in loans to cover their margins and to meet panic withdrawals by customers, the borrowers couldn't pay up. The Bank of England had learned its lesson by then from the great Wall Street crash, and implemented a lifeboat fund. If banks can be kept afloat, the rest of the market has a chance. If banks are allowed to fail, we all go together.

Any crash will hurt the short-term trader far more than the long-term investor. Indeed, for the person with a pension in mind, share price crashes present an ideal opportunity to pick up cheap stock. The big Footsie stocks will be unable to resist the sudden downturn, but given five or ten years will be far stronger than just before the crash.

All of this makes sense as long as inflation is kept under control. Dividend payments are usually a lot less in percentage terms than the return offered on long-term bonds. This is because bonds are redeemed at par value, whereas share prices can double or treble in value as well as paying a dividend.

One of the warning signs to look for is the yield offered on long-term bonds. Large investment institutions tend to bankroll any excess of government expenditure over income. The Treasury does the dirty work by issuing government bills, better known as gilt-edged stock or, more simply, as just gilts. These can have a maturity period of up to thirty years. Now, if inflation is starting to gather pace, there is a stronger chance of economic growth ultimately becoming stilted by the efforts taken to reduce inflation. Furthermore, as industrial output declines and unemployment rises, governments find less money coming in and more money going out. The resulting need is for more money to be borrowed.

But investors are unlikely to be in a hurry to lend money only to see it eaten away by inflation and bad economic management. As a result, the Treasury has to increase the rate of return on

the city
the press
webcraft
the old way
sleuthing
fund managers
short termers
crash!
new economy
telecoms
smokestacks
economics
tax

the city
the press
webcraft
the old way
sleuthing
fund managers
short termers
crash!
new economy
telecoms
smokestacks
economics
tax

longer-dated bonds. This is the warning sign, when the yield on long bonds starts to look more attractive than lower-yielding equities with share prices that look overvalued. There are mini-crashes from time to time as a result of this, when investors start to reduce the percentage of their portfolio in equities, and start increasing the percentage of funds held in gilts and good old cash deposits. These are just ripples, and you should not be overly concerned about them.

Company valuations based on projections comprise another little pointer to be watched. All companies borrow money in order to expand. Growth through acquisitions and expanded markets is the norm. Some companies resort to expansion through organic growth, and these are usually the victims of predatory moves by another company. An example is an outfit that makes milk bottle tops. There is only a finite amount of these that will ever be needed, and after saturation point is reached growth can only come through higher prices, assuming efficiency peaks of production have already been achieved. The result is weak growth. It is much better to borrow some money and buy another company that makes beer bottle tops, for example, thereby increasing the spread of products.

But this can be taken too far. In the 1970s, the situation reached absurd proportions. The joke at the time concerned the little man who went to see his bank manager and asked for a loan of £12 billion. When asked what the loan was for, the little man said he needed it to finance a takeover bid for the bank.

So Could It All Happen Again?

While there is nobody who can put their hand on their heart and say another crash will never happen, we can at least hope that some of the causes have been identified and are being avoided.

Bearing in mind the various factors discussed above, it is fairly safe to say that a bust has to be preceded by a boom. Perhaps, then, if we could identify and recognise a boom we would at least be in a position to prepare for the bust. It should be that easy, but trying to pin down an exact definition of a boom is almost as hard as attempting to quantify what constitutes a crash in share prices. Removing upward excesses in economic activity also removes the need for a downward correction, and in the last decade the Group of Seven nations has done just that. Japan is perhaps the exception to the rule, and even here the lessons have been mostly learned, although recovery is going to take a long time.

In an attempt to prevent a drama turning into a crisis, stock markets have introduced a number of checks and balances that prevent anything from sliding into oblivion in one hit. This works in much the same way as a sin-bin in ice hockey. People getting out of control are taken out of the game, and are given time to cool down and think things through.

The finer points vary from exchange to exchange, but the principle is the same – whereby limits are placed on the amount a stock or index can move without trading being suspended. Of course, there is nothing to stop the whole process continuing once trading is resumed, but at this point the big stick can be brought out and trading suspended altogether.

There is some merit in this. When the Nasdaq performed the

the city
the press
webcraft
the old way
sleuthing
fund managers
short termers
crash!
new economy
telecoms
smokestacks
economics
tax

swallow-dive that we mentioned at the start, dealers in London were bracing themselves for a similar test of confidence when UK markets opened the next day. But the stock market did not open, on this occasion because of technical problems. Now all sorts of conspiracy theories were freely floated, but the point is that by the time trading actually resumed late in the afternoon, the Nasdaq had started its next trading session and the index was up. So, the closure, although not intended, actually saved what could have been a violent and, as it turned out, unnecessary rollercoaster ride.

Changes in technology are going to make the lifestyle that we currently know very different in as little as ten years from now. And the resulting advances in communication should allow a greater degree of transparency. We should be able to let off steam little and often, rather than allowing it to build up.

Furthermore, thanks to these changes in technology, selling shares nowadays when there is a panic is somewhat harder than it used to be in the past. Back then, a broker could always walk around the stock exchange floor and pin a sell order on a stockjobber, whereas now we are reduced to relying on a piece of fibre optic cable and someone's willingness to pick up the telephone at the other end.

And this is the get-out clause. When there is a panic and share prices are crashing, market makers concentrate on marking down the price on the screen and put the telephone in the top drawer. They are obliged to deal at the price shown on the screen and up to the number of shares indicated, but there is nothing in the rule book about picking up the telephone. Furthermore, in today's market, with the flexibility offered by the Internet, there is almost no doubt at all that a real run on shares would see the Internet trading systems grind to a halt in a matter of hours. Besides, the orders still have to go through a market maker, and there is nothing simpler than just going off-line for an hour or two.

Not only have lessons been learned from the 1970s, but the mechanics of the economy have also been digested and understood. Share prices cannot crash on their own. A sharp slide in prices is not the cause of economic malaise, it is one of the symptoms. And for shares to be badly hit on anything more than a temporary basis, the underlying framework has to be in place first.

The circumstances that led to a sharp correction in prices in 1997 simply confirm this. In the US at that time, inflation was under control and relatively weak. Growth levels were strong – in fact too strong for the comfort of some. Unemployment was very low, and while there was little sign of skilled labour shortages pushing up wages, the circumstances were ripe for just such a thing to happen. Meanwhile, investors had been piling into shares as companies continued to reel off quarter-year after quarter-year of rising profits.

At that time Alan Greenspan made his infamous reference to the 'irrational exuberance' of the market. This is a comment that has been misinterpreted and misquoted several times since. No matter, the effect was instantaneous, and share prices collapsed 10 per cent in no time at all.

But this was only a shot across the bows. The message that Greenspan was trying to get across was that share prices can continue to rise as long as the basic economic criteria are supportive. They were at the time and they still are. If inflation were starting to rise and consumer spending rose too fast, Greenspan's message would have been, I told you to be careful. But these factors never came

the city
the press
webcraft
the old way
sleuthing
fund managers
short termers
crash!
new economy
telecoms
smokestacks
economics
tax

the city
the press
webcraft
the old way
sleuthing
fund managers
short termers
crash!
new economy
telecoms
smokestacks
economics
tax

into play, and it was not long before share prices were well ahead of the levels seen when he gave that warning.

There is a worry, however, and it is more a case of the unknown than the known. What is the value of an Internet-related stock? Is it based on assets or potential? If it's assets, then everything is vastly overvalued. There are no great factories with plant and equipment, no vast tracts of land or massive ships. There are no assets in the ground to be dug up. So the value is in the potential. And who can quantify that?

Dot.Com Gambling

Have investors been buying tech stocks because they are so impressed with the company's five-year game plan? We don't think so. Most of them make a loss and have never paid a dividend. Perhaps the shares have been bought for a short-term gain, and because this is where all the hot money is going. Fine. Buy some dot.com shares, watch the price go up and then clear out. But very few people do.

Trying to establish the true value of shares should be quite easy. But from time to time the value is based on expectations rather than reality. And this is what makes stock markets such a dangerous place to be.

If a share price can rise from 70p to £70 in two years, why can't it rise to £700 in the next five? It's when greed and the casino mentality take over from rational appraisal that the sensible investor starts buying gold before the whole situation explodes.

People became very excited about the Nasdaq and the way in which, by early April 2000, it had fallen 20 per cent in four weeks to 4,100. Oh dear, was this a crash? Was this the beginning of the end? Well, not really, when you consider that the previous August the index stood at 2,500.

As this chapter has shown, stock market crashes are not only the result of a given set of economic circumstances, they also require one essential ingredient, and that is the willingness of most investors to panic. Someone without any grasp of human nature, when asked to comment on a rapidly falling market, would be excused for asking, 'Why did you push the share prices up there in the first place?'

And this is where the differences between the situation in October 1987 and the situation in April 2000 become clear. The April slide was not a departure from reality, it was a return to reality.

At the very best, you could call the tech decline a crash within a more orderly market. After all, the old economy stocks did a lot better by and large immediately after the fall. It is when these are abandoned as well, and the money starts to find a different home altogether, that it is worth sitting up and taking note. Having said that, the movement of the tech stocks provides a valuable lesson in learning to look out for a fall.

Without actually becoming a full-blown crash, the US Nasdaq offered a great example of how speculators can behave like mad animals in a self-perpetuating orgy of buying until it all ends. In August 1999, the Nasdaq index stood at 2,500. Six months later it broke through 5,000. The rise was supported, or rather the reasoning behind the buying that pushed it this high was supported, by projected profits.

Some people adopted the phrase new economy stocks. One

the city
the press
webcraft
the old way
sleuthing
fund managers
short termers
crash!
new economy
telecoms
smokestacks
economics
tax

the city
the press
webcraft
the old way
sleuthing
fund managers
short termers
crash!
new economy
telecoms
smokestacks
economics
tax

cynic immediately countered by calling them No Economy stocks. And up to a point he was right. But of course, the lesson we must learn here is how to interpret the noises coming out of the market.

When a spectacular rise like this takes place, some investors will shake their heads and say that it will all end in tears. Some of these people are very clever, but a majority are simply trying to justify why they have no tech shares, when the truth is that they missed the first rush and are frightened to get on board once the bandwagon has started to move.

Then there are the guys who will tell you that tech stocks are the way forward and the only place to be. This is sometimes a subconscious plea for someone else to agree with them, because they are quietly getting more and more scared, having put all their money in the techies.

But remember this. A 20 per cent return on an annual investment is very nice money. The doubling of the technology-laden Nasdaq between October 1999 and March 2000 was highly unusual. Even when it fell from 5,000 to 4,000 – a decline of 20% – it was still up strongly on the previous year.

It's nice to be able to watch one sector of the market going through this sort of trauma because it gives us all a valuable lesson in how dangerous the whole business of stock trading is, without having to suffer the effects of a full-blown crash.

However, we must be careful here. Some will argue that this is not a crash but a correction to more realistic levels. But isn't that what causes a crash anyway? The point here is that this is a sector problem and not a fundamental economic problem. If instead we saw all sectors falling sharply and the economy showing signs of overheating, then we would be worried. And signs of overheating do not constitute one month's retail price inflation distorted by oil price rises, as was the case in that same April.

Spotting the Signs

So, what can we learn from all this? Advances in technology and communications, a reduction in class barriers, peace, political middle ground – all these are key reasons why the next crash will have to be something special to even take place. Look at the catalysts in recent years that would have been quite good enough to spark a crash if the other factors had been in place. South American debt caused more than a few sleepless nights and a stock market wobble, but there was no crash. The financial disintegration of the old Soviet Union had German bankers dusting off their pistols, but nobody was blown to bits. It's true that if there were a major conflict in the Middle East and oil prices rose fourfold, it would be reasonable to expect share prices to fall sharply. But this is an external factor, and stock prices would fall in such a situation whether they were anything between vastly overvalued and slightly undervalued.

The fundamental picture will never change. Economies will overheat only if inflation is allowed to rise too much; workers receive wage increases that output levels do not justify; consumers borrow too much money and live beyond their means; and money supply growth spirals out of control. Then you will see a stock market crash. Otherwise, the sudden corrections that can be equally nasty, and carry the same financial penalties as a sustained downturn for the short-term investor, will be followed by a recovery that is almost as violent.

the city
the press
webcraft
the old way
sleuthing
fund managers
short termers
crash!
new economy
telecoms
smokestacks
economics
tax

the city

the press

webcraft

the old way

sleuthing

fund managers

short termers

crash!

new economy

telecoms

smokestacks

economics

tax

So the secret is to remain agile, read the signs and not get too greedy.

Nigel Spall and Jonas Crosland

Chapter Nine

| **The New Economy** |

the city
the press
webcraft
the old way
sleuthing
fund managers
short termers
crash!
new economy
telecoms
smokestacks
economics
tax

Investing in the technology sector is pure, unbridled, white-knuckle excitement. It's about investing in the inventions and toys of the future, keeping your fingers crossed and your eyes shut, and praying your chosen stock will be the next Microsoft, the next Intel, the next IBM – or alternatively, praying that your stock will be bought out by Microsoft, Intel or IBM.

We've all heard the stories of the lucky punters who bought into a share at 10p a go and watched it fly up to £10. And we all want to live that dream. Imagine – you invest £1,000 of your hard-earned cash in Greatidea plc. The shares are trading at 10p a time so your £1,000 buys you around 9,800 shares after dealing costs and the like. Then, just one week later, the stock doubles to 20p, making your investment worth around £1,960. The next week it doubles again to 40p, and so on, until say, after three months, the shares are up at £10. You sell your 9,800 shares in Greatidea for £10 each and make £98,000, before tax. Then, after you sell, the shares fall to, say, £5 and stay there for the next six months. Pure bliss. And exactly the sort of rags-to-riches stories great investment tales are made of.

What you don't tend to hear are the stories about the unlucky investors who put their £1,000 into Greatidea shares when the stock was trading at £10 each. But someone must have invested at that level because, putting it very crudely, for every seller there has to be a buyer and vice versa. So imagine for a minute you are the unlucky one. You pay your £1,000 out and get around ninety-eight

the city
the press
webcraft
the old way
sleuthing
fund managers
short termers
crash!
new economy
telecoms
smokestacks
economics
tax

Greatidea shares, after dealing costs and so on. The very next week the stock has fallen sharply and is trading at £5 a time. Your £1,000 is now worth around £490. What do you do? Sell and cut your losses – after all, the stock could be heading back to 10p, which would value your £1,000 investment at £9.80. Or do you sit it out and hope the stock picks up? After all, this time next year it could be worth £20, which would make your ninety-eight shares worth around £1,960.

Clearly we all want to be in the lucky punters camp. While we all know that investing in technology shares is generally categorised as 'high risk', we are all hoping that that 'high risk' investment has the potential to translate into an extremely 'high reward'. The trouble is, in recent years, the success stories seem to have outweighed the horror stories. And that has made making money out of technology shares look easy.

By way of example, just before Christmas 1998 shares in On-Line, then a little-known Internet company, were trading at around 12.5p. Since the stock was so tightly held, mainly by the company's directors, it didn't take too much demand for the shares to force the stock price higher. Just a month later the shares were at £1.29. A year later, in January 2000, the shares were changing hands at £7. They went on to touch a high of almost £16 and fell back to a fiver.

But 1999 was key for the technology sector in the UK as a whole. Several events that year, including the On-Line phenomenon, really turned investors' heads – particularly private investors' heads.

While putting money into On-Line was like backing the 250 to 1 horse in the Grand National, shares in what many now regard as 'core' and 'stable' companies were also showing big gains in their share prices. The technology sector was beginning to look like a 'dead cert'. Take ARM Holdings, the chip designer, and Psion, the hand-held computer maker. ARM stock started 1999 at around 325p a share and closed the year at £41.77. Likewise Psion stock was quoted at 582p in early 1999 and finished the year at £27.

Private investors were also spurred on by flotations, or IPOs, which came back into fashion in a major way. The big example here is Freeserve, which started life as part of retail chain Dixons. Back in 1999, Dixons took the decision to float the Internet Service Provider (ISP) on the London Stock Exchange. It also took the more unusual step of offering shares in Freeserve to Freeserve's subscribers – partly as a way of rewarding them for their loyalty. The eXchange Holdings, a personal finance portal, also offered shares to the public when it floated shortly after Freeserve and a plethora of others have also followed suit, including, most famously, lastminute.com.

While tech stocks took a cold shower, like the rest of the stock market, over the summer months of 1999, all hell broke lose in autumn when the Stock Exchange launched techMARK – the technology market. FTSE launched two new indices in November – the FTSE techMARK 100 and the FTSE techMARK All Share – to help investors monitor the performance of the sector. And so the Internet/technology gold rush began in earnest.

The techMARK 100 launched at a base level of 2,000 index points in November. By the end of 1999 it stood at around 3,500 points, and by 6 March it was up at 5,743.3 points. This was driven partly by investors' appetite for Internet companies, and partly by the performance of the Nasdaq, a share market in the US dominated

the city
the press
webcraft
the old way
sleuthing
fund managers
short termers
crash!
new economy
telecoms
smokestacks
economics
tax

by technology companies. In November the Nasdaq Composite index was at around the 3,100 level; by the end of 1999 it was at around 4,000 points and by 10 March, it was up at 5,048.64 points.

The end result was that everyone started to forget about the dreaded Year 2000 computing issue, which had dogged the technology sector in the latter part of 1999, and began to look for the next big Internet/technology company. Indeed, by mid-March, thirteen techMARK stocks were also members of the FTSE 100 index. The massive gains in technology companies' share prices made investing in the sector look easy and exciting, and that proved to be the seductive catalyst for many new private investors. Everything seemed to be going up and everyone wanted a part of it.

No one was really ready for what many considered to be a bloodbath in the technology sector, which occurred at the end of March 2000 when tech share prices lost, on average, around 35 per cent over five weeks. At the end of March the techMARK 100 index stood at around 4,300 points while Nasdaq was back down to around 4,500 points.

If we can learn anything from this period, it is that the sector has been, is and most likely will continue to be extremely volatile. After all, market professionals are only human, and while everyone loves a good story you can only hear a good story so many times until it bores you to tears. Volatility comes with the tech stomping ground and is here to stay.

The Internet/Technology Gold Rush of 1999 and the Emerging Trends

This volatility is both terrifying and exciting. It is also fun – as long as you can cope with the rollercoaster ride of stress that accompanies it. And one of the main reasons, if not the main reason, the technology sector will always be characterised by volatility is that there will always be some new company claiming to be the next big thing – or some new cunning plan that will change the way we live.

When the technology good times started to roll in November 1999, there was indiscriminate buying of everything technology-related across the board. Likewise, when technology shares hit hard times in March 2000, there was indiscriminate selling of all technology-related shares. The best possible outcome of the volatility would be that investors began to analyse more carefully which stocks might make it and which might not. But that is only achievable up to a point. After all, one of the reasons technology investors love the sector is because they believe they are buying into what might be the next big thing. Since no one has a fully functioning and accurate crystal ball, much is taken on trust, hope and faith, and that sort of optimism can't really be analysed in a meaningful way.

The Internet/technology gold rush of 1999 is, however, entirely understandable. Suddenly, the Internet was really taking off. The price of personal computers came down, access to the Internet became free, telephone call charges started to fall, and so on. Suddenly you could access the Internet over a mobile phone and suddenly there was the prospect of getting the Web on your TV,

the city
the press
webcraft
the old way
sleuthing
fund managers
short termers
crash!
new economy
telecoms
smokestacks
economics
tax

too. People began to latch on to the fact that there really might be something in the Internet after all, and people wanted to invest in the companies shaping the future.

Undoubtedly the Internet was the key driver in the whole phenomenon simply because it was so wide-reaching. All companies, if they geared up to the Internet future, stood to benefit. Being able to access the Internet over next-generation mobile phones (see Chapter Ten), including WAP devices, through the TV, the PC and, indeed, through fridges, microwaves or other such appliances, meant a whole new market had opened up – the world of e-commerce, or buying over the Internet. Companies could suddenly talk directly to their customers over the Net, which meant they suddenly had access to an enormous and very valuable database of opinion.

To the investor, every Internet-related stock looked like the second coming. It also meant the Internet looked as important a development as the Industrial Revolution. Unsurprisingly everyone wanted in and they wanted in on the ground floor – simply because they couldn't see the ceiling.

Consequently, companies with cunning Web plans started springing up left, right and centre and dot.com mania truly began. And these companies were quick to realise that the magic words were Internet, portal, website and WAP. Put an announcement through the Stock Exchange peppered with those golden nuggets and the share price would rocket. Alternatively, if a company wanted to raise a bit of cash all it needed to do was whisper the Web word.

Take CMG, an IT company. It started talking about the opportunities in mobile phones in 1999 and began to put a few WAP announcements out into the public domain. Once word got round that it might be a beneficiary of the Internet-over-the-mobile-phone boom, its shares flew through the roof. At the beginning of November 1999, the shares were at around £24. Just three months later they had almost trebled in value to around £70. The company has since split its shares – that is, divided each share into several, so each share is worth less but investors hold more – and, at the time of writing they were back close to the levels reached in December.

Another major trend to emerge was the rise of the Internet/technology 'incubators'. The idea of the incubator (a company set up to take stakes in private businesses it hopes will morph into tech giants) was basically borrowed from the US. British-based stockbroker Durlacher was quick off the blocks to spot the potential in the idea and embraced it with glee. Its shares went through the roof. Masses of Internet incubators then followed suit and floated on London's markets. These included, to name just a few, NewMedia Spark, e-capital investments, JellyWorks and Legendary Investments.

Indeed the period was characterised by a plethora of flotations across the sector. From November to March, the markets were flooded with companies saying they were the next big thing, raising money and listing on the stock markets. At the time, it seemed standard for a couple of new companies a day to announce their flotation plans. The other phenomenon that came back into fashion was offering shares to the general public. The most famous example here, of course, is lastminute.com, where private investors famously got only thirty-five shares each for their trouble.

But the Internet/technology gold rush wasn't just the preserve of those already in or 'up and coming' in the technology sector –

the city
the press
webcraft
the old way
sleuthing
fund managers
short termers
crash!
new economy
telecoms
smokestacks
economics
tax

the city
the press
webcraft
the old way
sleuthing
fund managers
short termers
crash!
new economy
telecoms
smokestacks
economics
tax

or the New Economy companies as they have since been nick-named. As we demonstrated in the previous chapter, the Old Economy companies were cashing in too.

It looked dead easy for an Old Economy company to revive its flagging share price. All it had to do was either announce a Web plan of its own or sell off its old businesses, turn itself into a 'cash shell', and buy in someone else's Web plan. The magic formula seemed to be – sell old business, announce cunning Web plan, raise cash, buy new Web business and change name. Simple.

Villiers, formerly a small engineer, did more or less just that. It sold off all its engineering assets, talked about the Internet, bought a company called Ultramind for its Internet stress-management products, raised some cash and changed its name to Ultrasis. When the company was boring old engineer Villiers, the stock was at around 10p. Once the Web plan got out, the share price moved up to around 40p and then on further to around 70p.

One of the major ironies of the gold rush period was that unexciting and uninspiring businesses, or indeed businesses in trouble, could announce an Internet plan which would push the share price up. The company would then raise money at these higher levels and could buy in another company's profit stream – thereby disguising its own shortcomings.

The Internet/technology gold rush represented a unique window of opportunity for those willing to take it. While the market may not be so receptive to such goings-on again in our lifetimes, the point is that if the volatility in technology share prices is here to stay then we need to know how best to protect ourselves. And that means trying to decide which of our beloved Internet/technology investments might be around in five years' time.

How to Spot the Winners in the 'New Economy'

Trying to pick out the winners is obviously much easier said than done. Particularly since decent analysis on the technology sector is far more difficult to come by than, say, decent analysis on the supermarket sector. That is mainly because all supermakets sell food while there are many strings to the technology sector's bow, and very few technology companies are therefore comparable – i.e. they don't all make chips.

That aside, the same basic principles apply when investing in the tech sector as when investing in any other sector. Common sense is key, as is a healthy portion of cynicism and a sprinkling of luck for good measure. Get the hard facts, read the analysis and comment, and check out the gossip.

The starting point for any investment decision has to be in gathering as much information as possible. Get hold of a company's annual report and accounts, find out what it does, how big the marketplace is and who its competitors are.

Much of this information is available over the Internet, so get the hard facts from the horse's mouth. The company's own six- and twelve-month figures will usually be available on-line on its own website, as will a synopsis of what it actually does, how it is faring and where it is heading. Also read all the announcements the company delivers via the Stock Exchange's Regulatory News Service (RNS). These are now available free of charge on the Internet at websites like www.sharepages.com. See Chapter Three for more details.

What you're looking for are signs that your chosen company is dynamic. In an ideal world you'd see a well-balanced board of

the city
the press
webcraft
the old way
sleuthing
fund managers
short termers
crash!
new economy
telecoms
smokestacks
economics
tax

directors that included a stable old-timer as well as some techie experts, some serious businessmen, charismatic salesmen and an A-list market celebrity.

You'd also expect to see a decent product, idea or plan and, depending on the company's age, you'd look for signs of credibility – alliances and/or joint ventures with big, established, well-known names. You have to ask yourself how big the market is for the company's product, who its competitors are and whether it stands a cat's chance in hell of delivering and building a successful brand. Is there a story to tell, someone clever to tell it and sell it, and someone to buy it?

Collecting expert opinion is equally important, both from analysts in the investment community and from independent research houses. Find out what the City has to say on the stock, but bear in mind that the company's own broker will always produce research that leans towards the positive, since it obviously doesn't want to bite the hand that feeds. So find out what other investment analysts have to say about the company too. While a few years back your chances of getting access to this information would have been like gaining entry to the Magic Circle, the Internet has democratised the flow of information. Websites like multex and hemscott (again, see Chapter Three), as well as investment banks' own websites, tend to dish out a lot of info. The same sources will also provide crucial historic data as well as share price history.

In an ideal world, you'd be looking for the company to have secured a Premier League or Division 1–3 broker – often one of the big American banks – or, failing that, a respected broker with a decent history and a decent list of clients. Another important factor is the shareholder list. Better to rub shoulders with IBM or

Intel and some serious heavyweight institutional backers like 3i or Barclays than with just the chief executive, his mum, his granny and her poodle.

You'll also want to check that the company's profits or losses are moving in the right direction (increasing or decreasing respectively), that turnover is going up, that costs are being kept under control, that a decent but not too large sum is being spent on research and development, and that staff numbers are growing. Furthermore you'll need to know that there is a decent amount of cash in the bank in case the company hits hard times, or if it finds itself not making money and needs the cash to finance its activities. If that is the case, you need to know how long that cash will last and when the company will need to raise more money.

Knowing the opinions of independent-sector experts is vital too. Again these are available on the Web. Research houses like Forrester, IDC, Dataquest and Gartner offer the investor insight into current trends and thinking in the sector. Their research will give you an idea of a company's marketplace, how big it might be and who its competitors are.

It might sound obvious but read the financial press too. Try to get a consensus view on what they make of the business and read what the tipsters and commentators are saying. If you genuinely believe in a company when the whole world has united against it, there is no point burying your head in the sand. While you might ultimately be proven right over the long term, chances are that the poor sentiment towards the business will be damaging over the short term.

Finally read the gossip on the company. Your level-headed and serious sources of research should be the main ingredients for your

cake, but the gossip is the icing. Go to the Internet chat rooms and bulletin boards and read the market reports of the daily City press for those titbits of information which often drive prices.

To be honest, most company data can be used as a decent remedy for insomnia. Anything which spices it up a bit, drags it kicking and screaming into the twenty-first century, brings it to life and makes it fun, is just as valuable. That's what we at TheStreet.co.uk are trying to do.

Hopefully, after all your hard work you will end up with a well-rounded, balanced view of the company. And with any luck, your information will have given you a better idea of whether it will be around next year, in five and in ten years' time. You should also have a good idea of its goals, what it needs to do to achieve them, and what signs to look out for along the way. And, in case of emergency, who is likely to pick it up and support it if hard times hit.

Newcomers vs Old Hands

Bearing all of the above in mind, it is also important to draw a very thick line in the sand between the newcomers in the technology sector and the old hands, and likewise between those companies that are highly valued by the market and those that are worth just a couple of million.

It is easy to find masses of information about companies that have been around five years or more, and likewise for companies that are worth a lot of money. But for young and/or small technology companies, there is scant information available with which to make a sound judgment. Consequently, investing in these companies consists to a large extent of taking a lot on trust, shutting your eyes, and hoping for the best. Those back-of-cereal-packet risk warnings hidden in company documents are there for that very reason – to alert investors to the risks involved. The company could be the next Microsoft or it could be a complete dud. The only thing that will tell is time.

The trouble with newcomers is they are exactly that – new-comers. They are companies with an idea, a plan or a product, usually with an inexperienced management team, fighting for market share in a new and immature space.

And this is exactly the trouble with investing in anything Internet-based or anything new in technology. To put this another way, if you want to invest in the sci-fi companies of Tomorrow's World, you don't really know if you're at the wheel of a Ferrari, if you're getting into a trusty old Ford, or if you've accidentally climbed into the Trabant.

It is nigh on impossible to come up with a winning formula with which to evaluate these businesses. While we can look to the US and try to learn from their mistakes and successes, and while we can have a stab at identifying which subsectors of the technology sector might come out on top, at the end of the day the only way to judge a company is to put it under the microscope.

By this we mean judge each new situation entirely on its own merits, because some companies *will* go under – fact. While it's difficult to separate the winners from the losers when you have practically no information at your fingertips, you should still be guided by the principles you would apply to a more established company. At the end of the day, it's about deciding for yourself if the company has a decent plan and product, if it has a sufficiently

the city
the press
webcraft
the old way
sleuthing
fund managers
short termers
crash!
new economy
telecoms
smokestacks
economics
tax

the city

the press

webcraft

the old way

sleuthing

fund managers

short termers

crash!

new economy

telecoms

smokestacks

economics

tax

dynamic management team to promote its ideas, and if the market-place is sufficiently large to support several players.

Since with young companies there is usually no track record, no historic profit/loss data and nothing to compare it to, you need to use the information you have and use it wisely. Look at the management team carefully, look at what the company does and the market size, look at the sort of deals it has done and the sort it needs to pull off. And ask yourself if it can reach those milestones. Does it have a decent amount of cash to play with, does it have a decent broker and a list of quality shareholders? Will it be here next year, or in five years?

Sounds like guesswork. And, to a large degree, it is. Luck – bad or good – also goes with the territory. For example, what looks to be a decent company could run out of cash, try to raise some more, but fail because sentiment in the entire sector is adverse. Conversely something that looks like a rubbish company might also run out of money but succeed in raising more if market conditions are buoyant.

However, it is important to note that the entire sector is not a wild, out-of-control and poorly run lottery. There is a whole other tech world out there – that of the old hands. Some companies have driven round the block a few times already and clocked up a reassuring number of miles.

Now, investing in the Rolls-Royces of the sector might not be as exciting as taking the sports car for a spin, but at least with the Rollers you know you have quality, class and style.

Generally speaking the companies that the 'techxperts' reckon represent quality are those that make money, those that have a decent market share in a growing marketplace, those with a proven and quality management team, and those with tangible prospects.

We're talking the boring stocks here – the ones that rarely disappoint, the ones that have been there, done that, got the T-shirt, the ones that are in all the technology fund managers' portfolios under the 'stable' heading. These are the stocks that are in the FTSE 100 index or, at the very least, the FTSE 350. We're talking about Sage, Logica, CMG, Sema, and so on. They've been around for a long time (in tech years) and chances are – at least as things stand at the time of writing – they will be around for a good few years yet. Fortunately, there will always be demand for quality, or for what is perceived as quality.

Nowhere is this more evident than in the new issues arena. Of the companies floated on the market in the period of instability in March and April 2000, the ones that weathered the storm better were the ones perceived as having 'real' technology. Conversely those who took a beating tended to be the Internet stocks.

The market loathed lastminute.com (although in the unpredictable world of tech stocks, who is to say that the market won't revise its opinion?). While it got its flotation away in the nick of time and the shares registered an initial premium, it wasn't long before the market savaged it. Lastminute floated at 380p on 14 March. By mid May its shares were swapping hands at around 125p.

On the flipside, take Bookham Technology. It floated on the market at the worst possible time – right in the middle of the tech sector downturn – but, since it was perceived as quality, it rode the storm and continued to trade at a healthy premium throughout. It came to the market at £10 a share on 12 April, rose to a huge premium, and did not dip below its original price during the whole period of instability.

the city

the press

webcraft

the old way

sleuthing

fund managers

short termers

crash!

new economy

telecoms

smokestacks

economics

tax

the city
the press
webcraft
the old way
sleuthing
fund managers
short termers
crash!
new economy
telecoms
smokestacks
economics
tax

Investing in the technology sector is about doing your home-work, putting your money where your mouth is and, to an extent, luck. This may be in the form of an upbeat broker's assessment, an avaricious predator, a successful business model and a dynamic business team, or simply excellent market sentiment. But it is also, to a degree, about damage limitation and being aware of the danger signs.

Warning Signs to Look Out For

Not all technology stocks were created equal. This is why investing in the sector is fun. While the herd mentality of technology investors means the shares move together, it is crucial to be aware of the warning signs if your chosen stock is having trouble getting off the starting block.

How do you recognise if you've invested in the Trabant and not in the Ferrari before it's too late? It is very, very rare for a company to be doing okay one day and the next minute to go bust. It usually takes a good couple of years for a company to really fall apart.

So what are the warning signs and when should you jump ship?

There are key warning signs for when the technology sector as a whole is looking a bit 'toppy'. These include the river of IPOs – when companies first float on the stock market – slowing down to a stream, becoming a trickle and then drying up altogether. So when companies are still floating but not quite managing to raise as much money or get the kind of valuation they hoped for – take heed. The same applies to companies that are trying to raise money on the markets. When they raise cash, but not as much as they wanted, sit up and take note. To put it bluntly, it means investors are becoming less tolerant – even bored – and that is a worry.

Usually, by the time companies are cancelling or postponing flotations as well as cancelling fund-raising exercises, it is too late. By this point the market is normally being ripped apart. Take Yes Television by way of example. It stated its intention to float on 20 March 2000 and on 17 April, at the height of the sector's troubles, announced it was postponing its float owing to market conditions. Just two days later, on 19 April, the float was back on again as a result of market sentiment improving slightly, only to be cancelled in May.

As for the warning signs to look for in specific stocks, perhaps one of the initial signs is when your chosen stock fails to keep up with the herd – i.e., when the good times roll, it doesn't go up, or it doesn't go up as much as the others. This generally implies that when the hard times hit, it will be absolutely trashed.

☐ Watch out for periods of silence. It doesn't take a genius to figure out that when a company has good news it will be shouting it from the rooftops. Companies know this. So when they go quiet, the chances are it means there is nothing good to say.

☐ Scrutinise the company's figures. If turnover, profit and so on are going the wrong way without explanation – start worrying. If cash is running out, or there is none, start really worrying.

☐ Profit warnings. Companies tend to set themselves hurdles they believe they can easily clear, because they know the market loves a pleasant surprise. When a company issues a warning it's basically saying it has cocked up. If, after a warning, the company radically changes its ways, cuts costs, changes direction, changes management, reviews strategy and so on, it might deserve a second

the city
the press
webcraft
the old way
sleuthing
fund managers
short termers
crash!
new economy
telecoms
smokestacks
economics
tax

chance. If it carries on regardless, hoping market conditions will change for the better, be wary. It might be in denial.

☐ Fund-raisings. When a company raises money for no other purpose than to stay alive, it is in trouble. Big trouble. What you need to look out for in those raisings, is how well they are taken up. In other words, what percentage of existing investors were prepared to put their hands back into their pockets to help the company out? This is a very crude but pretty effective measure of how quickly patience is running out.

☐ Resignations. If any of the directors, brokers, accountants, advisers leave without proper explanation, take note. Either this is a sign that things might get better or it is a sign there is much worse to come.

Other indications that all is not well are when a company's major shareholders start selling, and when those shareholders aren't replaced. Likewise, if the company's own directors haven't bought any stock for a while, why should anyone else? If the directors believe in the business, then a falling share price should represent a massive buying opportunity. If no one is buying, why should you?

This list is by no means comprehensive – just a guide to some of the louder warning bells. The problem for the private investor, though, is not just recognising the warning signs, it is acting on them, and selling. This to a large extent is psychological – it's about admitting you're wrong and giving up hope.

And this is rarely going to be easy, since investing in technology shares is like planting acorns. You water them every day, give them the right amount of sunlight, do everything by the book, and wait for the day when they start showing new shoots of growth and turning into oak trees. It is very difficult to give up on your acorn, chuck it on the compost heap and walk away without looking over your shoulder. But sometimes this is exactly what you need to do. The temptation is to cling on to your investment, believe what the management tells its shareholders – that it really is turning the corner this time and that things really will get better – and ride out the storm.

Again, the only thing to do is judge each company on its own merits – listen to what the company says, listen to what the experts say, and read the gossip. It could be that the company might be about to stage a comeback, or it could be that it's dead in the water.

It is vital to understand that not all technology stocks will make it. Some won't. So if you think for one moment that you've invested in a Trabant – get out before the engine falls off.

Tactics for the More Cautious Investor and Tactics for the Gambler

If investing in the technology sector all sounds like a bit too much effort and stress, there are a number of ways to 'play ball' but with a reduced risk.

If you're going it alone, the old rule of 'never invest more than you're prepared to lose' has to be ringing in your ears. If you want to take less risk, don't just put your entire lump sum into Greatidea.com. Spread it among a portfolio of technology shares that includes the good, the bad and the ugly. Buy shares in the old hands, shares in those who occupy the middle ground, and shares in the rank outsiders.

If you want someone to take the decisions for you, invest in a

the city
the press
webcraft
the old way
sleuthing
fund managers
short termers
crash!
new economy
telecoms
smokestacks
economics
tax

the city

the press

webcraft

the old way

sleuthing

fund managers

short termers

crash!

new economy

telecoms

smokestacks

economics

tax

technology fund. That way the fund manager has the stress of picking the stocks, and the stress of taking the buy and sell decisions, while you, fingers crossed and sentiment permitting, enjoy the upside.

Technology incubators are also worth considering. Basically they are a way of investing in unquoted technology companies. In principle, the idea is a great one. The incubator invests money in a selection of unquoted technology companies and in return receives a stake in those businesses. The hope is that the unquoted companies are bought, or float on the stock market, so that the incubator realises its investment. This enables the private investor to enjoy the potentially large gains to be had in private companies. As ever, though, it is vital to be very selective in the choice of incubator, simply because there are so many. Some will prove to be successes and others will be out-and-out failures. Analysing the flow of deals and the members of the management team is vital.

Staying with the incubator theme, perhaps a less risky way of investing is to buy shares in a profitable business with an incubator attached to it as well. Two companies that spring to mind at the time of writing are both stockbrokers – Durlacher and Beeson Gregory. Both have the safety net of a profitable broking business and both offer the upside of the incubator. However, there is a plethora of similar stocks out there following the same model. Even ICL, a major information technology company, which is expected to float on the market at some point over 2000, has an incubator business. 3i – a traditional venture-capital fund – should also be considered. It is an experienced investment fund, and looks widely across the technology sector.

Since the biotechnology sector is, in some ways, similar to

the technology sector, it can only be a matter of time before biotechnology incubators start mushrooming at the same speed as the technology incubators. Again the same warnings apply, and scrutinising the flow of deals will be crucial.

If, on the other hand, risk is your game and you want to increase it, then spread betting has to be for you (see Chapter One). The advantage in this is that while you increase your risk, if your bet comes off there is no Capital Gains Tax to pay. It also gives you a relatively uncomplicated way of being able to 'short' shares on the market – in other words, make money out of the market if you think it is going to fall. However, while the gains can be spectacular (there are well-known stories of folk retiring on winnings they made in just a few weeks) the losses can be monstrous too.

In the technology sector, the risks and rewards of stockmarket investment are multiplied. You will never get a supermarket share increasing ten, fifty, one hundred times in value over a one-month, six-month, one-year period. This is the potential excitement that the technology sector offers. Likewise, those same supermarket shares are unlikely to lose all their value as quickly as they gained it. This is the rollercoaster of volatility the technology sector offers.

Don't invest more than you can afford to lose and enjoy the thrill of the chase. It might take you to the moon and back, and if you're really lucky, back to the moon again and then on to Mars. Investing in the technology sector is about playing with fireworks in a sauna. Not about watching paint dry.

Liz Vaughan-Adams

the city
the press
webcraft
the old way
sleuthing
fund managers
short termers
crash!
new economy
telecoms
smokestacks
economics
tax

Chapter Ten

It's Good to Talk A Brief Foray into Telecommunications

the city
the press
webcraft
the old way
sleuthing
fund managers
short termers
crash!
new economy
telecoms
smokestacks
economics
tax

Like the technology sector, the world of telecoms is frenetic, exciting and constantly changing. Driven by the trend away from fixed towards mobile communication, and the growth of data communications via the Internet, the industry is converging fast, and its formerly bureaucratic incumbents are constantly being challenged by new entrants and new technologies.

The rate of all this change is so great that any analysis we offer today will be out of date by tomorrow. What we can do, however, is take you on a whistlestop tour of the industry and its terminology so that at the very least you will know your IP from your ISP and be able to recognise the main telecoms players.

The Landscape

In Europe, telecom operators vary from the large European incumbents who own extensive networks within their national borders to pure resellers with little or no infrastructure. The former embrace such giants as BT and Deutsche Telekom, and the latter include smaller start-ups like Spain's Jazztel and Scotland's Thus and Atlantic Telecom.

Sandwiched in between is a plethora of operators who lease or own some or all of their telecom infrastructure. Most of these 'new entrants', or alternative telcos, as they are known, focus on the

the city
the press
webcraft
the old way
sleuthing
fund managers
short termers
crash!
new economy
telecoms
smokestacks
economics
tax

business sector. However, in the residential sector, BT's competitors, namely the cable companies, have built dense local networks to exploit several revenue streams – cable, telecom and Internet – from the residential customer base.

As we have said, the telecom industry is experiencing phenomenal technological change. Historically, telecom traffic was primarily voice-related, and the networks were originally designed to meet this demand. Increasingly, however, the bulk of traffic is – or is soon expected to be – data, driven by the burgeoning use of the Internet. Telecoms analysts predict that the emergence of new technology will eventually lead to a single network architecture suited for both voice and data traffic.

Finding Your Way

Figuring out how to invest in the telecoms sector can be tricky. For a start, while segmenting the market by type of company was a relatively easy thing to do in the past, the boundaries between the players are becoming increasingly blurred as the sector converges. Furthermore, like Internet companies, many of the players in the telecoms industry defy traditional valuation tools as their value often depends on future usage. Are most telcos overvalued? The answer really depends on your view of the future.

If you believe the networked home will be with us soon and your family will be doing lots of 'gee-whiz' multimedia, interactive things on multiple devices; that we will all be walking around with webphones sending video clips to each other and reading electronic newspapers on hand-held devices rather than the old-fashioned paper versions – then most business plans look quite conservative.

However, if you subscribe to the view that it will be a long time before these things are truly part of everyday life, then, yes, you will want to think carefully about valuations of telecom conpanies.

What is certain is that the incumbents must keep pace with acquisitions and investments if they are to remain competitive alongside the new alternative operators, and consolidation in the industry is likely to continue.

If you are looking to invest in the telecoms sector then you too will need to move swiftly and keep abreast of the different types of players. It is interesting to note that a portfolio of new entrants, taken out at the beginning of 1997, would by now have significantly outperformed a portfolio of incumbents over the same time period. This is partly because the established PTOs (Public Telephone Operators) have been buying the relatively new players – witness Deutsche Telekom snapping up One-2-One, and France Telecom's purchase of Orange – and, as a result, increasing the share prices of those players.

It is also vital that you watch developments carefully if you are to successfully navigate the choppy waters of changing technology, regulation and the ever mutating ownership of the main players. In terms of technology, be warned that the biggest uncertainty often revolves around not whether a new technology will work, but how long it will take for market and customer acceptance of that new technology to come to fruition.

Bearing this in mind, it is worth having a quick look at some of the technological developments that have already revolutionised the telecoms industry, if only to equip yourself with the knowhow to translate the many acronyms that pepper this sector.

the city
the press
webcraft
the old way
sleuthing
fund managers
short termers
crash!
new economy
telecoms
smokestacks
economics
tax

Fixed Wire Networks

Today, the bulk of telecom traffic is still carried over fixed wire networks. For long-distance transmission, most of the traffic is carried over fibre-based networks. Fibre is the technology used by the cable operators and is significantly superior to the old copper wire network owned by BT. BT is spending a considerable amount of capital upgrading its networks.

The final mile of the local area networks is still predominantly copper-based. This mile is known in the industry as the 'golden mile', since crucially it enters home and office buildings.

Fibre

In the next few years network capacity demands will grow explosively as more people are connected to the Internet, increasingly through mobile devices as well as fixed terminals. They will spend more time on-line and access higher-bandwidth, interactive multimedia services. Long-haul fibre capacities will need to keep pace with the growing demand for bandwidth. Those companies that can satisfy ever increasing demand for bandwidth will certainly enjoy success.

The good news is that, if anything, developments in fibre capacity technology are outpacing the growth in demand. Dense Wave Division Multiplexing (DWDM) works by splitting the light wave in the fibre into different wavelengths (like colours), each able to carry a separate stream of information. At the same time, advanced high-speed electronics can squeeze more data on to each wavelength.

Apart from the backbone carriers, the other principal users of fibre have been the cable companies that have built fibre-rich local loop networks. With the advent of cable modems offering very high-speed Internet access, these cable networks seem attractively positioned. But a potential threat to the cable companies is ADSL.

ADSL

ADSL (Asynchronous Digital Subscriber Line) allows high-speed data transfer using traditional copper voice telephony lines. It is not a particularly new technology, but it seems finally to be coming of age as technical developments have made it more reliable and less expensive to install.

ADSL is principally being rolled out by incumbent PTOs to compete with high-speed cable fibre networks. BT has a multi-billion-pound ADSL roll-out programme in the UK.

Rolling out ADSL is an expensive exercise as incumbents will need to invest significant sums to replace switches throughout the network to be able to provide multimedia services to customers.

Mobile

As mentioned earlier, the other key driver on the telecoms scene – apart from the trend towards high-speed data communications – is the trend towards mobility.

The first round of Global Standard for Mobile (GSM) communication licences was issued around 1990 in the UK to two operators, Vodafone and BTCellnet, and are operative in the 900MHz frequency area. In all European countries, two or more 900MHz

the city
the press
webcraft
the old way
sleuthing
fund managers
short termers
crash!
new economy
telecoms
smokestacks
economics
tax

the city
the press
webcraft
the old way
sleuthing
fund managers
short termers
crash!
new economy
telecoms
smokestacks
economics
tax

licences have been awarded for a period of fifteen to twenty years.

The UK was the first European country to issue additional 1800MHz licences (DCS or GSM-1800) to Orange and One-2-One, which became operational in 1993. Germany followed in 1994 with E-Plus, and France in 1996 with Bouygues. Subsequently, all European countries have issued two or more 1800MHz.

In layman's terms, GSM-900 frequencies are 'wider' than GSM-1800. They therefore travel farther and cover a bigger geographic area. Consequently, achieving full coverage of a country will require fewer cell stations with a GSM-900 network than with a GSM-1800.

Wireless data opportunities have been touted as the next big thing for operators in European mobile telecom markets hoping to cream off much of the revenue generated by Internet access and data transmission. In the past, wireless transmission speed has been a limiting factor. However, the new wireless technologies are improving wireless data speeds all the time. There are two main ways of increasing the speed. The first is through General Packet Radio Service (GPRS), which introduces packet switching capabilities to GSM. The second is through Third Generation (3G) technologies.

3G

3G mobile telecommunications are more often known as UMTS (Universal Mobile Telecommunications System). The UK was the first country to hold an auction for 3G licences. This auction, held in April 2000, raised a mammoth £22.5 billion for the UK government and was won by TIW of Canada and the four incumbents, Vodafone, BT, One-2-One and Orange.

UMTS is a new communications standard, providing data rates at speeds up to two hundred times faster than GSM (up to 2Mbps). These very high data rates open up the possibility of transmitting information in a number of formats – voice, pictures, text, audio and video clips, and software applications. Here are just some of the potential uses:

☐ Internet and intranet access
☐ News
☐ E-commerce, on-line banking, shopping
☐ Video conferencing
☐ Access to radio and TV broadcasts and video-on-demand
☐ Interactive games

WAP

WAP (Wireless Application Protocol) is another very important technological breakthrough, which opens up countless possibilities for the future of telephony. WAP is a clever new system that recognises the type of device that is asking for information and configures the data to suit – for example, putting it into a format suitable for display on a mobile phone screen.

Already there are joint ventures being put into place, such as the one between Ericsson and Reuters, to develop personalised news and information services. Some analysts have speculated that these services could be financed by advertising rather than paid for by the subscriber.

the city
the press
webcraft
the old way
sleuthing
fund managers
short termers
crash!
new economy
telecoms
smokestacks
economics
tax

Internet Protocol (IP)

Internet Protocol, as the name suggests, was designed for Internet use – basically transmitting data. Although IP is hardly new, the convergence of telecoms and computers is now actually happening, driven by the widespread adoption of digital standards – the 0s and 1s of binary computer language – and the growing acceptance of the packet-switched technology underpinning Internet-based data communications.

But as voice and data communications converge, the logic of combining separate networks becomes compelling. Voice over IP used to be of poor quality, but technical improvements now mean it is hard to distinguish it from a normal circuit-switched call. Today, it is possible to eliminate these potential voice quality problems using a virtual private network or managed network, whereby the IP network can ensure that capacity is available between the starting and ending points of the call so that the 'packets' (small lumps of information) arrive on time and in order.

Traditional telecoms operators are aware of this threat to their voice business, which is why they are developing their data and Internet businesses as rapidly as possible. Low-cost IP telephony is growing rapidly, and is one of the drivers behind falling tariffs on the traditional voice business of the PTOs.

Satellite

Satellite seems to have fallen out of favour, in particular with financiers, especially since the well-publicised problems of Iridium and ICO. Satellite mobile phone services have also failed to take off, although this is mainly because of the expense involved. However, satellite-delivered TV services continue to be an important sector; BSkyB is the leading provider of digital TV services in the UK using satellite technology.

Bluetooth

According to a certain investment banker, the name was not, as Bluetooth's website suggests, derived from that of an eleventh-century Viking; it was, in fact, conjured up in a bar in Denmark by a bunch of geeks who were fed up with all the annoying acronyms used in the telecom market.

Bluetooth is a new short-range radio connectivity standard that will basically allow us to get rid of wires. No longer will those irritating mobile telephone earpiece wires dangle from your ear. You will simply pop a little device in your ear and it will communicate with your phone – even if it is in your pocket or handbag.

In the office, computers, mice, printers, keyboards, phones, organisers will all work together without a jungle of cables. But according to some analysts, the most revolutionary impact of this technology may be in the home – Bluetooth will allow domestic appliances to communicate with each other without the need for ugly wiring.

The vision is of a New Age home where your mobile phone acts like a central server connecting all domestic appliances. You will be able to switch on the kettle, turn on the TV, the lights, set the burglar alarm, turn on the heating, draw the curtains and set the video just by pressing buttons on your phone.

★   ★   ★

the city
the press
webcraft
the old way
sleuthing
fund managers
short termers
crash!
new economy
telecoms
smokestacks
economics
tax

The above provides only a snapshot of the technology developments taking place within the telecoms industry. To take the plunge into this sector it is vital that you, as an investor, stay as well informed and up to date as possible. Apply the same rigorous criteria you would use in assessing a dotcom company to telecoms companies that attract your attention. There is a host of information readily available in all kinds of formats, from the trade press and the Internet to industry reports and newspaper features. Don't be afraid to immerse yourself in it. The telecoms industry is fascinating, fast-moving and full of potential stock market winners – the difficulty, as ever, lies in picking the right ones.

Annemarie Quill

Chapter Eleven

Smokestacks – Why You Shouldn't Ignore the Old Economy

the city
the press
webcraft
the old way
sleuthing
fund managers
short termers
crash!
new economy
telecoms
smokestacks
economics
tax

This chapter is about investing in so-called Old Economy stocks. The normal reaction of many a private investor on reading these words is to turn the page. Hardly surprising, given that conventional wisdom, or whatever passes for it in today's Net-crazed markets, dictates 'New Age good, Old Age bad'. On this basis, anything with dot.com, dot.co.uk or dot.net in its company name is worth a punt. On the other hand, anything with 'metals', 'engineering' or 'manufacturing' in its name is to be treated with scepticism.

Such sweeping generalisations are, of course, a lot of tosh. Fads come and go but, as any idiot knows, the one thing that sustains share prices over the long term is a solid earnings stream. You need profits to do this – and this chapter will look at a sector that has made plenty of them in the past and continues to make them today. Industrial stocks may not be sexy, but they can be a lot safer than some here-today-who-knows-what-tomorrow tech stocks. There, we've held your attention long enough – hopefully – to interest you in the subject.

Back to Basics

So if tech stocks are flaky, risky and basically a bit of a nightmare for the uninitiated, why have they been so popular?

There is no simple answer to this, other than to point out that

stock market bubbles seldom require a logical explanation. Some people, of course, made a lot of money simply by buying shares in companies they knew nothing about – a lemming's delight. Indeed, logic doesn't really come into the equation at all when one considers the tech sector boom on the stock market.

Investors could quite reasonably have looked at the heady ratings commanded by some tech stocks in early 2000 and the seemingly inexorable rise in their share prices and wondered why they would ever want to invest in an industrial stock again.

Even some institutional investors – exceedingly well paid for their stock-picking skills but usually happy just to follow the pack for fear of missing out on the Next Big Thing – agreed. It was only the intervention of common sense in the form of limits on the percentage that a fund can put into a single stock that prevented more fund managers piling willy-nilly into the tech sector.

The flight of money into the tech sector had serious implications for the so-called smokestacks, not least in the way it demoralised chief executives throughout the sector and made them question the rationale behind their companies' stock market listings altogether. Asked by journalists what they thought of the tech sector boom, most engineering company directors simply shrugged and wrote it off as 'City madness'. The City, they believed, had never truly understood their business, so why should they pretend to understand the City's?

It was a reasonable answer in the circumstances, but ignorance of the reasons for the City's disdain for their shares simply compounded the problem. In short, if company directors don't know what the problem is they are hardly likely to be able to do something about it.

Some, however, were philosophical, including Allen Yurko, ebullient chief executive of Invensys, the controls and automation systems group formed by the merger of Siebe and BTR, the one-time Birmingham Tyre & Rubber. In his usual forthright manner, he declared: 'If you slit your wrists every time the share price dropped, you'd have pretty scarred wrists.'

Yurko believes that valuations will inevitably come back in line with the performance of the business. Industrial stocks go in and out of favour – they have before, they will again. The important thing, he believes, is for executives not to get too distracted by the issue.

A lot of other industrial company directors share this view. Most readily seize the opportunity to point out the blindingly obvious – that it is important to think of fundamentals when investing. You know, things like profits, earnings and other such old-fashioned concepts. It's easy to forget about the basics, of course. Many of the most sought-after shares in 1999 and early 2000 were little more than concepts themselves – companies that boasted a business plan, a fancy name and, er, little else. Of course, the plan – usually the best an expensive MBA education can buy – contained details of proposed future levels of business, but no real guarantee that the company could actually achieve them.

Value investors – those who buy undervalued stocks in anticipation of an eventual rise – would agree with this perception. As the so-called TMT (telecom, media and technology) stocks shot up into the stratosphere, many active investors reckoned that the time had come to move back into the Old Economy.

After all, how could they turn down a quality player like Rolls-Royce on a price-to-earnings ratio – basically the price of the share

the city
the press
webcraft
the old way
sleuthing
fund managers
short termers
crash!
new economy
telecoms
smokestacks
economics
tax

compared to the profits a company makes each year – of just 11.8, electricity generator PowerGen on 9.3, or National Power on 7.7? Many more rational stock market analysts reason that when the TMT sector runs out of steam there will be a rush back into the undervalued smokestacks. An important lesson here is not to be confused between undervalued stocks and cheap ones. Cheap ones are those on low, single-figure price-to-earnings ratings that are there because they deserve to be – commodity manufacturers with antiquated plant and no real idea about how to get out of their predicament. They should be avoided.

The theory that TMT hiccups will see a mass return to smoke-stack stocks is therefore only partly true, however. Some Old Economy stocks are likely to remain in the doldrums, particularly those stuck in low-value metal fabricating activities or those who allow the e-commerce revolution to pass them by. Many smoke-stacks are ideally placed to leverage the strength of their bricks-and-mortar operation and leapfrog e-upstarts – the evidence so far, however, suggests that many of them are only doing this slowly, and this means some stocks represent less of an opportunity for investors than others.

Challenges for Industry

Some people may see manufacturing as the bedrock of the economy – the one sector that actually makes tangible products that are sold in the open market for cold, hard cash. It's not an unreasonable starting point.

But look back to the origins of the London stock market and you'll see that the biggest quoted companies were all involved in the construction and maintenance of the railway network – companies whose time has been and gone. Say what you like about Railtrack, but the railway maintenance business simply isn't there any more in the way it once was. The world has moved on – and companies that fail to move with it will get left behind.

British manufacturing may have enjoyed a world-class reputation but the simple fact is that it has become a commodity activity. Metal bashing can be done more cheaply in sweatshops across the Far East than it could ever be done in Birmingham, Sheffield or Doncaster.

The oft-stated mantra for estate agents and successful property investors is that only three things matter: location, location, location. In a similar way, the route to success for industrial stocks is innovation, innovation, innovation.

What UK Manufacturing plc has had to do is adapt, add value and move with the times. While Far Eastern sweatshops may sweep street kids up to work for 8p an hour, they do not have the resources or technical knowhow to automate processes and increase the specialist engineering content of the products they churn out. They may make great widgets, but an automated high-tech sub-assembly? Not likely. The ability to make such products in the UK gives producers the ability to charge a premium price – that is where the future of the manufacturing industry and engineering lies.

One thing industrial company directors have still found it hard to get to grips with, however, is the double standards they perceive City analysts to have used in working out valuations of their businesses.

Conventional wisdom – and there is something to be said for convention because it's safe – has it that businesses should be

the city
the press
webcraft
the old way
sleuthing
fund managers
short termers
crash!
new economy
telecoms
smokestacks
economics
tax

valued on a multiple of either historic or projected earnings. That convention was thrown quickly out of the window by the emergence of the dot.coms in the late 1990s. Many of these businesses, however well run and well organised, did not just make a loss but in many cases had very little revenue either.

Dodgy arithmetic was the least of the punters' problems – sometimes the valuations had more to do with the enthusiasm of investors for the stock than any actual calculations. To overcome the problem of having businesses that couldn't be valued conventionally on earnings, some analysts simply looked at revenues – but this has had serious problems of its own. Even if the ratios described – sometimes they were many hundreds of times predicted future revenues – were vaguely justifiable, important questions about future profitability were just skated over as though they didn't matter.

Engineers, of course, had to justify every point of their price-to-earnings ratio – even if it was a lowly 6 or 7. In days of old, when knights were bold and monkeys chewed tobacco, it would never have occurred to investors to put money into a company they didn't understand.

But such was the frenzy for dot.com stocks that punters neither knew nor cared what the companies they were investing in actually did.

'It's some sort of Internet company' was usually reason enough to persuade people to spend their hard-earned – or hard-speculated – cash buying up shares. Investors overlooked the adage that fools and their money are soon parted – and splashed out. Barely a week went by in late 1999 and early 2000 without some dot.com Initial Public Offering (IPO) getting off to a rip-roaring start.

The way in which the tech stocks sucked in money reminded

many in the market of a previous boom which saw punters indiscriminately investing in biotech companies. Investors saw these companies as a good risk. They might come up with a must-have drug – cures for AIDS were a particular favourite as were various cancer remedies. In the end, of course, it only ended up proving that the companies were a long way from successfully concluding their research, and when the City realised this it pulled the plug.

One of the most serious challenges facing industry has been the extent to which the engineering and manufacturing sectors have been hit by exchange rate fluctuations. The pound's appreciation against the dollar and the Deutschmark was a major factor behind the falling valuations of industrial stocks, because a stronger pound makes your exports more expensive and rival imports cheaper at home. Analysts and fund managers took one look at the export exposure of a company and took fright. Not without reason – the pound gained 25 per cent against the mark between September 1996 and July 1997, and British manufacturers felt the pain as they struggled to export and witnessed a flood of cheaper imports pouring into their home market. They were caught between a rock and a hard place.

The impasse was not exactly helped by the fact that the new Labour government handed over control of monetary policy to a committee of the Bank of England. In the past politicians used interest rates as a political tool, bringing them down ahead of an election and sticking them up afterwards. Had politicians still been able to control rates they might well have brought them down now, since the constituencies in and around Birmingham are all

the city
the press
webcraft
the old way
sleuthing
fund managers
short termers
crash!
new economy
telecoms
smokestacks
economics
tax

the city
the press
webcraft
the old way
sleuthing
fund managers
short termers
crash!
new economy
telecoms
smokestacks
economics
tax

mostly marginal parliamentary seats and it doesn't take too many disheartened car workers in the West Midlands to help change the face of the House of Commons.

At the same time as foreign exchange rates changed, so too did the City's attitude to smaller companies, many of them industrial stocks, to boot. Fund managers, under increasing pressure to match their rivals' performance levels, went for bigger and bigger companies, at least guaranteeing to track the major stock market indices. In the process, they dumped dozens of smaller companies from their portfolios.

The rationale was simple enough. If they had £1 billion to invest, it was simply not worth their while buying 2 to 3 per cent of a company that was valued by the market at just £50 million.

Never mind the hassle of trying to find spare stock in some pretty illiquid companies – administering the holding and keeping tabs on what the business was up to was just too much hard work. Why bother when, instead, they could invest £100 million quite easily in HSBC, SmithKline Beecham or Vodafone AirTouch?

Short-Term Solutions to Lowly Valuations

This combination of factors led to a flight of equity out of SmallCap companies – those valued by the market at less than £50 million. The pace at which funds dumped them accelerated sharply in 1999, prompting many of these businesses to reconsider their position on the market.

If they couldn't attract the interest and enthusiasm of fund managers in their shares, they couldn't use their quoted status to raise funds for growth – and therefore faced a difficult future as an unloved stock incapable of doing anything to change the City's perception of it.

It was a Catch-22 situation, and chief executives throughout the lower echelons of the stock market watched incredulously as the value of their share option packages continued its inexorable decline.

One leading smaller companies fund manager summed up the situation neatly: 'I have to match my rivals' performance. I'm not going to be able to do this by investing in engineering, so I'm looking for small tech companies that look like they're on to a winner. I've only got to pick one really good stock and the rest of the portfolio can do what it likes.'

If this sounds like lunacy, it certainly looked like it to the smokestacks. Tired after a round of meetings with City financiers, the chief executive of one of the engineering sector's best-known mid-sized players conceded: 'They tell us to grow organically, so we grow. They tell us to become more efficient, so we cut millions of pounds of costs. They tell us to get rid of low-tech metal bashing, so we do that too. Now they tell us to get into high-tech – well, we can only do that by acquisition and our share price won't stand much more fund-raising. It's like they're asking for the impossible.'

Howle Holdings is an example of an engineering firm that did what its advisers recommended – and paid the price.

In April 1999 the Gloucester-based engineering tiddler – valued by the market at just £7.75 million – launched a surprise hostile bid for Sheffield toolmaker Brooke Industrial. The bid, which as an 'all-paper' bid offered only shares in Howle in exchange for shares in Brooke, followed some four years of merger discussions, all fruitless. The offer valued each Brooke share at 82.5p, a premium

the city
the press
webcraft
the old way
sleuthing
fund managers
short termers
crash!
new economy
telecoms
smokestacks
economics
tax

of almost 18 per cent on the closing price of 70p the day before the offer was made.

Howle's chairman and chief executive, plain-speaking Scottish Presbyterian George Govan, said: 'To be blunt, if you ask some lassie to dance for four years but they never come to the party, you either have to give up or do something different.'

On paper at least the bid made perfect sense. Both companies had been deserted by large investors. Both operated in similar markets. Howle, which floated on the stock market in 1997, specialises in cutting tools and tungsten carbide components for the woodworking, construction and automotive industries.

Brooke also has cutting tools and tungsten carbide businesses, but it had underperformed. Howle's margins – i.e. profit as a percentage of sales – were noticeably better than Brooke's – 13 per cent against 7 per cent. Brooke had even put out a profit warning earlier in 1999, and its shares were not likely to go anywhere without bid interest.

Despite gaining support from some Brooke shareholders, Howle ultimately lost the bid battle. The situation was complicated after Brooke bought a toolmaking business in South Africa, effectively a poison pill for Howle, and Govan pulled out. He freely admitted to frustration, pointing out that it was potentially a win–win situation for both sides.

Brooke shareholders were reluctant to trade their shares for stock in another small engineering company. A bit of cash might have made all the difference, but Govan stuck to his guns – prompting accusations in Brooke's defence document that he had made a stingy Presbyterian bid. Govan has a thick skin, but even he was probably taken aback by the ferocity of the counter-attack and by the scale of the advisers' fees – well north of £500,000 – incurred in the battle.

If Howle's experience says anything about investors, it is that cash speaks louder than shares and makes a far more compelling argument for accepting a bid than any talk of synergies and cost savings.

As the engineering sector's difficulties continued throughout 1999, analysts warned that the sector itself would disappear from the stock market by about 2002 as companies gave up waiting for the City to value them appropriately.

If the stock market's view of the smokestacks was bad news for the companies themselves, it was extremely good news for certain parts of the financial community – specifically the money men: consultants, bean-counters and legal eagles who found themselves poring over company books in support of management buy-out teams. In the Midlands, where once barely a month had gone by without news of a company flotation, now barely a week seemed to pass before someone, somewhere was announcing that the management was attempting to buy the company from shareholders.

Public to private bids soared in popularity in the first quarter of 2000. According to figures from the accountants KPMG, they increased 67 per cent in number in the last quarter of 1999, although their average value dropped by almost a quarter. In late 1999, it was hard to find any SmallCap industrial company that had not given serious thought to the possibility of mounting a management buy-out (MBO). The large number of deals either completed or under way by early 2000 indicated that many chief executives had lost patience with the City and had given up trying to wait for a U-turn in investor sentiment.

the city
the press
webcraft
the old way
sleuthing
fund managers
short termers
crash!
new economy
telecoms
smokestacks
economics
tax

the city

the press

webcraft

the old way

sleuthing

fund managers

short termers

crash!

new economy

telecoms

smokestacks

economics

tax

One company that highlighted the extent to which industrial stocks had fallen out of favour was Apollo Metals, a Birmingham-based supplier of materials to the aerospace sector. The company's name was something of a handicap in itself. Although metals accurately described the company's original activities, it had transformed itself through acquisitions and organic expansion into newer, more high-tech materials. Exploiting demand for materials supply and logistics on an outsourced basis, the company won numerous major contracts with blue chip manufacturers.

In 1999 Apollo, which turned over £90 million a year, won a deal that looked set to transform its prospects – a £500 million, ten-year contract to handle materials supply for British Aerospace's military aircraft and aerostructures division.

Winning the contract could have propelled Apollo into a different league, putting it in a position to win other major deals. With aerospace industry consolidation looming, most analysts were upbeat about the company's prospects.

Yet the shares stubbornly refused to reflect this. Investors had some reason to be cautious about Apollo since it faced a major challenge financing the development work necessary to gear up for the contract. At the same time it experienced a slowdown in its traditional engineering markets. The downturn led to a profit warning and saw full-year profits drop from £6 million to £4 million – Apollo shares slid accordingly below 100p, giving it a single-figure price-to-earnings rating.

Repeated tips in the engineering press failed to lift the shares. In the end it all became irrelevant. After more than a year of trading between 88–100p a share, a management team bought the company itself and took the company private – at 166p a share.

Apollo was by no means the only undervalued engineering outfit on the stock market. Another was Senior. It dropped the word 'engineering' from its name and even changed its financial PR advisers in a clear bid to revamp its City image in 1999. It was to no effect. Despite taking all the right steps throughout that year, a succession of profit warnings did for the stock and no amount of moves into higher-value flexible tubes businesses or overseas expansion could save the share price from spiralling downwards.

Low ratings may annoy and depress the directors of companies that attract them, but they're a blessing for other, larger industrial stocks that can afford to buy them. Many have deep pockets and large war chests amassed to help add to specific parts of their business – Smiths Industries, at the last count, had some £1 billion to spend.

Invensys, for example, announced a £2.5 billion disposals programme back in 1999 – the sales would leave it focused on controls and automation systems, well focused and sufficiently well funded to buy sizable companies in its target markets. This is an opportunity for middle-sized engineers that continue to trade at a level substantially below fair value. Analysts have singled out the likes of IMI as a company with unique products and well-run businesses that can be fitted into a much larger group.

Overseas buyers have not been slow to recognise the buying opportunity. Apollo Metals was stalked by US-based Reliance Steel & Aluminum before it went private. Numerous other engineers have had similar overtures made to them.

You can make money by buying shares in seriously undervalued businesses – but it is a gamble. Unless the company concerned is a quality operation with a spread of activities in high-growth markets, it may well prove totally resistible as a takeover target. Today's

the city

the press

webcraft

the old way

sleuthing

fund managers

short termers

crash!

new economy

telecoms

smokestacks

economics

tax

undervalued engineer could thus simply become tomorrow's undervalued engineer. The trick is to identify those businesses which have something out of the ordinary. The key differentiator is technology – metal bashing is out, high-tech is in. And nowhere is this more evident than in the engineering sector.

What the City wants to see is activities that cannot easily be replicated in the cheap labour-intensive sweatshops of the Far East. The secret is to get into sophisticated metals, introduce complex computerised distribution systems, run major manufacturers' materials needs on an outsourced basis. Add value.

Long-Term Solutions to Lowly Valuations

If you take a short-term view of the engineering sector, say from 1997 to 2000, few stocks would have produced performances over and above their peers. The deterioration in stock valuations was across almost all the companies in the sector, with very few exceptions.

Look back somewhat farther, say over the ten years from 1990, and a number of factors emerge to give investors a better picture of what is more or less likely to succeed in the sector.

The stocks that have performed better than their peers during the 1990s have been those companies that identified major industry trends they could exploit. It is important to assess each of these trends and their relative significance.

Key Factors to Look for in Industrial Companies

☐ Outsourcing – perhaps the biggest trend to affect the engineering and manufacturing industries. Companies are eager to contract out whole swathes of non-essential functions within their business. By taking on such work, engineers can provide entire sub-assemblies to production lines instead of single components. Major manufacturers are keen to deal with fewer and larger suppliers.

☐ Technology exploitation – the growth of e-commerce will be significant for the engineering sector, making the distribution chain more efficient, improving purchasing information and ensuring that the cost of doing business is reduced.

☐ High-tech versus low-tech – metal bashers are low value. High-tech electronics and electromechanical processes add value, so companies that specialise in these areas instead of metal forming represent the future of the industry.

☐ High-growth markets – while the automotive industry may be big, its products tend to be of a commodity nature (i.e. the vast majority of people own, or want to own, a car) and so price competition can be intense. Companies that look for profitable, higher-margin niches (off-highway vehicles, agricultural machinery, and so on) instead of the mainstream bread and butter have more chance of making a go of what can otherwise be perceived as a low-growth market. Barriers to entry in the aerospace sector (making successful competition less likely) and the high degree of sophisticated electronic componentry make operating here a good idea. Although the aerospace sector's fortunes move in sympathy with economic cycles – in other

words are 'cyclical' – its lows are never as dismal as those in the automotive sector, which suffers from severe overcapacity and margin pressure.

☐ Bigger is better – in 1990 the FTSE 100 accounted for 72 per cent of the All Share index by market capitalisation, rising to 80 per cent in 1999. Tighter asset allocations and a shift towards investing in larger companies have had a negative effect on smaller stocks. Although 1999 saw a revival in the fortunes of SmallCap engineers, this was against the background of a two-year underperformance – few analysts expect small companies to outperform their larger competitors in stock market terms.

Examples of High-Tech, High-Growth Engineers

Cobham – specialises in avionics technologies and services. It will benefit from outsourcing, has products on many major military aerospace programmes, including the Eurofighter, the Joint Strike Fighter, the Apache helicopter programme and air support services for the Ministry of Defence.

GKN – active in the defence sector, automotive drive lines, powder metallurgy and helicopters/aerospace. It has been a beneficiary of the trend towards outsourcing and has acquired extensively in the powdered metals field. It is also using the Internet as an enabling technology throughout the business.

Ford – in the automotive industry the concept of outsourcing has been taken to heart, helped along the way by the principle of just-in-time delivery, an idea brought to this country by the Japanese. Ford, like many other car-makers always looking to cut production costs, has gone farther than most by suggesting that it could simply become a design, marketing and after-sales service company. The manufacture of cars could mostly be contracted out – since the best margins are in the service activities delivered alongside the basic car production.

Rolls-Royce – the manufacturer of engines for the aerospace industry (not to be confused with the manufacturer of the famous cars) is in many ways a British success story. It was rescued from ruin and has developed new aero-engines widely recognised as world-beaters. Last year it delivered double-digit earnings growth and has expanded into marine power and energy, giving it strong positions in growth markets. None of this has yet been recognised in the City and the company is widely perceived to be undervalued. Analysts' big worry is that it doesn't make enough on the supply of engines but only reaps rewards from high-margin servicing work much later.

Meggitt – a high-tech electronics and controls engineer where profits growth is strongest in the electronics division. Aerospace accounts for just over half of profits, with Boeing representing about 6–7 per cent of turnover. Its products find their way on to several major defence programmes, including the Eurofighter.

Ultra Electronics – not strictly an industrial stock but its high-tech electronics systems are found in many defence environments, from military aerospace to submarine hunting to land systems. Its shares have roared ahead since floating at 250p in 1996. The company has made its name by achieving a dominant position in very high value-added defence and aerospace operations.

Invensys – heavily re-engineered since the merger of BTR and Siebe, the company specialises in high-tech controls and automation systems. Massive reorganisation has obscured the underlying

the city
the press
webcraft
the old way
sleuthing
fund managers
short termers
crash!
new economy
telecoms
smokestacks
economics
tax

the city
the press
webcraft
the old way
sleuthing
fund managers
short termers
crash!
new economy
telecoms
smokestacks
economics
tax

growth story but the company is well run, and although it tells a rather boring story it's only boring because Invensys is a solid performer.

IMI – another reorganised engineering group, IMI focuses on controls and systems, including drinks dispensers. It bought Polypipe last year and now has a sizable presence in the plastic pipes business. Its shares have been undervalued and the company is frequently identified as a potential bid target.

TI Group – has invested almost £1.5 billion on acquisitions in the past two years. Aero components account for 18 per cent of turnover, with power train fluid system and auto brake and fuel components 46 per cent. The company supplies every major aero-engine manufacturer yet its rating reflects lack of interest in its lower-growth activities.

The Internet and Engineering

It would be easy to write off the engineering and manufacturing sectors as unworthy of your interest. At one point in late 1999 and early 2000 it was difficult to convince anyone, even analysts and fund managers, of the merits of investing in anything other than tech stocks.

That period has now passed, and not before time. Fund managers, who did briefly enjoy the fact that they only needed to spot one Baltimore Technologies, one ARM Holdings or one Sage to make the rest of the portfolio's performance totally irrelevant, have now gone back to relying on investment analysis to guide their decisions.

You, as an investor, want to see evidence that the companies whose shares you buy are taking the New Age economy seriously.

E-commerce will have an impact whatever sector of the economy the business operates in – even engineers use Internet sites to buy commodity products.

The City's predilection for dot.com stocks, however, had one rather undesirable consequence in early 2000 – all the engineering sector's directors were clearly briefed as to the advisability of coming up with detailed e-commerce plans. Some made more sense than others.

It was, admittedly, a difficult situation for these companies. Never mind their millions of pounds of turnover, their 15 per cent margins and their blue chip customer base. All the City seemed to want to know was: 'What's your Internet strategy?'

And so the public at large was subjected to the unseemly and ridiculous sight of engineers and manufacturers coming up with their own dot.com plans – mostly in the foolish belief that they could pull the wool over the investment community's eyes. Of course, that wasn't such a foolish notion – the dot.coms having mostly succeeded in doing that already. But as the frenzy for dot.com stocks wore off, so too did the market's willingness to believe what they were being told – and the announcements had progressively less effect.

City financial PR advisers, those mysterious spin-doctors who craft the press releases that accompany financial results statements, are largely responsible for the flood of superficial e-commerce announcements in early 2000. You can't blame them for trying, but many missed the boat.

Glynwed became an early victim of the rush to climb into the Internet business. The metal basher of old is now a high-tech pipe systems company, with operations in the food service and consumer

the city
the press
webcraft
the old way
sleuthing
fund managers
short termers
crash!
new economy
telecoms
smokestacks
economics
tax

goods markets. Its products include the Aga, beloved of country kitchens everywhere, and it has expanded acquisitively into new, higher-growth markets.

Glynwed's e-commerce strategy was agacookshop.com, an e-commerce extension of its Aga shops. It may also launch a lifestyle portal later in 2000, aimed 'at the interests and needs of the Aga household'. As diversions from the core business go, this looked like a pretty startling example.

Car leasing and servicing company Lex Service, which took over the RAC last year, unveiled a two-pronged Internet strategy to set up motoring portals. Its £5 million investment in a 30 per cent stake in Autohit and several million pounds more in the RAC website appeared to make good sense, at first sight. But some onlookers wondered why, having spent so much buying the RAC and making such a success of integrating it within the Lex group, the company would want to spend millions more developing a rival Internet brand.

Lex claims that both sites will be complementary made some sense, but having two businesses in a related market sounded strange, even schizophrenic, to some who felt that the chief executive's analogy 'we will have two complementary irons in the fire' was somewhat wide of the mark. 'It's akin to putting two starving cannibals on a desert island and hoping they don't go for each other,' commented one wag.

So what next? Old Age stocks can dabble in the Internet all they like, but it's going to mean less and less for the share price.

The importance of e-commerce can't be underestimated, but neither should it be seen as a panacea for the underperformance of an industrial company's share price. There is already sufficient evidence to suggest that the investment community is waking up to the dangers of piling regardless into tech stocks. This does not mean there will simply be a flight of equity back into Old Economy stocks but, rather, that there will be a selective return.

Small industrial stocks look set to continue underperforming – because they can't become leaders in their field and are too small to afford the repositioning many require. A lot of companies floated for tax reasons and with the original founding family still holding a lot of the shares are best avoided. One analyst, commenting acerbically on one small Midlands engineer, said: 'All they need the business for is to pay the mortgage and keep the family Jaguar on the road. It's a lifestyle business, no more, no less.'

So now you've seen that the emperor was not, after all, wearing any clothes, what are the key things to look for in Old Economy stocks?

☐ Good positions in high-tech, high-growth markets
☐ High barriers to entry to prevent others copying the company's success
☐ A sound e-commerce strategy. Remember, if it sounds spurious it usually is: leave lifestyle portals to the consumer goods companies because engineers usually lack the expertise needed to run them
☐ High-dividend yields that can compensate for the possible lack of capital appreciation
☐ Moves away from low-growth, commodity activities

The importance of understanding research and amassing a detailed

the city
the press
webcraft
the old way
sleuthing
fund managers
short termers
crash!
new economy
telecoms
smokestacks
economics
tax

the city

the press

webcraft

the old way

sleuthing

fund managers

short termers

crash!

new economy

telecoms

smokestacks

economics

tax

knowledge of the company and the markets in which it operates cannot be understated. The sceptics, day traders who seem to rely on gut instinct and large doses of nicotine or caffeine, may scoff, but the frenzied dot.com boom has gone. In its place there is a more rational approach to stock-picking, and that has to be a good thing. Don't be disappointed if industrial stocks fail to show the sort of stratospheric growth enjoyed by the techs in the boom – there are plenty of other compelling reasons for investing in them and enjoying a long-term return.

Guy Dresser

Chapter Twelve

‘In the Long Run We're All Dead’ How to Understand Economics

the city

the press

webcraft

the old way

sleuthing

fund managers

short termers

crash!

new economy

telecoms

smokestacks

economics

tax

Putting Together the Jigsaw

When it comes to economics, the trick for you, the informed investor, is to be able to identify which economic indicators are important for your investment decisions. The ability to forecast economic trends is one of the essential skills of any active or passive investor. Rules of thumb, hunches and gossip you have picked up in the pub may all be good ways to predict future economic trends. But sooner or later you will trip up and have to resort to a more rational and scientific approach.

There is no such thing as a dead cert in economic forecasting – witness the endless lists of 'expert' economists in end-of-year Sunday supplements who got the economy wrong every year. The objective in the game of forecasting is to cut the odds on being wrong. And to do this you need to know how to interpret economic data. How do you distinguish between 'good' news and 'bad' news? For example, a fall in unemployment is often portrayed as good news for the man in the street, but it could lead to higher interest rates – 'bad' for the economy and quite often for the stock market.

To some, the nitty-gritty of economics provides the key to predicting both the short- and long-term stock market trends. It is an essential tool in any investor's kit. To others, the Office for National Statistics' (ONS) long list of economic indicators, not to mention the vast array of private and governmental surveys and forecasts, are just plain boring and should be left for the professionals

the city
the press
webcraft
the old way
sleuthing
fund managers
short termers
crash!
new economy
telecoms
smokestacks
economics
tax

and back-room economists – an unwelcome distraction from the overriding objective of making a quick buck or two. In our view, this is a risky camp in which to place yourself.

How often have you heard: 'Oh, the economy is ticking along quite nicely', or 'the Bank of England will look after us'? This recipe for complacency is also a recipe for disaster. It relies on the Bank of England and its policy-setting committee to do the right thing. Of course their remit is to respond to government policy and objectives, but they do not in effect control monetary policy. The assumption that they do is based on (misplaced) trust, and is likely to lead to 'blind' investment decisions for the serious small-time investor. Would you ignore a company's fundamentals when making an investment decision? Probably not. So why ignore the wider macroeconomic picture?

So, is it only in times of hardship that we resort to the worship of what has been called 'the dismal science'? Like religion, economics seems to provide a basic framework for our society, which, after a few lessons at school or mandatory visits to the local church, are quickly forgotten.

Of course, you don't have to be an academic to understand how economics affects our everyday lives, and perhaps more importantly our portfolios. Actually, it's probably best not to be confined to the ivory towers of academia to *really* understand what is happening to the economy.

The essence of economics for you, the investor, is the ability to predict interest rate changes and judge government policy decisions accurately – something which even esteemed City experts often fail to do. But of course, the reaction of the stock market to interest rates changes is not always rational and depends a lot on expectations, as well as at what stage of the economic cycle we are in, and what has followed before. Indeed, the science of economics would not be complete without a whole volume of work on expectations and how they affect the formulation of economic policy.

It is virtually impossible, and certainly beyond the scope of this chapter, to provide an inexhaustible checklist of economic indicators and the likely reaction of the stock or bond market to any particular move. Market psychology often clouds the picture, and markets are sometimes strange and illogical places.

First, we need an understanding of regular economic releases – the pieces of the jigsaw – and how these are constructed, as well as their implications for government policy and your own forecasts. And hopefully, we can destroy a few fallacies dear to our hearts.

Inflation

Inflation is the cornerstone of the government's economic policy and is probably the most important indicator to watch every month.

There is an endless list of inflation indicators to get your head around. The rate of change in retail prices is the key economic indicator, but probably not the most accurate. Released every month by the ONS, the Retail Price Index (RPI) is the standard method of measuring price rises for a basket of goods. The index is constructed by averaging the increase in the prices of consumer goods and weighting each price by the average amount bought by each consumer.

The RPI is based on a detailed survey of prices across the whole country – the index measures the price movement of more than

the city
the press
webcraft
the old way
sleuthing
fund managers
short termers
crash!
new economy
telecoms
smokestacks
economics
tax

600 goods and services in 146 regions. Each month, around 120,000 prices are used to calculate the overall index and the result is published on the second Tuesday of every month.

The second, and probably more important, gauge of inflation is the RPI-X – often called the underlying rate of inflation. This measure is the headline RPI we have already talked about, but excluding mortgage interest payments. Internationally, this is the most common method of calculating inflation.

Third, RPI-Y, which is the RPI-X but excluding indirect taxes, is probably an even better measure of *true* price movements, since it excludes, for example, rises in VAT and duty on items such as tobacco and alcohol.

Even these three measures have been deemed inadequate in the past. Back in the days when income taxes were being sharply reduced, it was argued that none of the RPI measures properly reflected the better standard of living permitted by those income tax cuts and increases in allowances. This resulted in the invention of the Tax and Price Index, which included an adjustment to allow for the effect of direct tax cuts, so that the TPI was lower than any of the RPI measures. In later years the pattern changed, and the TPI began to run higher than RPI-X or RPI-Y, and so it was dropped.

Why does inflation matter?

If all costs and all prices were going to rise at some predetermined rate for ever, then inflation would not matter one iota. We could adjust our investment decisions to take account of these fully anticipated price changes. So it is easy to see why policy-makers aim for price *stability*. There is really no absolute target for inflation

– the government's target of 2.5 per cent for the RPI-X is, if you like, a convenient number. Indeed, since it is quite often the case that the RPI overstates inflation by one or two percentage points, most governments' definition of price stability equates to zero.

Difficulties are posed by wide fluctuations in price levels. Inflation reduces economic efficiency since it distorts relative price signals – it is hard to distinguish between relative price changes and the changes in the overall price level.

Another argument for stability is that when prices and costs accelerate unabated, consumers and investors tend to act in anticipation of further rises, resulting in what is called a price spiral. This leads to uncertainties, and illogical decisions are made across the board, resulting in economic inefficiency.

As a consequence, policy-makers aim to achieve a stable, low-inflation environment in which we all come to expect a continuation of limited and steady changes in costs and prices. Once that climate is established, accurately communicated and duly anticipated by consumers and investors, they can all make logical and sound decisions. Sound economic decisions lead to a healthy economy, which will tend to grow. So low and stable inflation encourages a positive outcome, or the nirvana of sustainable growth.

Of course, some policies aimed at fighting inflation in the long term are counterproductive. As the headline RPI includes mortgage interest payments, and higher interest rates lead to higher mortgage repayments, rising rates tend to cause higher headline inflation. The same can be said of higher indirect taxes and duties. So, it can be argued that measures of inflation used to determine policy should exclude the short-term effects of previous policies aimed at lower inflation in the longer term. A hike in interest rates designed to

slow an economy that is overheating results in higher mortgage rates, which may push investors and consumers to demand higher wages to compensate. So, finding a true and accurate measure of inflation is fraught with difficulties.

Inputs

Enough of retail prices – there are other, equally important inflation measures to review, namely prices faced by, and ultimately passed on to, consumers by producers. Generally speaking, if producer prices are rising, sooner or later the rises will be passed on to consumers, although a lot depends on what kind of market demands retailers are facing. Producers may well face sharply rising commodity prices – as in 1999 – that are passed on to retailers and not to the consumers, since the market would not tolerate higher prices. Accordingly, retailers felt the pinch.

The ONS publishes producer prices data once a month, ahead of the RPI release, and therefore great emphasis is placed on this release. This data is considered to be a good leading indicator of cost pressures, and useful in analysing how producers are behaving.

The PPI is compiled on basically the same principle as the CPI (Consumer Price Index) – based on a basket of goods that are assigned weightings in the index reflecting the output of each contributor relative to the total.

Generally, a growing world economy means increasing demand for raw materials to make goods – and hence rising international prices. Given that the UK imports most commodities and is heavily dependent on raw materials – we have a high propensity to import them – the exchange rate is of vital importance. In periods when the pound is strong, imported commodities tend to be cheaper.

Strengthening sterling is at least good news for inflation hawks – those keen to keep inflation down, and the government has fought to keep sterling at high levels.

Earnings: A Warning Flag

While we're on the subject of inputs to inflation, it would be remiss not to review what is probably one of the most closely observed sets of input price inflation data: earnings. Average earnings in the UK are calculated in three-monthly periods and then annualised, but tend to lag behind the current periods by at least two months. For example, average earnings data for the three months to February are released in the middle of April. In the United States, hourly earnings data are compiled alongside what are know as non-farm payrolls data, and are released monthly. The US Labor Department also releases the much watched, and much feared, Employment Cost Index every quarter.

The average earnings index is the most comprehensive measure of pay. The figures are seasonally adjusted – meaning they take into account the rises and dips that occur at times like, say, the end of the year, when people tend to receive bonuses – and released with the employment and unemployment statistics. Calculating earnings growth is a complicated task because it is difficult to track movements in the settlement and payment of wage increases. Each month, the ONS conducts a survey of eight thousand companies and organisations in both the public and private sector, representing 40 per cent of employees in the country. The seasonally adjusted earnings index is volatile because of differences that occur in the timing of payments from year to year. For example, earnings in the three months to February 2000 raced ahead by 6 per cent when

the city
the press
webcraft
the old way
sleuthing
fund managers
short termers
crash!
new economy
telecoms
smokestacks
economics
tax

compared to the same time the year before – setting off alarm bells back in the spring of 2000. But many economists dismissed this as spurious since it covered a time when massive bonuses were paid to City workers.

Acceleration in earnings growth is the reddest of red warning flags for monetary authorities.

In the UK, it is generally accepted that an annualised growth rate of 4.5 per cent is consistent with the government's inflation target of 2.5 per cent. Earlier in 2000, average earnings growth, at around 6 per cent, was moving towards its fastest rate since the middle of July, a red-hot warning flag for the Bank of England and a stimulus to raise interest rates further to prevent inflation from picking up in the future. At the same time, there were increasing signs that the labour market remained tight – meaning there were less unemployed workers available to take up new jobs – as the monthly unemployment count was falling consistently. Again, this is a case of 'good' and 'bad' news. Bad news for those seeking a sustainable economic growth path, accompanied by low interest rates, but quite clearly good news for those seeking to invest in cyclical consumer stocks, because consumers had more money in their pockets to spend.

Economic Growth

Gross Domestic Product (GDP) is the most commonly used gauge of national income and measures the aggregate of incomes received by various segments of the economy. Because of the complexity of compiling it, GDP data often lags, and is published and revised every three months. Essentially it tells us how much wealth was created in the economy over a certain period of time.

The figures are grossed because GDP does not allow for the depreciation of capital – in other words, wear and tear on factory machines. When the value of income from abroad is included – what domestic companies earn abroad and send home minus what foreign companies earn here and send back overseas – then the GDP becomes the Gross National Product (GNP), a lesser-used gauge.

The GDP deflator, one of the most important indicators of inflation and often the most accurate measure, assesses the difference between current and constant price GDP and its components. For example, if an economy grows at a nominal rate of 4 per cent and at 2 per cent in real terms, the implicit price deflator is 2%. This is often a better benchmark of inflation when comparing different economies.

The List Continues

There are many economic indicators to assess from month to month and quarter to quarter, and the jigsaw would be far from complete with merely a review of inflation and growth. But there is no question that these are the two most important indicators to watch out for. Others can be assessed for their impact on both of these fundamentals. Regular economic releases are downloadable from the ONS's website (www.ons.gov.uk).

Industrial and Manufacturing Production Broadly speaking, this is indicative of the state of the economic cycle. Manufacturing output is, simply, the amount of goods produced by a nation's factories and is a component of industrial production, which includes the supply of energy and water and the output of raw

the city
the press
webcraft
the old way
sleuthing
fund managers
short termers
crash!
new economy
telecoms
smokestacks
economics
tax

the city
the press
webcraft
the old way
sleuthing
fund managers
short termers
crash!
new economy
telecoms
smokestacks
economics
tax

materials. Industrial output generally excludes agriculture, trade and services. These figures are released once a month by the ONS. In addition, the Confederation of British Industry (CBI) releases its Industrial Trends survey – both monthly and quarterly – the latter giving qualitative opinion from senior manufacturing executives, on past and expected trends in output, exports, prices, costs, investment intentions, business confidence and capacity utilisation. The monthly survey provides an interim health check on orders, stocks, price and output expectations. Both are thought to be closely watched by the Bank of England's Monetary Policy Committee, which is responsible for setting base interest rates.

Retail Sales Clearly these should not be forgotten in any assessment of the economy as they are a good indicator of consumer confidence and demand. Most countries release this data as an index. As with industrial and manufacturing data, the CBI releases its Retail and Distributive Trades survey – considered to be an authoritative indicator of short-term trends in the UK distribution sector and of consumer demand – every month. It too carries significant weight in the formulation of economic policy at the Bank of England.

Trade Balance This represents the difference between exports and imports; it may measure visible trade only, or trade in both goods and services. It can tell us a lot about how the economy is performing and about future prospects. For example, the UK has a large propensity to import – as income grows, goods are likely to be sucked in. As past experience has shown, this has led to periods of inflation. In contrast, Japan's imports tend to grow at a relatively low rate when income expands, and at the same time its exports rise relatively rapidly if other economies are growing. If Japan grows at the same rate as its trading partners, then its trade surplus will tend to increase.

Money Supply Important as an indicator of the level of financial transactions in an economy, and, if you belong to a certain school of economics, controlling money supply is the key to controlling inflation. Indeed, governments during the 1980s and early 1990s adopted targets for monetary aggregates and believed that pure monetary policy could have a considerable effect on national income (and by implication a considerable effect on unemployment or inflation). This view is associated with Milton Friedman (born in New York, 1912). On the other hand, the Keynesian view (John Maynard Keynes – born 1883 in Cambridge) is that pure monetary policy has little effect on national income (and so can have little effect on unemployment or inflation).

the city
the press
webcraft
the old way
sleuthing
fund managers
short termers
crash!
new economy
telecoms
smokestacks
economics
tax

The Basis for the Understanding of Money:

If M is the money stock in any economy and V is the number of times it changes hands, or velocity of circulation, then:

$M \times V$ = the amount of money spent, which must equal real output Y multiplied by the price index P; $M \times V = Y \times P$

Monetarists argue that controlling the money supply controls money GDP (that is $Y \times P$) and therefore inflation can be controlled and the trend in real output can be predicted. This is if the velocity of money is assumed to be constant. Their opponents argue that money GDP fixes the demand for money – that the cause and effect run in the opposite direction – and there is nothing a government can do to prevent this.

the city
the press
webcraft
the old way
sleuthing
fund managers
short termers
crash!
new economy
telecoms
smokestacks
economics
tax

The measures of money are released weekly by the Bank of England in the UK and the Federal Reserve in the US. Narrow money – called M0 in the UK and M1 in the US – is defined as currency in circulation, plus sight deposits (current accounts where money is available on demand). Broad money – M2 – consists of M0 plus savings deposits and time deposits. The even broader definition of money is called M4 – there is no M3 in the UK – which consists of M0 plus sterling deposits held at British banks by the non-bank private sector. During the 1980s and 1990s, many monetary authorities had targets for these monetary aggregates, but now they have moved to targets for inflation instead.

Policy Formulation

It is generally accepted that, in some form or another, there is a clear trade-off between employment and inflation. The Phillips curve (named after New Zealand economist A.W.H. Phillips) was formulated to support this proposition – that, at least in the short term, higher inflation will reduce the level of unemployment. However, this was undermined by the 'stagflation' of the 1970s – stagflation being a period in which there was a combination of increasing unemployment and rising inflation.

Such a trade-off has been proven to be a short-run phenomenon, but the debate still rages on. A later reformulation of the trade-off argued that the long-run rate of unemployment is fixed at a natural level, and attempts to reduce it below this would result in accelerating inflation. But even this has been brought into contention by recent evidence, especially in the US, where inflation has been hovering around 2.5 per cent while the unemployment rate has fallen way below what is thought to be its natural rate. (When Phillips first formulated his theorem in the late 1950s, he found that the rate of increase of money wages would be zero if approximately 5 per cent of the workforce were unemployed – clearly inappropriate for modern times.)

The natural rate of unemployment is also known as the non-accelerating inflation rate of unemployment, or NAIRU. In recent years, unemployment both here and abroad has been below most estimates of what was thought to be the NAIRU without producing accelerating inflation.

The original Phillips curve implied that there was a long-run trade-off between inflation and unemployment, but that view has long since been abandoned, on empirical as well as theoretical grounds. Nonetheless, the Phillips curve trade-off between inflation and unemployment in the *short run* remains central to the formulation of monetary policy. Does the long run matter? Probably not – as John Maynard Keynes said: 'In the long run, we are all dead.'

Setting Interest Rates

Setting interest rates at the appropriate level depends on a whole host of both domestic and external economic and political factors. The trick for us as private investors is to be able to forecast interest rates within reasonable limits – no mean feat in this day and age.

John Taylor, economics professor at Stanford University, created a rule for calculating the optimum level of interest rates. Of course, rules always seem to be broken in this fast-changing world, but it can be a useful guide to what the optimal level of interest rates is. Although it was formulated for the US, it is appropriate for most modern western economies.

the city
the press
webcraft
the old way
sleuthing
fund managers
short termers
crash!
new economy
telecoms
smokestacks
economics
tax

According to the Taylor Rule, the Fed should adjust short-term rates – in this case the overnight rate, or the Federal funds target – to respond to differences between actual and desired performance in its dual objectives of price stability and full employment. It is best treated as a formulaic explanation attempting to quantify the behaviour of the Fed. That is, if interest rates, inflation and GDP are analysed, one can determine a rule that describes the Fed's behaviour.

This is done by setting the real Fed funds rate equal to a nominal 2 per cent plus one half of the difference between actual and targeted inflation and one half of the percentage difference between actual and potential GDP (assuming potential real GDP growth of 3.5 per cent). The nominal funds rate should be set equal to the targeted real funds rate plus actual inflation.

In practice, of course, setting interest rates, or forecasting them, is not as easy as all that.

The Bank of England and the Monetary Policy Committee

In May 1997, the Chancellor of the Exchequer, Gordon Brown, announced that the government was giving the Bank of England operational responsibility for setting interest rates. In fact it was the first major policy move he made in the New Labour government. According to the Treasury: 'The Bank's monetary policy objective is to deliver *price stability* (as defined by the government's inflation target) and, without prejudice to that objective, to support the government's economic policy, including its objectives for growth and employment.'

There were many reasons why the Chancellor handed over this

responsibility. The UK had a very poor inflation record compared to Germany, where the success of the Bundesbank could be directly attributed to its independence from political control. The US Fed had been similarly praised.

Decisions on interest rates are made by the Bank of England's Monetary Policy Committee, which meets on a monthly basis, by a vote of the MPC on a one-person, one-vote basis, with the Governor of the Bank of England, Eddie George, having the casting vote if there is no majority.

Much time and effort are expended every month predicting the outcome of the MPC meeting, but the bottom line is that it does not generally have more information on the economy than the average, well-informed investor. Yes, they are experts in their fields – members include the two deputy governors (one being the Bank of England's chief economist, Mervyn King), respected City economists and academics.

There are, of course, many conspiracy theories regarding the independence of the MPC and indeed the Bank of England (is it really as independent as it is meant to be?), but for the moment we will disregard those. Further, the MPC publishes the minutes of their meetings – a very important event for any bank-watcher – on the Wednesday of the second week after the meetings take place. From these, the investor can ascertain, for example, how many MPC members voted for an interest rates rise, which economic factors led them to do this, and what their general view of the economy is. It is vital for any interest rate detective to avidly follow the minutes, which can be found on the Bank of England's website. (Another useful publication for the avid MPC-watcher is the Bank's guide to economic modelling tools used by the MPC. You can

the city
the press
webcraft
the old way
sleuthing
fund managers
short termers
crash!
new economy
telecoms
smokestacks
economics
tax

the city
the press
webcraft
the old way
sleuthing
fund managers
short termers
crash!
new economy
telecoms
smokestacks
economics
tax

order it from the Bank's website: http://www.bankofengland. co.uk/mpc/index.html.)

Here are a few pointers to forecasting interest rates:

☐ *The MPC seldom switches back and forth from month to month.* As we have seen in recent years, once the Bank of England starts raising interest rates it is likely to continue to do so for quite a few months. Switching back and forth is likely to cause too much volatility in already volatile markets. So, look for recent patterns in interest rates.

☐ *The MPC is unlikely to vote for an aggressive move in interest rates.* Rather, if an aggressive move is needed, the committee is likely to opt for a series of moves over a longer period; not the short, sharp shock that is often feared. It is only during times of economic crisis, or external shocks, that a central banker would risk losing face, or even risk jeopardising the stability of financial markets – for example, when sterling left the ERM, or when the South-East Asian economies plunged into crisis. And it is probably a good idea to give up forecasting interest rates altogether at times like these.

☐ *The MPC will not in general respond to, or want to be seen to be responding to, one set of data.* For example, a sharp rise in inflation ahead of a committee meeting will be interpreted as a sure sign that the members will vote for a larger-than-expected corrective tightening of policy. This is rarely the case.

☐ *Remember that any move in interest rates will take time to have an effect on the economy.* The extent of the lag is again subject to debate and depends a lot on the extent of structural reforms and the state of the economy. The initial effects of interest rate changes are seen on economic output and then subsequently on inflation. Interest rates therefore have to be set today in order to influence inflation on average *two years on*, which means building a picture of what the economy will look like beyond the time horizon typically seen.

☐ *Compare interest rates with the current rate of inflation.* They are rarely as low as inflation and will be pushed three to five percentage points above inflation if the Bank wants to slow the economy and tame inflation.

☐ *Try to ascertain which economic indicators are the ones that the MPC consider to be important.* For example, if GDP is running over 3 per cent per quarter for four consecutive quarters, the MPC is probably going to vote for further rate rises, unless unemployment is high, or the economy is emerging from recession. Look at more general indicators of economic growth and inflation, such as house prices. The MPC may want to quash a sharp rise in house prices to prevent an inflationary spiral.

☐ *Listen to their words of wisdom.* A good way to predict which way the MPC will be swayed is to look for coverage of speeches by Eddie George and members of the MPC, since they will often tacitly warn of future rate rises so investors and the markets are not taken by surprise.

There is a tendency in all of us – from small-time investors to City hotshots – to be over-influenced by what is happening today, or rather what today's data are telling us happened a few months ago. Even members of the MPC are human and may, either consciously or subconsciously, respond to the current economic climate. Ideally, interest rates would rise as output strengthens to forestall

the city
the press
webcraft
the old way
sleuthing
fund managers
short termers
crash!
new economy
telecoms
smokestacks
economics
tax

the city
the press
webcraft
the old way
sleuthing
fund managers
short termers
crash!
new economy
telecoms
smokestacks
economics
tax

any potential increase in inflation; and they would fall as output weakens without waiting for inflation to fall first. But any cursory examination of the past will show a close correlation between interest rates and the path of inflation.

Don't be lulled into a false sense of security by low inflation. Inflation often remains low in the early stages of an economy's recovery. People often get over-optimistic about prospects for inflation in the early stages of recovery and similarly get over-pessimistic at the other end of the cycle. The period of over-optimism is particularly dangerous as it is a difficult environment in which to tighten monetary policy.

Don't Worry; It's Logical

Up to May 2000, a Schroders Investment Management computer model predicted nine out of ten of the MPC's rate decisions and claims an 85 per cent long-term success rate, compared with 70 per cent for opinion polls of City economists. Schroders reckons that its computer model could have run the country's monetary policy better than the committee itself.

Each month, the computer is fed the annual growth rates of thirteen key economic indicators. The formula is simple: it subtracts the percentage that has risen from the percentage that has fallen, and the result is smoothed to take account of trends in previous data. The model predicted in May that interest rates had peaked.

Economic Forecasting – Cutting the Odds on Being Wrong

Now comes the real challenge: forecasting the economy and economic trends and profiting from these forecasts. Of course, it's difficult enough forecasting the stock market these days, let alone the economy, so why complicate the picture? Well, as we will discover, it is a lot easier to forecast where the economy is heading these days than where stock prices will be at a certain point in the future.

For investors, the ultimate goal is to forecast what the economy will do in the context of their individual investments. Economic forecasting depends on a mix of economic understanding, complex statistical methods – beyond the scope of this chapter – and, of course, common sense.

After gaining a basic knowledge of everyday economic indicators and seeing how all the pieces of the jigsaw fit, we now have to use this information to look into the future. The hitch is that once the jigsaw has been completed, along comes a little earth tremor to upset your neatly completed puzzle and you have to start all over again – but with different rules!

So the rules of economics are not set in stone, then? Some science! If economics is not a science, then how can it be of any use when constructing economic forecasts? Well, nobody said you had to be 100 per cent correct 100 per cent of the time, did they, and anyone claiming they are is either deluded or lying. The best an investor can do is cut the odds on being wrong. It must be better than following your hunches or listening to your mates in the pub.

Throughout history there have been many times when econom-

ists have been tripped up, outfoxed and humiliated. It's a continually changing world out there, and sometimes the basic tenets of economics prove to be entirely inappropriate. Admittedly, there have been many external shocks which have moved the corner flags.

Forecasting has clearly become easier. As we moved through the eighties, the idea of being able to actually manage the economy emerged. The policy-makers and advisers ushered in by Margaret Thatcher in the UK and Ronald Reagan in the US during the eighties were a different breed to those populating the ivory towers in the seventies. Many people saw it as a return to the 'no pain, no gain' school of classical economics (see Chapter Eight). As Thatcher said: 'Economics are the method; the object is to change the soul.'

After the mismanagement and disarray of the Seventies, central bankers on both sides of the Atlantic inherited extraordinarily high inflation rates, which they set out to fight. The economy quickly hit back, delivering two punishing recessions, which brought with them unemployment rates not seen since the Thirties. The cure was painful, but delivered much lower inflation levels as the decade wore on. Central bankers showed that some of the old ideas about the trade-off between inflation and unemployment were true.

The central bankers were back in the driving seat and steering their economies on a straight and even course through the Nineties. There are two points here. First, the government and central banks became much better at forecasting the economy in order to effectively manage it. Second, it became much easier for the investor and the man in the street to understand where the economy was heading and how it was behaving.

Listening to the Chatter

Other people's forecasts can be a useful tool for any serious investor. Of course, some people are better at forecasting than others, and the trick is to be able to separate the less reliable soothsayers from those who are more often right than wrong. The big problem is, the less reliable forecasters seem to keep cropping up! Good forecasters will, of course, admit to being wrong, or at least deliver a health warning with their predictions. So it is often better to take more notice of the humble forecaster than the one with the biggest head.

Forecasters tend to fall into three main groups. Private forecasting firms and consultants are usually expensive to use and hence beyond the reach of the private investor. More useful for us are government and central bank forecasts. The Treasury publishes economic forecasts alongside the Budget in March, which usually waver on the conservative side, but nonetheless provide a useful guide for the investor. The Bank of England, in its quarterly inflation report, forecasts whether inflation is expected to fall above or below the government's target. And third, numerous forecasts are produced by research departments of the large brokerages. Indeed, most of these are freely available on the Internet or for the asking. One thing about City economists is that they will, and are paid to, seek as much media attention as possible. Most forecasters will want to make their predictions available, just in case they're right!

So what are the questions that need to be answered before the investor can effectively use other people's forecasts?

the city
the press
webcraft
the old way
sleuthing
fund managers
short termers
crash!
new economy
telecoms
smokestacks
economics
tax

Should the forecast be believed?

Everybody has his or her own idea of where the economy is heading. It's a matter of comparing what you think with the forecaster's prediction, and maybe giving the expert a little more credit for his insight, since he or she is just that – an expert. After all, he or she has probably devoted his or her life to the dismal science. If in doubt, err on the side of caution, remembering that quite a few 'forecasters' like to consider themselves to be mavericks or contrarians.

What type of investments should I opt for given the economic forecasts?

The type of investment instruments you opt for will depend heavily on your expectations. For example, if you are thinking of putting some of your money into gilts, the two key factors you will need to consider are inflation and interest rates. If you expect inflation to fall in the coming year, interest rates are also likely to fall, or at least not rise from current levels. If interest rates fall, then bonds are likely to be more expensive next year than this year. A forecast of strong employment might be useful too, since it may imply the economy is strengthening and would tend to suggest that interest rates might need to be tightened in the future to quash inflation and keep the economy on a sustainable growth path. A forecast of strong economic growth means, for instance, that cyclical stocks would pay dividends, whereas companies that have heavy interest payments would be unlikely to. Common sense, spiced with a little economic knowledge, can go a long way.

The two economic issues you need to consider before investing in stocks are earnings and interest rates. Take an example – you are thinking of investing in a company that makes household furniture. As you look at a whole host of economic factors, you will want to see how they affect the company's earnings. Higher interest rates would certainly take their toll on furniture-makers, since people would be less likely to move house, and first-time buyers would be less likely to step into the market. Furniture owners would be less likely to borrow money to replace existing furniture. Conclusion: rising interest rates don't look very helpful for furniture-makers.

What economic factors might affect furniture-makers' earnings? A forecast of a strong housing market might suggest that furniture stocks are presently a good buy. Consumer sentiment is also a key issue in furniture buying. Two major factors that drive consumer sentiment are unemployment and inflation. During periods of high unemployment, you are more likely to save money for the eventuality of losing your job. Inflation is a trickier factor to get your head round. Higher inflation would probably mean higher interest rates in the future. A big jump in inflation these days is more likely to be followed by a swift move from the Bank of England, which would hurt furniture-makers' earnings. However, steadily rising inflation is likely to encourage purchases, convincing people to buy now rather than later. Conclusion: rising inflation would on balance be a boom to furniture makers.

Knowledge Is King

There is no question about it – economics is a useful tool for any serious investor in this fast-changing financial world. To forget economics would be clearly misguided, but to overstress its importance would also be foolish. Economic data releases should be

the city

the press

webcraft

the old way

sleuthing

fund managers

short termers

crash!

new economy

telecoms

smokestacks

economics

tax

watched closely by the serious investor, but what is more important is being able to interpret them accurately and apply them appropriately. The same can be said of other people's forecasts and of course media pronouncements on the world of economics.

It really is a case of knowledge is king.

Oliver Wagg

Chapter Thirteen

Tax – How Not to Let It Ruin Your Life

the city
the press
webcraft
the old way
sleuthing
fund managers
short termers
crash!
new economy
telecoms
smokestacks
economics
tax

None of us wants to give the taxman a penny more than necessary, but you shouldn't allow tax to become an obsession. While tax-efficient investments can add an extra sparkle to your portfolio, never allow this to blind you to the real value of the underlying assets. After all, the real purpose of managing your investments is to make money, not reduce your tax bill. So, if the most lucrative investment isn't possible without paying tax, don't worry. Provided the end result will maximise your money, it's a good decision.

Tax-Efficient Investments

If you want to minimise your tax bill – whether you're talking income or capital gains – there is a whole host of opportunities available. Among the most common tax-efficient investments available in the UK are Individual Savings Accounts (ISAs), their forefathers Peps and Tessas, and many of the National Savings products and friendly society plans. Many of these have been discussed in Chapter Four.

The problem with some of these investments is that in order to maximise their benefits you have to leave your money tied up for years. For example, although Tessas are no longer available, existing ones will still be running for the next four years. They have a lock-in period of five years, during which if any capital, or more than 75 per cent of the interest, is withdrawn, the tax-free advantages are lost. Similarly, National Savings certificates, whether fixed

the city
the press
webcraft
the old way
sleuthing
fund managers
short termers
crash!
new economy
telecoms
smokestacks
economics
tax

interest or index-linked, have terms of either two or five years. If these are cashed, interest is still paid tax-free, but at a lower rate.

However, the worst offenders are the friendly society plans. These generally have ten-year terms, and if you stop making payments or need to cash in the investment you forfeit the tax benefits. But ten years is a long time and circumstances, whether your own or the investment's, can easily change. This could mean that disposing of the assets, and the tax benefits, is your best policy.

Although some of these financial commitments are only small, and should become even smaller relative to future earnings, you may want to consider the value of some of these tax-efficient guarantees if you have to stop saving and cash the plan in early. On the friendly society plans in particular, the hardest forfeits affect anyone who has to surrender in the early years. Because the charges on these products tend to be high, you can find that despite a couple of years of investment growth you don't even get your money back. And even if you can continue to make payments, the nature of the investment might change. What was once a top-performing investment could all too easily turn into the type of product that needs regular premiums just to keep its value at a stable level.

The art of picking an investment winner is further complicated by the advertising used to promote these products. Nobody wants to advertise a mediocre fund, so the top performers will always have a high profile. But top performance is hard to maintain, and many of yesterday's star performers are soon at the bottom of the league tables. And, unfortunately, if you've bought a dog, even if it's the most tax-efficient breed going, you're on to a loser.

Additionally, in spite of the huge perceived benefits of avoiding income and Capital Gains Tax, there are times when the tax savings that can be made on these types of investment are irrelevant. If you are a non-taxpayer unlikely to face a Capital Gains Tax bill, then a decision to invest in an ISA or directly in the underlying, and taxable, unit trust is pointless. Similarly, if you want to invest in a growth ISA that doesn't pay any income, then the only tax advantage you will have over the same investment without an ISA is shelter from Capital Gains Tax.

Charges

Check what you're being charged. Although many ISAs do not impose any extra charges on top of investing in the underlying vehicle, some managers will charge extra. This can mean, particularly for the smaller investor, that any tax savings are wiped out by charges. In the same way, with regard to pensions, you may be taking advantage of the tax breaks the government passes on to people saving for their retirement, but check these aren't just camouflaging the high charges and inflexibility of the plan.

Interest Rates

Banks and building societies have a strange habit concerning interest rates on deposit accounts. When the advertising campaign is launched, the rates are often the highest in the market. Then, when the punters have signed up and the posters have come down, down comes the rate, too. Unfortunately, this habit also applies to rates for the deposit-style tax-efficient products, notably the cash ISA and the now defunct Tessa.

the city
the press
webcraft
the old way
sleuthing
fund managers
short termers
crash!
new economy
telecoms
smokestacks
economics
tax

Although both Tessas and ISAs are transferable, this can often be more hassle than it's worth. With Tessas, especially since they have ceased to be offered, and competitive rates can no longer be used to attract new business, savers may be trapped in a low-interest rate product by the promise of a loyalty bonus at the end of the five-year term. And cashing in the investment, or even part of it, will only lead to the loss of the tax advantages you have already built up.

If you haven't got the time, or the inclination, to follow the rates on the tax-efficient products, you may be better placing your money in a normal savings account with a more visible presence in the market. The rate may initially be lower, and the taxman will take his cut of the interest, but if the provider wants to be known as one of the best in the market, it will stay competitive.

And, after all, the amount of tax that can be saved is only 20 per cent of the interest. So if there is an interest rate of 6 per cent, this will only represent a reduction of 1.2 per cent in the total return.

Alternatives

The emphasis placed on making the maximum ISA investment each year means it is very easy to make this a mission and lose sight of other areas of your finances. But there's no point making tax savings if your finances could benefit more from cash gains. For example, if you have any type of debt, particularly uncleared credit cards bills, it is madness to face an annual interest bill in the region of 20 per cent just to benefit from the tax savings on your ISA.

Capital Gains Tax aside, the amount you will gain from the tax-free environment of an equity ISA is just 10 per cent of the dividend. Dividends paid on non-ISA investments are subject to a

20 per cent tax charge; under the ISA rules this is reduced to 10 per cent. So if a unit trust ISA has a yield of 5 per cent, on a £5,000 investment you would save just £25 in a year. But if you've also got some form of debt, you might easily find yourself paying more than £25 in accumulated interest charges over a short space of time.

Other ways of using your money may also be more lucrative. For example, if you are buying property and have taken advantage of one of the flexible mortgages now available, you could be better off increasing the repayments, rather than saving. This not only clears the mortgage loan earlier, but it also reduces the size of the interest bill. Figures will vary between accounts and according to interest rates, but on an average mortgage you could save around £12,000 and reduce a twenty-five-year mortgage term by around five years, simply by increasing your mortgage repayments by £50 each month. And all without saving a penny in tax.

Capital Gains Tax

If you make a lot of money from your investments, then the taxman will want to share in your success by levying a Capital Gains Tax charge. Once your annual Capital Gains Tax allowance has been used up, any excess gains you've made will be taxed as income. If you're a higher-rate taxpayer you will have to stomach a higher Capital Gains Tax charge, too.

There are several ways to juggle your money around to avoid this tax: pass assets on to your spouse (known as bed and spouse), use ISAs to shelter the gain, and – for the more adventurous – balance your losses against your gains.

These techniques, although saving money, do take some of the thrill out of investing. Additionally, the whole concept of making losses to allow for gains just prompts the question 'Why did you invest in the first place?' If you've made a large gain on your investment, rather than water this down with a poor performer, it may be better to spread the gain over two years by holding on to some of the assets. Or take it on the chin, and be smug in the knowledge that you invested well. It is also reassuring to know that only about one person in five hundred is ever hit with a Capital Gains Tax bill.

Setting Up a Company

Keeping the taxman's sticky fingers off your assets and income also comes into play when people set themselves up as companies. A low income coupled with decent expenses and a large dividend is a neat formula for minimising tax. This may avoid the taxman but it may also mean avoiding other areas of finance, particularly where income is important.

Pension contributions in particular may suffer. As these are based on income, with a refund based on the person's tax band, a low income carries a double penalty. What's more, many pension companies charge a fixed amount for each contribution made, also penalising anyone paying in low premiums.

Because of the emphasis on income, mortgage applications can also prove problematic. In a bid to reduce the tax bill, you can find yourself restricted in your choice of mortgage deals and inadvertently paying a higher rate.

Inheritance Tax

Avoiding Inheritance Tax has become a hot issue in recent years, and not surprisingly. Anyone who dies with an estate totalling little more than a little property and a small portfolio of investments may also leave their beneficiaries an Inheritance Tax bill for 40 per cent of the excess. However, some of the methods of avoiding this liability can be as expensive as paying the bill.

A 'whole of life' insurance policy is a common way to ensure that the funds are available to pay any tax bills. It does guarantee that if you die, even the day after it's taken out, the bill will be met, but it needs regular checks and can be expensive. The expense is the result of two factors. First, thoughts of mortality and the prospect of leaving an inheritance do not tend to trouble us until we are older, at exactly the age when life assurance premiums become prohibitively expensive. Second, unlike straightforward term assurance where death must occur within a predetermined term, 'whole of life' cover will always pay out at some point provided premium payments are maintained. These two factors mean that someone in their sixties looking to take out 'whole of life' insurance for Inheritance Tax purposes can easily pay in excess of £1,000 a year.

The second problem with this type of product is that you need to make regular checks on your finances and keep an eye on how the government is treating Inheritance Tax. The size of your estate could shrink, or the government could increase the threshold for Inheritance Tax, reducing the need for an insurance product to meet the tax liability. While it will still pay out, increasing the money left to your benefactors, it is an expensive way to boost your estate.

the city
the press
webcraft
the old way
sleuthing
fund managers
short termers
crash!
new economy
telecoms
smokestacks
economics
tax

At the End of the Day . . .

Although most of the money we spend or invest has already been taxed as income, this doesn't mean that you should shun any investment strategy that will also make the taxman's coffers a little fuller. If you can avoid paying any additional tax, providing it is with a solid investment that suits your lifestyle, then take the tax benefits. But if the tax savings mean the performance of the investment is compromised, or you may need to make sacrifices to retain the tax advantages, forget it.

Sam Barrett

Summing Up

By now, you should have gained a reasonable basic understanding of the stock market, the part it plays in providing capital for companies and its role in general wealth-creation. You will also have a good grasp of the basic principles of investment, the relationship between risk and reward and the best way to use various sources of financial information.

There remains one major area that we haven't dealt with yet – personal finance. Now we know that personal finance may seem boring or mundane, but its importance cannot be over-stated: if your personal finances are under control you'll sleep more soundly at night. The two biggest investments that most people make in their lifetime relate to their housing and their pension. Get either of them wrong and you can end up paying the penalty for years.

The following section, therefore, takes us away from stock markets and into the realm of decisions that everybody has to make, whether they invest in shares or not. This applies to everyone with a bank account, a credit card, a mortgage or a tax bill. In other words, almost everybody at some time in his or her life.

We start by giving you some golden rules, or what to do and what not to do. If you follow these principles you will not go too far wrong. Then, under the heading *The Seven Ages of Money*, we describe the ways in which financial planning needs change over the lifetime of an individual. Few people move smoothly from one stage to the next – but most of us would be better off if we did.

Finally, we give you more detail on those twin giants of personal finance – mortgages and pensions – before concluding with a jargon-free glossary of financial and technical terms. With all of that under your belt, you should be a fully-rounded, confident investor, ready to go out and make your money do some work.

Nils Pratley

Investor Basics
The Building Blocks for Making
and Keeping Your Money

Golden Money Rules

Dealing effectively with your finances is probably one of the most important life skills. Nobody will look after your money as well as you can so it is up to you to take an interest in your financial affairs. Here are TheStreet.co.uk's golden rules to help you do just that:

- ☐ Don't bury your head in the sand – money problems will not go away unless you deal with them.
- ☐ Keep control of your finances. Work out a budget and try to stick to it. If you are bad with money, do not have a credit card which might encourage you to overspend. Use only your debit card, cash and cheques.
- ☐ Always shop around for the best deal, and where necessary, take independent financial advice.
- ☐ Review your overall financial situation regularly.
- ☐ Never let your bank current account go into the red without having arranged an overdraft facility. Interest charges on unauthorised overdrafts are at penalty rates as high as 30 per cent – plus charges of £25 a time to tell you that you are overdrawn.
- ☐ Always check your bank, credit card and savings account statements – mistakes do happen.
- ☐ Keep a record of the numbers of credit/debit/cash/cheque/store account and charge cards and make sure you know where to find the emergency number in case they are lost or stolen. (It is

on the back of your statement but you probably will not have it with you so make a note in your diary or address book.)

☐ Keep a record of the renewal dates of your household buildings and contents and car insurance so that the policies do not inadvertently lapse. Make a diary entry a few weeks before the renewal date so you have plenty of time to shop around for a cheaper alternative before the renewal notice comes in.

☐ Buy straight protection policies (like term assurance to provide a lump sum should you die with young dependants) as soon as you marry. Protection is very cheap when you are young. The older you get the more expensive it becomes.

☐ Life assurance is about providing for your dependants in the event that you die, or are sick and unable to work – it has little or nothing to do with savings. Savings-type endowments are a hangover from the days when you were eligible for tax relief on all types of life policy. This was abolished in 1984.

☐ If something looks too good to be true – it probably is.

☐ Keep a record of all your financial commitments and investments and file them all in one place – preferably in a fireproof filing cabinet

☐ Do not invest in anything that is likely to give you sleepless nights.

☐ Always make full use of your ISA allowance (maximum £7,000 for 2000/01, £5,000 for the next eight years) before you consider putting money into a personal pension scheme. ISAs are more flexible than pensions and you do not have to wait until you retire to get at your money.

☐ Start to save for a pension as soon as you possibly can – the earlier you start the greater the benefit (but invest the maximum in ISAs first).

- ☐ Higher rate taxpayers should not forget that National Savings Certificates provide a tax-free return.
- ☐ Complete your tax returns on time. If you don't, there are automatic fines and penalties which can really hurt.
- ☐ Do not forget to make a will. If you die intestate only a proportion of your assets will pass automatically to your spouse. Remember that marriage and divorce negate a will.

Lorna Bourke

The Seven Ages of Money

Few of us stop to think about money until we are forced to do so by a practical problem. A child is given money for Christmas and needs to put it somewhere safe. A teenager going to college or university needs a bank current account and an overdraft to finance further education. A young couple decide to get married and need a mortgage to purchase their first home. It is usually at these times that we think about our finances. So what are the essentials at each stage of your life?

Childhood

As soon as a child has money to save you will need some sort of savings account. There are hundreds to choose from, with most high-street banks and building societies offering a variety of accounts, including the most popular instant access account with minimum deposits of as little as £10. A child can pay in and withdraw cash on their own signature from the age of seven.

Many of them allow you to access your cash through cash machines using a cash card. You can pay in cash and cheques through the branches, unless it is a postal-only account, and withdraw cash over the counter or through the cash machine. Savings accounts may or may not have cheque facilities.

The advantage of a savings account is that your money is secure and earns interest. Most individuals choose a savings account for the best rate of interest combined with easy access. Generally there are no charges for running a savings account, although there may be for services like 'third-party cheques' where the bank or building society writes a one-off cheque made payable to a person designated by the account-holder.

Starting Work/Student

As soon as you earn money, or have to manage your own finances, you need a bank current account. Over 80 per cent of the adult population have a bank current account with cheque book facilities, cash machine card and debit card – usually combined in one piece of plastic. The vast majority of employers pay wages by direct credit through the banking system, so it is difficult to operate without a current account. A current account may pay interest on credit balances but more commonly does not.

Transactions like writing cheques are free, as are direct debits, standing orders and transfers between accounts – but only so long as the account is in credit. If the account is overdrawn, these transactions will usually incur charges as well as interest on the amount borrowed on overdraft. Some banks impose flat quarterly charges when the account is overdrawn, others charge for each transaction.

Overdrafts

If you need to borrow on your current account – and most young people do – you should arrange an overdraft facility. You will be charged interest on the amount you borrow, calculated on a daily basis. Some accounts include an automatic overdraft facility – typically around £250. Students are frequently offered free overdraft facilities up to a certain limit. Unauthorised overdrafts incur hefty penalty interest charges, which can be as high as 30 per cent or more, as well as penalty charges for writing letters or returning cheques unpaid of around £25 a time. Avoid being inadvertently overdrawn as it can be very expensive.

Cheque Guarantee Card

All banks issue a cheque guarantee card which ensures payment on cheques you write usually up to a value of £50, although some 'premium' accounts offer higher guarantee limits of up to £250 or more. Banks will delay issuing the card for a few weeks or months if you are a first-time account-holder to see how you conduct the account. Few retailers will accept a cheque without the guarantee, which is why cheques are rapidly being replaced by debit and credit cards for most retail purchases.

Cash Machine Cards

Most cheque guarantee cards will also operate Automated Teller Machines (ATMs) for cash withdrawals. There is usually a daily limit imposed on the amount you can withdraw – often £100. If you use the machines of your chosen bank there is usually no charge for accessing cash through an ATM. Many banks and building societies belong to the Link, Maestro or Cirrus networks, which allow you to access cash from a variety of bank and building society machines. There may be a charge for using another bank's machines.

Debit Cards

This is also incorporated in the cheque guarantee and cash card facility and is identifiable by the Switch or Delta logo. Your debit card can be used to pay for goods and services at most major retail outlets and the amount of the purchase will be debited to your current account.

If you do not have enough money in the account to complete the transaction or the amount of the purchase would push you above your authorised overdraft limit, the transaction will be refused. This can be embarrassing, so it pays to keep tabs on your cash position.

Credit Cards

If you are a spendthrift it is probably better to avoid credit cards. It is worth remembering that around 80 per cent of actions brought to magistrates' courts are for non-payment of credit card debt. Do not think you will get away with it. The credit card companies nearly always sue.

There are currently around four hundred credit cards on offer, and fierce competition in the credit card market is currently forcing charges down. Interest rates range from a hefty 22 per cent to as little as 5.9 per cent on some of the newer cards which have concessionary introductory rates. Clearly it pays to shop around. Do not just accept the credit card offered by your bank.

Some credit cards charge an annual fee as well as interest on uncleared balances. You may be charged interest from the day of purchase or from the statement date. With the latter you can avoid interest charges entirely by settling the account in full by the required date. There are many loyalty schemes in operation such as bonus points or Air Miles. Generally it pays to go for the lowest interest rate.

Some credit card issuers offer a cheque-book facility which allows you to pay for services for which you might not otherwise be able to use your credit card – such as medical or dental fees, accountancy and legal charges.

One major advantage of using a credit card for major purchases is that should the supplier or retailer fail, you can claim compensation from the credit card company provided the amount of credit involved is at least £100 and not more than £30,000.

Charge Cards

Charge cards like American Express, Diners and some Mastercards do not offer a credit facility. The bill must be settled in full each month. But they are a convenient, secure and widely accepted payment method. Some, like American Express, have an annual charge. Others do not.

The main advantage of charge cards is that there is no limit on the amount you can spend – in theory you could buy a £20,000 new car on an Amex card if the retailer was authorised to accept it. In practice, the retailer will have a floor limit, and if you used your card for a very expensive purchase it would be queried – although not necessarily turned down. Charge cards, like credit cards, offer security – you do not have to carry large sums of cash or a cheque book and cheque guarantee card.

Personal Belongings and/or Contents Insurance

Although as a student or a young person you may not have anything more valuable than a mobile phone, camera, hi-fi/CD player or TV, these are precisely the items thieves go for. If losing the lot in one go would be devastating, cover yourself with personal belongings and/or household contents policies.

A personal belongings insurance policy provides compensation up to an agreed limit if your valuables such as jewellery, cameras and so on are lost, stolen, accidentally damaged or destroyed. They are annual policies and have to be renewed each year. If you are a bad risk and make a large number of claims, you may find it difficult to get cover.

Typically cover is offered for a pre-agreed amount at a fixed percentage rate according to the type of risk. All cover for theft of personal valuables such as jewellery or cameras will pay the full replacement value of your belongings. The rate may range from around £3 a year for every £100 of cover to as much as £20 a year per £100.

The terms and conditions vary widely and you may be required to give a specific value for each item covered above a certain amount. The policy may alternatively have a 'single item limit' of 5 per cent of the total sum insured. Discounts are typically available if you are prepared to accept an excess for the first £50 or £100 of any claim. Many package policies have fixed limits for different categories of cover.

Car Insurance

You are legally obliged to have motor insurance if you own and drive a car. Motor insurance is an annual policy and it pays to shop around before buying and on renewal as there are wide differences in premium rates. Cover can be 'third party, fire and theft' only or fully comprehensive, which is more expensive. The latter covers you for all accidental damage to your car – the former does not. Both types of policy provide legal fees protection and compensation should you be sued by a passenger, another driver or a pedestrian who has been injured in a motor accident where you are the driver.

Marriage and Children

Marriage, like measles, is something that happens to most people. It is still popular in spite of the rising incidence of cohabitation. Estimates from the Office of Population Censuses and Surveys reveal that 93 per cent of fifty-year-old men have been married at least once, as have 95 per cent of women, and more men than women remarry. Every year, nearly 300,000 people marry, many for the second or third time, but there are over 165,000 divorces. These cheery statistics mean that anyone marrying today should be aware that he or she has little better than a 50–50 chance of remaining married to the same person.

Life Assurance

It is arguable that if you are single, and intend remaining so, you do not need life assurance at all. But since most of us get married it is worth bearing in mind that you are likely to have dependants. The younger you are when you buy life assurance, the cheaper it is. This should be an important priority as soon as you marry – even if you intend delaying starting a family.

Life assurance protection policies, like mortgage protection, term assurance, convertible term cover, and whole life, provide a pre-agreed tax-free lump sum if you die during the term of the policy. In the case of whole life it pays out at whatever age death occurs.

If you do not die during the term of the life cover, these policies will pay nothing. For this reason, many individuals decide to have a savings-type endowment with some life protection thrown in. This is not a good idea because the life cover will be wholly inadequate.

It is generally agreed that the average breadwinner (and these days it is likely to be both partners) needs at least three times their gross salary as straight protection. The most sensible way to provide this is to add this amount to the cash sum covering your mortgage. So if you have a £100,000 home loan and you earn £35,000 a year you should probably insure your life for the next twenty-five years – the period when you are likely to have young dependants – for at least £200,000.

Where both partners work, both lives should be insured. Non-working mothers need cover too. The cost of hiring full-time help to look after young children should the mother die is around £200 a week. Joint life cover may be slightly cheaper than two separate policies, but they will have to be discontinued and separate cover purchased if the worst happens and you get divorced.

Many employees do not bother to insure their lives because they have cover of three times gross salary as an employee benefit. This is fine – but do bear in mind that if you are made redundant or become self-employed, you will be purchasing life cover at a later stage in your life when you are older and the cover is therefore more expensive, or you may not be in good health, in which case your premiums will be loaded, or, in a worst-case scenario, you may be unable to obtain cover at all.

Term assurance is cheap but the younger you are when you buy it the better. It costs only around £8 a month for £100,000 worth of twenty-five-year term cover when you are twenty-five. But by the time you are forty the premium goes up to over £35 a month.

Suitable protection policies for married couples include:

- ☐ Term assurance
- ☐ Mortgage Protection
- ☐ Convertible Term Assurance
- ☐ Whole Life
- ☐ Joint Life – first death (for mortgage protection)
- ☐ Joint Life – second death (for inheritance tax planning)
- ☐ Dread Disease or Critical Illness
- ☐ Permanent Health Insurance

Critical Illness policies provide a tax-free lump sum if you develop any of a list of diseases. If you are critically ill, you may be forced to give up work and a lump sum can help ease the situation. This should be perhaps second on your list of life cover priorities.

Illnesses covered usually include heart disease, liver, lung or kidney disease or failure, and some cancers. Be aware that the exclusions are numerous and Sod's law will probably dictate that the illness that actually lays you low is not on the list.

Permanent Health policies provide replacement income to age sixty or sixty-five if you are sick or disabled and unable to work. Most employed people can manage without this cover as they will probably be paid their full salary for up to six months of sickness and half salary for a further six months. You can, however, buy cover with a twelve-month deferral period if you feel it is necessary.

Terms and conditions for PHI vary widely, and anyone wanting this type of protection should take independent advice as there are many exclusions. Some policies will pay out if you are unable to do your normal work. Others will only pay out if you are unable to work at all. Because of the incentive to malinger, premiums for PHI can be expensive. However, for anyone who is self-employed it is worth considering either PHI or Payment Protection cover, which is much cheaper but does not pay benefits for the rest of your life. However, if you are still unable to work when the Payment Protection benefits end, you will probably have to completely rethink your life anyway.

When Children Arrive

Children, bless them, are expensive, and if you intend educating them at fee-paying schools you will either need deep pockets or should start saving at birth. Of the seven million children currently of school age, an estimated 425,000 are educated at fee-paying schools. With student grants being a thing of the past, even if you intend sending your children to state schools, you will need to save for their further education. The sooner you start the better.

There are a number of suitable savings products ranging from a low-risk straightforward savings account at the bank or building society to unit and investment trust savings plans. Provided you have at least five to ten years before the money will be required, an equity-based investment is likely to produce the best return. Unit trust regular savings schemes are probably the most flexible and have the lowest charges.

There are a number of packaged 'school fees' products, which are frequently nothing more than a with-profits or unit-linked endowment or a mixture of a deferred annuity and an endowment. You can generally get a better deal and lower charges by putting together your own portfolio of investments – which may include endowments – with the help of an independent adviser.

One popular low-risk method of providing school fees is to buy a succession of with-profit endowments, maturing in successive years, which are encashed to provide the fees. The child should be at least seven years off requiring fees in order that the endowments remain qualifying policies. Bear in mind, however, that no savings plan can guarantee to pay school fees in full since you are saving for an unknown commitment.

Remember too that a child is entitled to a personal tax allowance (£4,385 for 2000–2001), so it may be more tax-efficient to hold the investment in the child's name (where this is possible) than holding it in the name of a wealthy grandparent or godparent who may be a 40 per cent taxpayer. If the money invested has come from a parent, any income generated will be treated as though it is the parents' income once it exceeds £100 a year.

Where large sums of money are involved, it will probably be worthwhile setting up a trust with the children (and perhaps others) as beneficiaries. Any of the following investment products or a combination of several would be suitable for school fees provision:

☐ Unit or Investment Trust Regular Savings Scheme or lump sum investment

☐ With-profit endowment – regular saving or lump sum bond

☐ Unit-linked endowment – regular saving or lump sum bond

☐ A portfolio of individual shares

☐ A series of equity-based Isa investments

☐ Deferred annuities

☐ Guaranteed-growth bonds

☐ Zero coupon investment trust shares

☐ Capital shares of split capital investment trusts

☐ Gilts (government stock) or corporate bonds (these could be held directly or through mutual funds)

☐ National Savings products

☐ Bank or building society savings schemes.

Finally, if it has not been possible to save for school fees, as a last resort you could consider remortgaging the family home with a 'flexible mortgage'. This type of mortgage allows you to borrow up to a pre-agreed limit – usually 75 per cent of the value of the property – and repay the borrowing as and when you can afford to do so, provided it is over the normal term of the loan. If you have to borrow to finance education, this will be the cheapest way of doing it.

Divorce and Single Parenthood

As we have already pointed out, with almost 50 per cent of marriages ending in divorce, this is unfortunately not a possibility anyone can afford to ignore, and it inevitably brings financial problems. The statistics show that 50 per cent of divorced men remarry and the majority find themselves paying maintenance and trying to support two households on one income.

With the establishment in 1993 of the Child Support Agency, which sets minimum maintenance payments for children, it is more difficult for fathers to avoid their responsibilities. But the vast majority of divorced or single mothers will find themselves bringing up children on far less money than when they were married. Frequently they are totally dependent on social security payments such as income support and housing benefit.

Of the 1.3 million single parents in the UK caring for 2.1 million children, the vast majority are single mothers. Fewer than 10 per cent are single fathers. In 1998 well over a million single parents were dependent on income support or family credit. Less than one in three single mothers receive any financial support at all from their former partner. Where maintenance is paid the average amount is around £16 a week per child, or £30 a week where there are three or more children.

With money so short, the most important financial considerations are:

Who gets what on divorce? – Where there are children the wife usually gets half the joint assets (including any pension fund assets) plus one-third of the joint incomes. This is a very rough rule of thumb, and where family trusts are involved the eventual settlement can be very different. Similarly, if the wife is the higher earner, the settlement may be a lump-sum clean break. The provisions for splitting pensions are still not decided and it may be either a transfer of funds or 'earmarking', where a proportion of a former spouse's pension entitlement (usually the former husband's) is earmarked and paid to the former wife at retirement.

If there are no children the general formula is that both partners keep assets owned in their sole name before marriage. Assets acquired during the marriage and jointly owned will generally be divided, the exact proportions depending on the relative contributions.

Life assurance – Where one partner, usually the wife, is dependent on the former husband for maintenance for herself and children, she should make sure that this maintenance includes a sum sufficient to cover premiums on the former husband's life. If he dies, their income disappears also. Do not rely on a former spouse to maintain existing life policies. Inevitably, if money is short it is all too easy to cancel the policy without the other person knowing.

Joint life policies will have to be discontinued and both partners will need to take out individual cover. During marriage, if one partner dies, any assets passing to the spouse are free of Inheritance Tax. This is no longer the case after divorce, and where the former partner or the children are the beneficiaries of the life policies they should be written in trust to ensure that they are outside your estate and received by the beneficiaries free from any potential Inheritance Tax charge.

On divorce a wife will lose all entitlement to a state widow's pension. Divorce negates a will and both partners should make new ones.

Retirement

Retirement is a profound change in life and for the vast majority of individuals involves a drop in income at a time when they have more time on their hands to spend money. Naturally, much thought should be given to pensions, which is covered in detail later.

Buying an Annuity

For anyone with less than £100,000 in a personal pension fund or the old Self-Employed Retirement Annuities, at retirement you will be more or less obliged to buy an annuity because of the relatively high cost of administering income drawdown (see p. 287). You will have to decide what type of annuity to buy – with profits or a straight income for life. The return on a straight annuity is dependent on several factors:

☐ Interest rates at the time of retirement
☐ Your age when you buy the annuity
☐ Your sex (women have a longer life expectancy than men and therefore suffer lower annuity rates)
☐ Whether the income is paid monthly, quarterly, half-yearly or annually
☐ Whether the income is paid in advance or in arrears
☐ Whether some return of capital is guaranteed if you die within five years of retirement (capital-protected annuities)
☐ Whether the income increases or is index-linked

Investing for Income in Retirement

There are a number of investment products that will provide income in retirement. The following could all be part of an income portfolio:

☐ Bank and building society deposit accounts
☐ Government stock (gilts)
☐ Permanent Interest Bearing shares (PIBs)
☐ Guaranteed income bonds

- [ ] National Savings products
- [ ] Income shares of split capital investment trusts
- [ ] Income Unit Trusts
- [ ] Corporate Bond Funds (if held within a Pep or Isa the income can be taken tax free)
- [ ] Life company with-profit bonds
- [ ] Life company distribution bonds.

With yields on investments currently low, it is also worth considering taking the capital growth from investments as income. This has the added advantage that the first £7,200 (2000/2001) is tax free.

Inheritance Tax Planning

If your assets, including the family home, exceed £234,000 (2000/2001) you will be liable for Inheritance Tax at 40 per cent on your death unless you leave everything to your spouse. Transfers between husband and wife both during your lifetime and on death are free of IHT.

To make good use of both partners' nil rate band, it pays to split assets between husband and wife, with each leaving up to the nil rate ceiling (£234,000) to children, grandchildren or other beneficiaries. This way you can avoid IHT on up to £468,000 of your assets. The only other way to avoid IHT is to give assets away during your lifetime and live for a further seven years. These assets are then outside your estate for IHT purposes. However, you cannot give away the family house to your children or other beneficiaries, and remain living in it, unless you pay a commercial rent. This is deemed to be a 'gift with reservation' by the Inland Revenue and does not avoid IHT. Be careful about passing on assets to children or other beneficiaries where there are significant Capital Gains Tax liabilities. You could suffer double taxation – CGT on the gift and IHT on death.

You should, however, consider the following avoiding action:

☐ Transfer or write life policies (both protection and savings type) in trust for the benefit of named beneficiaries so that they are outside your estate.

☐ Insure your life with a term policy for the seven years after you have given assets away for sufficient to cover any potential IHT liability.

☐ Insure your life with a whole life policy to cover any potential IHT liability which will arise on your death. For married couples, a joint life, last-survivor policy might be more suitable.

☐ Consider leaving your mortgage outstanding at retirement to reduce the net value of your estate. The value of any associated endowment policy could be passed on to children.

☐ Your children might consider insuring your life to cover any potential IHT liability. This is cheap if you are still relatively young.

☐ Transfer assets into a trust with you continuing to receive the income.

☐ If you are operating income drawdown on your pension, make sure any remaining fund on death before age seventy-five (when you will be obliged to buy an annuity) is written in trust for the benefit of named individuals.

☐ Make a will trust leaving assets up to the nil rate band threshold to your children, grandchildren or other beneficiaries, with your spouse as the 'life tenant'.

☐ Leave your share of the family home to the children with the express wish that your spouse continues to remain living in the property during their lifetime.

☐ Take independent professional advice from both a solicitor and an accountant. Solicitors are not always clued up on the more sophisticated ways of avoiding IHT. The Society of Trusts and Estate Practitioner's members are all professionals qualified in IHT planning.

Lorna Bourke

Buying a Home
A Helping Hand up the
Property Ladder

Most people need to borrow money to buy a house or flat and the vast majority of homebuyers – some 10.9 million – take out a mortgage. Since this is likely to be the biggest financial transaction you will ever make, it is worth taking time to understand the different types of mortgages available and which is likely to be the most suitable for you. With over three thousand mortgage products on offer, picking a 'best buy' is not easy, and you will probably need professional advice from a reputable mortgage broker – preferably one who is registered with the Financial Services Authority, and who is able to advise on all aspects of house buying including associated savings products and insurance.

What Is a Mortgage?

A mortgage is a loan secured against property – usually your home. The loan is commonly used to buy the property but it can be used for other purposes. If you are already an owner-occupier you can remortgage your home and use the extra funds for school fees, home improvements, etc. In the event that you default on repayments on the loan, the lender is entitled to repossess the property and sell it in order to settle the outstanding debt. As the advertisements say, 'Your Home Is at Risk if You Do Not Keep Up the Repayments'.

Repayment or Interest Only?

When you buy a property you will be given the choice of a straight repayment loan or an interest-only mortgage, which will generally be linked to an associated savings scheme.

Repayment – With a straight repayment loan, each monthly payment consists of part interest and part repayment of the original sum borrowed. At the end of the term the loan will be completely paid off and you will own your home outright. It is arguable that everyone should have a straight repayment loan, particularly at times when the net cost of borrowing is greater than house price inflation.

Interest-only – Interest-only mortgages are sold in conjunction with some kind of savings scheme. Each month you pay the interest on the outstanding home loan, plus a monthly payment to a regular savings scheme – probably a with-profits endowment policy, a unit-linked endowment, a unit trust regular savings scheme, a personal pension (if you are self-employed or in non-pensionable employment) or a regular savings Individual Savings Account.

You may be able to arrange an interest-only mortgage with no associated savings scheme, if you can show, for example, that you have a portfolio of shares sufficient to cover the loan, or you stand to benefit at a later date from some kind of trust fund or share option scheme, or you are the beneficiary of a will and expect to inherit money or other assets. At the end of the mortgage term, the money invested in the savings vehicle pays off the outstanding debt. There may also be a surplus, or in a worst possible situation a deficit. The money saved may not be enough to pay off the outstanding home loan. This is why you should regularly review any savings vehicle used to pay off a mortgage. (More details of the various savings vehicles associated with interest-only mortgages later.)

An interest-only mortgage is an attractive proposition if the after-tax return on the savings vehicle over the term of the loan is greater than the net cost of borrowing. In other words, if the net return on your with-profits endowment is 9 per cent a year, and the average cost of your mortgage borrowing throughout the term of the loan is 8 per cent or less, it pays you to leave the debt outstanding, paying interest only, and invest the money in the endowment.

Remember – paying off a loan has little or nothing to do with long-term savings. The only reason lenders promote endowment-linked loans is because they earn hefty commissions of anything up to eighteen months' premiums when they sell you an endowment policy. If you can afford to do so, your best bet is to go for a 'belt and braces' approach. Take out a repayment loan, and if you can also put money away in a long-term savings scheme like an ISA or unit trust regular savings scheme, then you are well covered.

How Much Can I Borrow?

The general rule is that you can borrow up to three and a half times your gross earnings, plus the earnings of a partner. If, for example, you earn £50,000 a year, you will be able to borrow up to £175,000. Buying jointly with your partner who earns, say, £30,000 a year, total borrowing rises to £205,000. When interest rates are low, it may be possible to borrow a larger multiple of your earnings – say four times gross income – if you are in secure employment in one of the professions such as the law or accountancy where there is a recognised career structure and you can expect regular pay increases.

How Much of the Purchase Price Can I Borrow?

You can usually borrow up to 95 per cent of the purchase valuation – not to be confused with the asking price or the price you are actually paying. In an overheated property market it is not unusual for the lender's valuer to put a valuation on the property which is lower than the asking price. It may also be considerably lower than the price you are prepared to pay if you find yourself in a bid battle with another potential buyer.

It is possible to borrow 100 per cent of the purchase price, but there is not much choice of lenders in this market and you will probably find that the mortgage package offered is not competitive compared with the wide range on offer for 95 per cent loans.

How Much Will It Cost?

Not such a daft question, and most homebuyers have very little idea of what to expect. The table shows the monthly cost of each £1,000 borrowed at varying interest rates over ten and twenty-five years.

Interest Rate	25-year repayment loan	10-year repayment loan
3.0%	£4.79	£9.77
3.5%	£5.06	£10.03
4.0%	£5.34	£10.28
4.5%	£5.62	£10.54

5.0%	£5.92	£10.80
5.5%	£6.22	£11.06
6.0%	£6.52	£11.33
6.5%	£6.84	£11.60
7.0%	£7.16	£11.87
7.5%	£7.48	£12.15
8.0%	£7.81	£12.42
8.5%	£8.15	£12.71
9.0%	£8.49	£12.99
9.5%	£8.83	£13.28
10.0%	£9.19	£13.57

So, for example, monthly repayments on a £67,000 ten-year mortgage at 7 per cent are 67 × £11.87 = £795.29

What Types of Mortgage are Available?

Standard Variable-Rate Loans

The standard variable rate of interest is the benchmark against which other mortgage products are measured. With this type of loan, your monthly mortgage payments go up and down in line with changes in the variable rate. Mortgage lenders adjust their variable rate, usually when the Bank of England changes the bank base rate. The standard variable rate is typically around 1.5 per cent above bank base rate, but it can be more or less. However, different lenders will have slightly different standard variable rates, although the differential between major lenders is seldom much more than 0.25 per cent. Monthly mortgage payments are usually collected by the lender on a direct debit mandate so you do not have to rearrange payments every time there is a mortgage rate adjustment.

The advantage of this type of loan is that if you borrow at a time of high mortgage rates – as in 1990/91, when the mortgage rate stood at 15.4 per cent – as interest rates come down, you derive full benefit from the reductions. The disadvantage is, obviously, that the reverse is also true. When interest rates rise, you will find yourself with higher monthly payments. First-time buyers have been caught out by unexpected rate increases in the past, leaving them unable to meet the higher monthly mortgage payments.

Fixed-Rate Mortgages

Fixed-rate mortgages are now widely available, although this is a relatively recent innovation. Your interest charges are fixed at a pre-agreed level for a number of years – typically two to five years although longer-term fixes of ten years or more are on offer from time to time.

During the term of the fix, your interest charges cannot rise above the agreed rate – but neither can they fall below it. If the variable interest rate rises above the fixed rate, you will be saving money on interest charges. If they fall below the fixed rate, you will be paying more than is necessary for your borrowing. The timing of taking out a fixed-rate mortgage is therefore important.

The advantage of fixed-rate mortgages is that you know absolutely what your monthly payments will be during the fixed-rate period, and if you have borrowed a large amount relative to your income, this is an important consideration. Much of the negative equity that homebuyers suffered in the early nineties came about because borrowers on variable rate loans were caught out by rapidly rising interest rates. (They went from 9.5 per cent in May 1988 to

15.4 per cent by February 1990.) Many borrowers were unable to meet their mortgage commitments in full. If they had borrowed 95 per cent of the purchase price, they soon found that the original borrowing, plus unpaid interest, was greater than the value of the property – otherwise known as 'negative equity'.

Watch Out for Penalties

To cover fixed-rate lending on your mortgage, the bank or building society frequently borrows in the money markets – also at a fixed rate. If you redeem your mortgage during the fixed-rate period, and interest rates have fallen, the lender will be out of pocket because he will not be able to relend the money repaid by you at the same rate, so there is usually a penalty to pay – typically three to six months' gross interest at the standard variable rate.

Some lenders impose the penalty for one or two years after the fixed rate has expired. Avoid mortgages with these 'penalty overhangs'. It is impossible to calculate the true cost of such a loan because you will be locked into the variable rate after the fixed rate expires, possibly three or five years down the line, and nobody can predict what the variable rate will be at that time. However, it is possible that the government will ban penalty overhangs.

When to Fix?

Try to lock into a fixed-rate mortgage when interest rates are low but expected to rise. Often the best fixed-rate deals are available just before interest rates finally bottom out. Fixed-rate remortgages are also widely available from most lenders.

Capped-Rate Mortgages

The best of all possible worlds is a capped mortgage. The 'cap' ensures that your interest charges can never rise above the capped rate for the agreed term. But if interest rates fall, you will derive full benefit from any interest rate reductions.

For example, the variable rate might stand at 6.99 per cent and you take out a mortgage capped at 7 per cent for five years. During the capped period, the mortgage interest charge will never be more than 7 per cent, however high the variable rate goes. But if interest rates come down, say to 6 per cent, you will see the full benefit of the reduction. This is a no-lose situation. Capped rates tend to be on offer for terms of two to five years.

However, some lenders impose a penalty if you come out of a capped-rate loan during the period of the cap. Given that you will benefit from any interest rate reductions and will not have to pay more than the capped rate, it is difficult to see very many situations where it will be advantageous to give up a capped-rate mortgage. Where penalties are imposed, they tend to be very similar to those on fixed-rate mortgages – three to five months' gross interest at the standard variable rate.

Discounted Mortgages

Many lenders offer discounted mortgages as an enticement – particularly for first-time buyers. The discounts may be anything from 0.5 per cent to 3 per cent or more below the standard variable rate, and can last for anything between six months and five years. A typical discounted loan might offer a reduction of 1.5 per cent on the standard variable rate for the first one or two years. The discounted rate will remain at a fixed differential below the standard variable rate but will otherwise go up and down in line with changes in the variable rate.

However, many discounted mortgages carry penalties for early redemption – usually for one to three years after the discounted period has expired. This enables the lender to recoup the cost of the loss-leader discounts by locking you into the standard variable rate for a fixed period after the discount expires. This prevents you moving to another lender – possibly with another concessionary rate.

Discounted rates are a good deal compared with the standard variable rate but may not be as good as a fixed- or capped-rate loan.

Cash-Back Loans

Cash-backs are a relatively recent innovation. The main mortgage may be a variable-rate or fixed-rate loan. But as a sweetener to entice you to become a customer, the lender offers a percentage of the loan as a cash-back 'gift'. Sometimes there is an upper limit placed on the amount that can be taken as a cash-back.

However, a free gift is never quite as free as it first appears, and usually you will end up paying more in interest charges on the mortgage, so that the lender can recoup the cost of the cash-back. These loans are very popular with first-time buyers who may need the cash to help with buying costs such as legal fees or furnishing the home, and cannot afford to borrow elsewhere.

If you redeem a cash-back loan within a certain number of years you usually have to repay all or part of the cash. Typically, you will be locked in for up to five years with a sliding scale of penalties. For example, with a 5 per cent cash-back on a £100,000 mortgage, you might be asked to repay the full £5,000 if you redeem the loan in the first two years, £3,000 for redemption in year three, £2,000 if you redeem in year four, and £1,000 if you redeem the mortgage in the fifth year.

Fee-Free Mortgages

As the name implies, with a fee-free mortgage the lender makes no arrangement charge and waives the valuation fee. This will typically save around £350 in up-front costs. Some lenders will also cover the costs of legal fees up to an agreed limit. There may be other concessions too, such as a discounted mortgage rate. These loans are popular with first-time buyers who are short of cash.

Flexible Mortgages

A recent innovation, flexible mortgages are now very popular. They are particularly attractive for the self-employed whose earnings may fluctuate, because they allow you to miss monthly repayments, increase or decrease monthly payments, pay off lump sums without penalty, or borrow more up to a pre-agreed limit – sometimes as much as 90 per cent of the property's valuation.

The best, like those offered by Virgin and First Active (at the time of writing), also combine current bank account facilities. This has the advantage of allowing you to borrow at the much lower secured mortgage rate, rather than using an overdraft facility or personal loan where the interest charge could easily be double. And because your salary is paid into the account, this also reduces the amount owed, at least temporarily, and can save considerable sums in interest charges over the life of a twenty-five-year home loan.

Most flexible mortgages do not incorporate your current account as part of the package and some offer very little beyond what you would expect from a conventional mortgage. They are simply jumping on the 'flexible' bandwagon. It pays to sit down and analyse what you want from a flexible loan.

Flexible mortgages are eminently suitable for the self-employed and anyone whose earnings fluctuate, career women whose earnings may be interrupted by the birth of children, commission- or bonus-earning salespeople who may want to make large capital repayments, and anyone raising finance for a new business.

The lenders generally do not ask you why you want to activate the extra borrowing facilities and flexible mortgages probably offer the cheapest finance available for new business start-ups, car finance, school fees and many other areas of expenditure where unsecured loans are relatively expensive.

But remember, borrowing against the family home to start a new business may be the cheapest option, but if the business fails you may lose your home – and very often your partner too.

Tracker Mortgages

One of the main criticisms of mortgage lenders is that they are very keen to increase their interest rates when the bank base rate goes up, but somewhat slow to bring them down when the base rate goes down. Tracker mortgages get round this problem by offering an interest rate at a fixed differential above bank base rate, and an automatic adjustment whenever the bank base rate moves up or down. A good tracker mortgage will have a differential of less than 1 per cent above the bank base rate and may have other attractive features as well – such as flexible repayments and additional borrowing.

But remember, tracker mortgages are fine when interest rates are coming down – not so good when rates are going up.

Conditional Lending

Many mortgage packages include compulsory insurances – endowments or pensions, mortgage protection, buildings and contents or mortgage payment protection. This is known as 'conditional lending' because you cannot have the loan without the additional insurances. Frequently these packages are a poor deal because what you save on the mortgage interest rate you lose on overpriced insurance. The trouble is that most unsophisticated homebuyers simply look at the headline mortgage rate and have no idea what they should be paying for the associated insurances. The government is looking at conditional lending, and it seems quite likely that it will be banned or restricted.

Tax and Your Home

The vast majority of homeowners have only one property which is their principal private residence and this is totally free from Capital Gains Tax on any profit you make when you sell. However, if you have more than one property – perhaps a holiday cottage or an investment property which you let – profits when you sell will be subject to Capital Gains Tax. There are complex rules concerning properties which have been your principal private residence which you subsequently let, and you will need professional advice from a qualified accountant on this. If you have more than one property, you must tell the Inland Revenue which is your principal private residence for CGT purposes.

Since April 2000, the residual benefit from mortgage interest income tax relief on the first £30,000 of borrowings to purchase your principal private residence has been abolished. If you let a property, all interest charges on money borrowed to acquire or improve and maintain the property can be offset against the rental income. You can also offset all the costs associated with renting the property – insurance, maintenance, replacement and so on against rental income before you are assessed for income tax.

Insurances

Mortgage lenders will generally try to sell you insurances with your home loan – savings-type policies, mortgage payment protection, buildings and contents, and mortgage term assurance – because they earn hefty commission on these policies. For example, on many with-profit endowments, the first eighteen months' premiums go straight into the pocket of the intermediary as commission. The intermediary is frequently the lender or estate agent.

Most insurances can generally be purchased more cheaply else-where with the possible exception of buildings and contents insurance. Because of the bargaining power of the big lenders, they are often able to negotiate better terms and conditions on these policies, for a lower premium than you can find on the open market. In the event of a claim on the buildings policy, the lender has a vested interest in ensuring that the claim is paid in full and your home restored, because the property is their security for the loan. This is particularly important if you have a big subsidence claim. The lender will fight on your behalf. It is also usually cheaper to buy both buildings and contents policy from the same insurer.

What Insurances Do I Really Need?

The only insurance that all housebuyers need is buildings insurance and arguably Mortgage Payment Protection Insurance (MPPI). Buildings insurance protects your property and the big investment you have made in it which you cannot afford to leave uninsured.

Mortgage Payment Protection

Mortgage Payment Protection Insurance pays a regular monthly sum sufficient to cover your monthly outgoings on mortgage payments should you be unable to pay through sickness, accident or redundancy. This is very important as, since 1995, state benefits no longer cover the first thirty-nine weeks' mortgage interest payments if you are out of work or ill. Most MPPI is sold by the lenders when a mortgage is arranged, but this may not be the cheapest deal.

In addition, most MPPI policies allow you to insure for a sum sufficient to cover outgoings on household utilities and any insurances such as buildings and contents, as well as endowment premiums. Social security benefits do not cover these essential payments at all.

MPPI monthly income payments generally last for one or two years, which will be sufficient for most eventualities. If you are still unemployed or sick after that time you are clearly going to have to rethink your entire life and finances. Permanent Health Insurance provides income up to age sixty or sixty-five should you be unable to work through sickness – but this is much more expensive than MPPI and it does not cover you for redundancy.

Costs for MPPI range from around £5 to £7 a month for every

£100 a month of mortgage and associated payments covered. You can buy MPPI cover as two separate elements – cover for accident, sickness and disability, or separate redundancy and unemployment cover. Most policies have a deferral period before benefits are paid, and this can be as long as six months if your employer will pay you during periods off work through sickness. However, it is not wise to have much more than a one-month deferral period on unemployment cover unless you have plenty of savings. You never know when you may find yourself out of a job. Generally speaking you will have to have been in employment for six months before you will be eligible for any benefits for redundancy.

The self-employed, who cannot rely on any income at all if they are unable to work, should definitely take out sickness MPPI cover. Terms and conditions on unemployment are often tough, so there may not be any point having this cover. Usually you have to have signed on for Job Seekers Allowance or have been made bankrupt before these policies will pay redundancy benefit to the self-employed.

Mortgage Protection Term Assurance

This policy pays a lump sum, sufficient to pay off the mortgage, on the death of the breadwinner before the end of the mortgage term. If the policy-holder survives until the end of the mortgage term, the policy lapses and there are no benefits paid. If both partners work, the policy can be arranged on a joint life first-death basis, so it pays out when the first partner dies, leaving the survivor with an unencumbered property.

Single homeowners do not need Mortgage Protection insurance unless they have dependants to whom they want to leave an unencumbered property. Many mortgage lenders will try to push you into buying cover even if you do not really need it, because it means that on your death the mortgage is immediately repaid. Do not be browbeaten into buying if you do not need it.

It is important to remember that all Mortgage Protection policies should be written in trust for the benefit of named individuals so that the proceeds are outside your estate for Inheritance Tax purposes. This is particularly important if you are a single parent with young dependent children, but not so important for married couples as transfers between married partners on death are free from IHT.

Premiums for Mortgage Protection policies are often included with payments to an endowment policy as part of a homebuyer's repayment package. It may be difficult to work out what proportion of the policy is buying you the mortgage protection death benefit, and how much is actually being invested in the endowment savings element which will eventually pay off the loan at the end of the mortgage term. Ask your mortgage lender to separate the two elements. It will almost always be cheaper to buy the Mortgage Protection policy by shopping around on the open market.

There are two types of Mortgage Protection policies – level term and decreasing term. Level term pays a fixed and guaranteed sum, sufficient to pay off the amount outstanding on an interest-only mortgage where the debt is not reduced during the term of the loan. Decreasing term policies are used in conjunction with repayment mortgages where the debt goes down as the monthly repayments are made. However, many homebuyers with repayment mortgages still opt for a level-term policy, preferring to know that the debt will be repaid in full in the event of the breadwinner's death and that there will be a surplus.

Both types of policy are cheap and you should not be deterred from buying this cover just because there are no benefits if you survive until the mortgage is paid off. For a thirty-year-old non-smoking male homebuyer, the cost of £100,000 of twenty-five-year level term mortgage protection cover should be no more than £12 a month.

With-Profit Endowments

Endowment-linked loans have fallen out of favour in recent years because lower returns from equity investments have reduced bonuses and therefore the returns from these savings schemes. However, the average return on endowment policies is still around 8 per cent a year – tax free. Although this is a big drop from the returns seen in the late eighties, when maturing endowments were yielding an average of 14 per cent a year, it is still perfectly acceptable.

The big attraction of a with-profits endowment as a repayment vehicle for a mortgage is that the value of your investment can only go up. Annual bonuses, once added to the policy, cannot be removed. But you must be prepared to hold the endowment to maturity to obtain the best return. As much as 60 per cent of the maturity value can be paid in the terminal bonus added to the policy at the end of the agreed term.

Unit-Linked Endowments

Unit-linked endowment policies are very different from with-profits policies. Unit-linked policies are very similar to unit trust regular savings schemes. The fund in which your money is invested is unitised and the value of each unit reflects the value of the underlying investments. If share prices rise, your units will increase in value. Conversely, if share prices fall, your units will decline in value.

This is a much more volatile investment and probably not suitable as a repayment vehicle for first-time housebuyers. If there were a stock market collapse just before your mortgage was due to be paid off, the maturity value of the endowment policy might not be sufficient to pay off the loan.

It is important to remember that most endowment-linked loans are sold by the lenders and you may have little or no choice of policy. This is a big mistake, as there are wide differences in the performance of different with-profits policies and even greater disparities in unit-linked funds' performance. If you choose to have an interest-only endowment loan you should take professional advice from an independent adviser who is registered with the Financial Services Authority.

Pension-Linked Home Loans

The main advantage of pension-linked home loans is that you are entitled to tax relief at your highest rate paid on contributions to a personal pension. The disadvantage is that you are using the tax-free lump sum – one quarter of your accumulated pension fund – that you are allowed to take from your pension scheme at retirement to pay off the mortgage. This will reduce the amount you have at retirement to buy a pension.

Only the self-employed or those employees in a job with no company pension will be eligible to invest in a personal pension. Like endowments, personal pensions come in with-profit or unit-linked form, and you will need advice on which pension policy to choose.

Isa-Linked Home Loans

You can use an Individual Savings Account (Isa) as the investment vehicle to repay a mortgage. This is a better bet than a unit-linked endowment because the charges are lower, and there are no penalties if you are forced to discontinue payments into the scheme. An Isa is a tax shelter and the investment is the shares, unit or investment trusts that you choose to put into it, so the choice is enormous. You will probably need advice from an independent intermediary in choosing a suitable Isa. If in doubt, go for an index-tracker fund. Only one in five professional mutual fund managers ever outperform the index, so if you buy a tracker fund you will, over the medium to long term, do better than the average actively managed fund.

Buy-to-Let

Buying property to let has become very popular in recent years for a number of reasons. First, in the early nineties, when property prices fell, many homeowners found themselves unable to sell their property, except at a loss, so they kept them and rented them out. This was particularly common among younger couples contemplating marriage, who would normally have sold their existing properties to purchase a larger shared home.

In the late nineties people bought properties to let as an alternative investment to a pension scheme. The collapse in annuity rates as interest rates fell made investment in rental property a more attractive option. This boom was fuelled by a number of new lenders who came into this field offering finance at only a small premium – usually no more than 0.5 per cent over the variable rate – to would-be investors.

The Association of Residential Letting Agents (ARLA) has a panel of major mortgage lenders and estate agents who specialise in this area.

Lorna Bourke

Pensions
Looking Forward to Life
after Work

Why Do I Need a Pension?

Only 50 per cent of the working population have any private pension provision – whether from a company pension or a personal pension. If you think you can rely on the state to take care of you in retirement, you had better think again.

The basic state pension at £3,471 a year for a single person or £5,548.40 for a married couple is insufficient to exist on. The government has said that it will guarantee income of £77 a week for a single person or £122 for married couples, but this is insufficient to do much more than allow you to survive. If this is your only income in retirement you will be obliged to depend on means-tested social security benefits like income support and housing benefit. Pensioners are the largest group of claimants for these benefits.

In the years before retirement there are a number of preparatory steps to be made. At least five years before retirement:

☐ Obtain an estimate from the Benefits Agency of your entitlement to the basic State pension and the State Earnings Related Pension Scheme. In order to qualify for the full amount you must have made National Insurance contributions, or have been credited with them, for thirty-nine years out of forty-four between the ages of sixteen and sixty if you are a woman, born before 6 April 1950, or forty-four years out of forty-nine between the ages of sixteen and sixty-five if you are a man.

- The retirement age for women born before 6 April 1950 remains at sixty but increases progressively until for those women born after 6 March 1955 it reaches sixty-five. Women born after this date therefore have to pay the same number of National Insurance contributions as men to qualify for a full state pension in their own right.

- Anyone who has been in higher education or had periods working abroad will have difficulty qualifying for the full pension. Women who have had career breaks to bring up children and those who did not work at all after becoming a mother will find it still harder to earn maximum benefits. Most will be better off claiming on their husband's NI contribution track record.

- Obtain up-to-date valuations on all your personal pensions, occupational pensions, AVCs (Additional Voluntary Contributions) and FSAVCs (Free-standing AVCs). If you have been or are a member of a 'final salary' occupational scheme, obtain an estimate of your benefits at retirement.

- If you have savings or pension schemes where you have a choice of investment funds, consider gradually moving into with-profits, fixed-interest and bond funds in the run-up to retirement to avoid the danger of having your accumulated funds severely reduced by an unexpected market crash just before retirement. Remember what happened in 1987 when the stock market fell by 30 per cent. A big setback could ruin all your retirement plans.

- If your accumulated personal pension funds are £100,000 or more, consider setting up a Small Self Invested Personal Pension from which you can operate income drawdown. This allows you to postpone buying an annuity until age seventy-five – useful if you retire at a time when annuity rates are poor. It also gives you complete freedom in terms of investment manager. The SIPP must be in place before you actually retire. Below £100,000, annual costs make income drawdown uneconomic.

☐ Consider commissioning a review of your pension provision from an independent pension consultant who will be able to give you a clear picture of what to expect in terms of income in retirement and what action must be taken to meet your target income. This should not cost more than £200 provided your affairs are reasonably straightforward, and is well worth the money spent.

At retirement you can take up to 25 per cent of the accumulated pension fund tax free. It almost always pays you to do so. The most likely exceptions are civil servants and others with index-linked pensions who may benefit by taking the maximum pension. You will of course have to decide where to invest any tax-free lump sum. The balance has to be taken as pension, and you must decide whether to purchase an annuity or operate income drawdown.

☐ Consider switching your accumulated investments in Peps and Isas into income-producing assets like corporate bond funds as the income can be taken tax free.

What Should I Do about Saving for Retirement?

Join Your Employer's Occupational Scheme

Some eleven million employees belong to company pension schemes, although not all employers offer an occupational pension. But if you are employed and have the opportunity to join the company scheme, this is almost always the right thing to do.

Typically an employer will contribute around 10 per cent of payroll to the occupational pension scheme, and the employee around 5 per cent. Because both employer and employee are contributing to the pension pot, it is almost certain to provide better benefits than if you are the only contributor to a personal pension. Even where the employer contributes only a small percentage of payroll, it is usually better to join the company scheme and top up benefits by putting any extra money you can save into an additional voluntary contributions scheme run by your employer, or a free-standing AVC if your employer does not run a suitable AVC.

The other advantage of joining a company scheme is that you will almost always be entitled to valuable 'death in service' benefits – typically three times your annual salary, plus dependants' benefits which would cost considerable sums to provide for yourself. About the only exception is where an employer has set up a group personal pension scheme for employees but makes no contribution at all to the scheme. (Most employers do make some contribution but it may be small.)

The new stakeholder pensions, which will be available from April 2001, may, in some cases, come into this category too if, as seems likely, the employer does not make any contribution to the scheme. Stakeholder pensions, for all the hype, are nothing more than group personal pensions where the maximum charges cannot be more than 1 per cent a year of the fund's value. There is no intention to compel employers to make contributions to a stakeholder scheme. In this situation you will probably be better off choosing your own personal pension.

You cannot contribute to a company pension and a personal

pension at the same time unless you have two sources of income (say from freelance consultancy) and one of them is non-pensionable.

Defined Benefit

The best company pension schemes are what are known as 'defined benefit' schemes, where the pension you receive in retirement is linked to your salary at the date you retire. Maximum benefits under Inland Revenue rules are two-thirds of your final salary.

The advantage of these schemes is that if the money in the pension scheme at the time you retire is insufficient to pay the promised benefits, your employer has to make good any shortfall. Typically a good 'final salary' scheme will provide 1/60th of final salary for each year of service. In order to earn the maximum benefits of two-thirds final salary, you would need to work for the same employer for forty years. Some schemes offer only 1/80th of final salary for each year of service.

At retirement you can take up to 25 per cent of the accumulated fund as a tax-free lump sum and it is usually in your interests to do so. The balance has to be used to purchase an annuity or income for life unless you opt for 'income drawdown'.

Income Drawdown

Until 1994, you had no option but to purchase an annuity at retirement. Since then income drawdown has been introduced. This allows you to defer buying an annuity until age seventy-five, and your fund can remain invested and continues to grow. You are allowed to draw down 'income' up to agreed Inland Revenue limits.

The advantage of this flexibility is that you are not forced to buy an annuity at a time when interest rates are low and the return from an annuity poor, thereby locking yourself into a low income for the rest of your life. Because income drawdown needs to be managed, and pension consultants charge a fee for this, it is not usually economic to operate income drawdown unless your fund at retirement is at least £100,000 or more. The big advantage with income drawdown is that your money remains invested and continues to grow. Should you die before age seventy-five, the balance of the pension fund is returned to your estate – albeit with a 35 per cent tax deduction.

Small Self-Invested Pension Schemes

If you intend operating income drawdown your best course of action is to switch your accumulated pension fund into a Small Self-Invested Pension scheme (SIPP) before retirement, where you can have complete freedom of investment management. If you operate income drawdown through your existing life assurance pension company, you will not be able to switch to another pension provider if the performance is poor. The switch into a SIPP must be made before you actually retire.

The best SIPPs offer complete investment freedom – you can use any fund manager or type of investment. Charges should be no more than £300–500 a year, plus a small percentage of the value of funds under management. Some charge a flat fee only, and if the fund is over £1 million charges are usually negotiable. Many SIPPs are run by private client stockbrokers, and the only other charge is normal commission on share dealing within your fund. SIPPs offered by life assurance companies invariably require you to invest all or part of your money with in-house funds.

You can, of course, take out a SIPP as soon as you start making pension contributions. Minimum investment per annum is usually £10,000, but it may be more. The advantage of a SIPP is that it gives you control of your investments.

What Is an Annuity?

An annuity is a lump-sum investment which buys you an income for life. The amount of the income will depend on your age at the time of purchase, your sex (women have a longer life expectancy than men and therefore receive a lower return), whether it is a joint life or single life policy, whether the income increases or is index-linked, and the frequency of payments. The younger you are when you buy an annuity, the lower the rate, because your life expectancy is longer. It is important to remember that once you have invested in an annuity your capital is gone – even if you die only a year after retirement.

Capital-protected annuities, which return a proportion of your investment to your estate if you die within, typically, five years of retirement, are available. But the return from these is lower than with a standard annuity. If you opt for an index-linked annuity, you will have to accept a cut of about 30 per cent in the starting rate to provide inflation proofing of 5 per cent a year. It will be about fifteen years before you break even compared with taking a flat-rate annuity. This is not a good idea if you are in poor health.

What Type of Annuity?

At retirement you may decide to buy an annuity. If you have invested in a packaged personal pension, the insurance company will probably offer you an annuity, but you also have the option to take your accumulated fund and buy an annuity on the open market.

There are specialist independent advisers like the Annuity Bureau or Annuity Trust – no website yet – which produce very good explanatory booklets on everything you need to know about annuities.

It pays to shop around – the difference in annuity rates between the best and the worst companies can easily be 10 per cent.

With-Profit Annuities and Invested Annuities

With current annuity rates historically low, an increasing number of life offices are offering with-profit or invested annuities. These allow your fund to remain invested while you draw an income. However, unlike a conventional annuity, income with an invested annuity may vary – which does not suit everyone. Will you be able to manage if your income falls? This option may be suitable for those with retirement funds of less than £100,000, below which income drawdown is not economic because of the charges.

Tax-Free Lump Sum

For personal pension investors, it pays to take the maximum tax-free lump sum at retirement. You never know when you might die, and a bird in the hand is worth two in the bush. With occupational pensions the decision is not so clear cut. Public sector employees usually enjoy index-linked pensions. This is very valuable, and you cannot generally invest the lump sum to provide better benefits than the index linking offers.

Retiring from an occupational pension scheme, you will have the option of accepting the 'compulsory purchase' annuity from your employer or taking the accumulated fund and buying a 'purchased annuity'. The tax treatment of compulsory annuities is less advantageous than for purchased annuities, and you are almost always better off shopping around on the open market.

What Happens if I Die before Retirement?

Not a happy thought, we know, but this is something that you need to think about now. There are a number of possibilities. Some old retirement annuity contracts offered higher benefits at retirement in return for which you simply received a return of contributions if you died before retirement. Others offered a return of contributions plus a flat interest rate.

Modern unit-linked policies tend to offer the full value of the accumulated units. With-profits policies have guaranteed death benefits but may pay more. All pension policies are written in trust but you should name the beneficiaries, in the event that you die before retirement, so that the proceeds are outside your estate for Inheritance Tax purposes. This is particularly important for single parents or anyone whose beneficiary is not a spouse.

And Finally . . .

If you are still unsure about what pension to choose or how to go about it, here is a quick guide to getting all the information you need from your personal pension adviser. Remember: this is the rest of your life we're talking about – a little advance planning can go a long way.

Twenty Questions to Ask Your Personal Pension Adviser

☐ What are the projected benefits from this policy for myself and/or dependants?

☐ What investment return have you assumed and how does this relate to actual returns?

☐ What are the risks and what type of policy is this? (unit-linked or with profits)

☐ What is the investment track record of this particular pension company, or the funds you are recommending?

☐ What has been the bonus history of this pension provider and how financially sound is it? (with-profits policies)

☐ Can I alter the benefits without penalty?

☐ What are the charges?

☐ Can I stop and start contributions without penalty?

☐ Can I take a contributions holiday without penalty, and if so for how long?

☐ Can I vary the level of contributions?

☐ Can I add lump sums?

☐ Is there a premium waiver if I am sick or unemployed?

☐ What are the benefits if I die before retirement?

☐ Can I transfer my pension fund to another pension company and if so are there penalties?

☐ Can the policy accept transfer payments from other personal or occupational schemes?

☐ What life cover can I include?

☐ What happens if I become employed and join a company scheme?

☐ Can I postpone retirement?

☐ Does this policy offer an income drawdown facility at retirement?

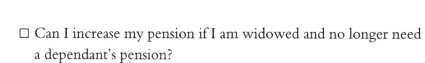

☐ Can I increase my pension if I am widowed and no longer need a dependant's pension?

Lorna Bourke

An Investor's Primer
A Glossary of Jargon and
Technical Terms

Accepting houses
Old collective term for the élite group of UK merchant banks, which were members of the Accepting Houses Committee.

Account day
In the now defunct equity market accounts system, an account ran from the Monday of one week to the Friday of the next. A share purchaser need not pay for their shares (settle their account) until the Friday which became known as account day, or settlement day. This system has been abolished, and when an investor buys a share there is now a ten-day rolling settlement system.

Accountants
Accountants play an important role in the financial community. Their main tasks include the auditing of company accounts, and tax work. However, they also serve valuable roles in the preparation of prospectuses, liquidation and winding-up work, and the provision of management advice services.

Accumulation units
When interest and dividends are combined or automatically re-invested to boost unit value. This term is usually associated with unit trusts.

Actively managed funds
With these funds, managers pick stocks or other securities with a certain goal in mind, like beating a particular index or achieving a certain level of return while assuming a certain level of risk. Because there's stock-picking going on, these funds tend to have higher expense ratios, and higher taxes, than passively managed funds.

Actuary
An actuary has a complex job, but the core function is to assess risk, value life assurance assets and liabilities, and advise on pension funding and pension fund performance statistics.

Administration
A procedure born out of the 1986 Insolvency Act as an alternative to liquidating an insolvent company. A court issues an administration order; an administrator is then installed to run the company in the hope of earning more proceeds than would have been the case if the company had been shut down.

Additional Voluntary Contribution scheme (AVC)
A pension designed to supplement a current company pension scheme.

ADR (American Depository Receipt)
A method through which foreign shares are bought and sold on the US Stock Exchange.

Allocation
The process of deciding who gets shares and how many they get at a new offering.

Allotment letters
Communiqués sent out to successful applicants to a new offering.

Alternative investment
Objects of value not usually categorised as financial assets, e.g. works of art.

Alternative Investment Market (AIM)
A small company market launched in 1995 to cater for the needs of young and developing companies (the costs are kept low and the rules to a minimum)

American Stock Exchange (AMEX)
Overshadowed by the NYSE and the Nasdaq, the AMEX is more noteworthy for its options trading than for its stock trading nowadays. Trading only about thirty million shares per day, AMEX volume averages less than 10 per cent of that on the NYSE or Nasdaq.

Annual General Meeting (AGM)
A general meeting at which directors are re-elected, the accounts are presented to shareholders, and routine matters are put forward to the assembled shareholders for a vote.

Annual Percentage Rate (APR)
Credit-granting outfits are required to quote the real cost of their terms of interest as an annual percentage rate.

Annual report
A statement of a publicly quoted company's yearly financial performance.

Annuity
A type of pension offered by an insurance company. A set income for life is received in return for an initial lump-sum payment.

Arbitrage
Using the differentials in the price of a security or currency in two different markets to your advantage.

Articles of association
A type of written constitution required by all UK companies which outlines subjects such as borrowing power, share issues, etc.

Ask
The ask is the price for which a seller is willing to sell a stock, while the bid is the price a buyer is willing to pay for a stock.

Asset-backed securities
The securitising of several forms of loan.

Asset stripping
The acquisition of a company in order to sell off its assets as opposed to taking its business forward.

Auction market preferred stock
A type of preference share issued by UK companies. While technically they are shares, they have similarities with floating-rate debt as the dividends vary with the money markets as opposed to being fixed.

Audit committee
A committee (usually of non-executive directors) responsible for overseeing checks of the financial governance of a company.

Autif
The Association of Unit Trusts and Investment Funds.

Back-end load
A load paid when you redeem your shares. Most funds drop the load if you hold for a specified period of time, usually several years.

Balance sheet
A periodical report, often at the end of the financial year, which includes a breakdown of a company's financial situation.

Baltic Exchange
The London-based market in which freight shipping is negotiated.

Bank of England (BoE)
The UK central bank which sets interest rates, lends money to the government, regulates the banking industry, prints and regulates the circulation of bank notes, and is the lender of last resort to financial institutions.

Bankruptcy
When an organisation or a person does not have the assets to repay their debts.

Base rates
The guiding rates of interest quoted by commercial banks.

Basic earnings
Earnings per share calculated as net income divided by the number of common shares. The number of common shares outstanding is usually easy to find in an income statement.

Basis point
Used to indicate changes in prices of shares and bonds – one base point is equivalent to a hundredth of a per cent.

Bear market
A contracting market, often the result of lower manufacturing output, rising inflation and interest rates and a weak currency. The opposite of a bull market.

Bear raid
Speculators trying to force the price of a company down (by short selling, spreading negative whispers) in the hope that they will be able to buy shares cheaply.

Bed & breakfast
The practice of selling a share one day and buying it back the next morning, normally employed to establish a loss for capital gains purposes.

Benchmark
An umbrella term for a comparative tool that measures performance.

Benchmark gilt
A government stock whose redemption yield is taken as the measure by which redemption yields on company bonds are set.

Bid
The bid is the price a buyer is willing to pay for a stock, while the ask is the price for which a seller is willing to sell.

Big Board
(See **New York Stock Exchange**).

Bilateral facility
A loan agreed with a single bank as opposed to one agreed with a syndicate of banks, enabling borrowers to set up several separate bilateral loans with a number of individual banks.

Black economy

Those shady areas of the economy where transactions are not officially recorded and are thus untaxed.

Board of directors

Those legally responsible for running a company. Executive directors are those employed by the company with management responsibilities. Those who just sit on the board are non-executive directors.

Bond

A type of IOU issued by companies, governments, etc. Usually medium- or long-term, bonds pay interest and can be traded on the market, and can either be secured or unsecured. UK bonds almost always have a face value of £100.

Book, book-building

Research often carried out by financial advisers before an issue of shares is made. It involves establishing the likely market and price for the issue and is used as a guide to price and probability of success.

Bottom line

Net income or earnings per share, found at the bottom of the quarterly or annual income statement. Earnings are the most important determinant of stock valuation. That's the bottom line.

Bottom-up investing
This describes an investing approach in which a manager focuses first and foremost on the prospects of an individual company, rather than overall economic or market trends.

Bought deal
When a company invites bids from securities houses for an entire share offer rather than placing the shares with a multitude of investors.

Bourse
Not just the French word for stock exchange, but also often used to refer to the French Stock Exchange.

British Venture Capital Association (BVCA)
The umbrella governing body for all venture capital funds.

Broker
A buyer and seller of financial products.

Bucket shop
Over-promoting shares which are often of low quality.

Building society
An institution traditionally created to hold savings for small individual depositors and lend money in the form of mortgages to individuals buying a house.

Bull market
A rising/growing market. The opposite of a bear market.

Buy-back
When a company buys back a proportion of its own shares. Often for the purpose of cancelling a proportion of the share capital in an attempt to improve the earnings or the asset backing of the remaining shares.

CAC 40
The major French stock market index tracking forty leading French companies.

Call options
Contracts stipulating but not obligating the purchaser to buy an agreed number of shares for an agreed price at a certain date in the future.

Capital Gains Distribution
When a fund sells securities it has owned for more than twelve months (eighteen months after 28 July 1997), the profits, or losses, are distributed among the shareholders. These gains are taxable at the capital gains rate. If the securities sold were held for less than one year, the distributions would be taken into ordinary income and taxed at your individual rate.

Capital Gains Tax (CGT)
The tax that is chargeable from the sale of assets that have increased in value since they were purchased.

Capitalise
A word with a myriad of meanings, but basically to 'turn something into capital'.

Cash cow
Part of a business which generates a substantial flow of cash.

Cash economy
(see **Black economy**)

Cash flow
The movement of money through an organisation over a given period of time.

Central bank
The core bank of a country, often linked in some way to the government, and usually responsible for implementing key financial strategy.

Charge to earnings
A change on the balance sheet must also flow through the income statement. If a balance sheet asset increases in value, the company realises a gain on its income statement, and if an asset decreases in value (or a new liability is created), a charge is taken against earnings. The most common charges are write-downs in inventory or plant

and equipment, often triggered by a merger or other corporate action. For instance: say a company thought its PCs were worth £1,000, and they've been carried on the books at that cost, but – lo and behold – they're really worth £100. Then it has to take a charge to earnings so the balance sheet can reflect the true asset value.

Chief executive
The key executive in a company, usually also a board member but always accountable to the board for the running of the company.

Chinese walls
Unseen barriers preventing information from being passed between certain arms/departments within a single institution.

Churning
A phrase use to suggest that a manager is buying and selling different shares too often, and usually just for commission.

The City
A square mile within London which forms the heart of the financial district.

Clearing bank
Also called high-street banks, these are the traditional deposit-taking and lending banks such as Lloyds and NatWest. They are part of the central clearing system which is the focal point of interbank payments.

Clearing house
The organisation that reconciles sales and purchases, arranges margins and settlements in the futures market.

Close a position
Selling a previous contract or position.

Close-ended
Close-ended investment vehicles have a fixed amount of share capital.

Closed out
Market authorities will close out a user of the futures market if s/he fails to maintain his/her position.

Collateral
Assets committed as security against a loan.

Coming to the market
Floating a share in a company on the stock market for the first time.

Commercial paper
A type of short-term IOU issued at a discount to investors in a company.

Commitment Fee
The fee paid by a borrower to a lender for arranging a loan.

Commodities
Orange juice, pork bellies, gold, etc.

Companies House
Where all information legally required to be submitted by all UK private and public companies is held. The building, in London, is open to the public and upon payment of a small fee any member of the public can search through these records on microfiche.

Compliance department
Those in charge of ensuring that there is no improper cross-fertilisation between different businesses within a securities house, thus ensuring compliance with the Financial Services Act.

Confidentiality clause
A clause in a contract which prevents the disclosure of any details of a deal.

Conglomerate
Usually a term describing a large company with a wide range of business interests.

Consideration
The price paid for something (not always in the form of cash).

Convertible share
Usually an unsecured loan stock which can be exchanged for ordinary shares according to an agreed process.

Corporate bond
Bonds issued by companies rather than governments.

Counter-party
Those on the other side of a transaction or agreement.

Counter-party risk
The risk that the counter-party may fail to deliver.

Covenant
The undertaking of certain conditions relating to a transaction or agreement.

Credit rating
A rating bestowed upon a company, a country or other issuer of debt securities by a credit ratings agency, giving investors an insight into how secure the issued debt should be.

CREST
Computerized share settlement system used within the London Stock Exchange.

Crowding out
When a government is borrowing so much money that there is not enough available for commercial businesses to borrow.

Cyclical stocks
Shares in companies whose business tends to follow a cyclical pattern of productivity and profitability, e.g. house building.

Datastream
Screen–based on–line information system for securities, commodities, currencies, etc.

Dax
Germany's leading market index equivalent of London's FTSE 100 and New York's Dow Jones Industrial Average.

Debenture stock
A secured company bond.

Deep-discounted bond
A bond issued at a price below its face value.

Deep-discounted rights issue
New shares offered at a price well below (more than 20 per cent) the existing price.

Deferred tax
Tax which may become payable, but is not so certain that it is provided for under current liabilities.

Demutualisation
The conversion process building societies go through to become a bank.

Derivatives
Financial instruments spun off from the basic set of market products (e.g. options and futures are derivatives as they are essentially spin-offs from shares and bonds).

Discretionary
When an investment manager makes his own decisions on someone else's investments.

Disintermediation
Lending directly to the end user.

Distressed securities
When a company encounters hard times and its stock and bonds fall in value, they are said to get into distressed level. These securities then become attractive to distressed investors, commonly called 'vultures', who hope to gain if the company's fortunes improve. (And a whole slew of bankruptcy lawyers who hope to gain if the company's fortunes don't improve.)

Distribution
A distribution of income – a phrase usually meaning dividend.

Diversification
Extending business activities away from core areas into new arenas.

Dividend
A sum paid out by a company to its shareholders in return simply for owning shares in that company.

Dogs of the Dow

Also known as the Dow Dividend theory. An investing strategy that entails rating Dow stocks by dividend yield from highest to lowest at the beginning of each year and then buying equal dollar amounts of the top ten. Each year, dividend yields are recalculated, new stocks in the top ten are added, and ones that don't make the cut any more are sold. Kinda kooky, but since it was first formulated in the book *Beating the Dow* back in 1972, has made investors enough money that the 'dogs of the Dow' theory puts buying and selling pressure on stocks at the beginning of each year.

Dow Jones Industrial Average

The dominant index of the New York Stock Exchange. It includes thirty, mainly industrial, stocks.

Downside

The potential for a share price to fall.

ECNs

Stands for Electronic Communications Networks – 'electronic stock exchanges' which automatically link buyers with sellers, thus removing the middleman and reducing the cost of a trade.

Employee Share Ownership Plan (ESOP)

A means of aiding employees to buy stock in their company.

Endowment

A life assurance and savings and investment policy often backing an interest-only mortgage.

Enterprise zones
Designated geographical zones with specially granted exemptions from certain restrictions (e.g. planning, tax, etc.).

EPS (Earnings per share)
The financial return of what a company makes for its investors (usually calculated by dividing profits after tax by the total number of ordinary shares issued).

Equity
The unit through which a part-owner holds an interest in an asset.

Euro
The single European currency introduced on 1 January 1999.

Eurobond
A strangely named international bond issued in markets outside the domestic market of the issuer by a syndicate of international banks in the domestic currency.

Euroland
Countries signed up to the European single currency scheme: Austria, Belgium, Finland, France, Germany, Ireland, Italy, Luxembourg, Netherlands, Portugal and Spain.

European Monetary Union (EMU)
A catch-all phrase for the introduction of a single European currency.

Ex-all (xa)
Appearing after a share price to signify a buyer acquires the share without rights to whatever the company is in the process of issuing.

Execution-only Stockbroker
Stockbrokers who merely buy and sell on an investor's instruction offering no advice. In the US they are known as discount brokers.

Extraordinary General Meeting (EGM)
A general meeting at which unusual or non-routine matters are put to the shareholders.

Factoring
A type of off-balance-sheet finance which has a similar effect to a loan. A factor will guarantee to collect debts owing to a company on that company's behalf and in the meantime it will make a prepayment to the company as a percentage of the sum it is due to receive.

Fixed-rate mortgage
The interest rate on the mortgage is set at an agreed level for an agreed period of time.

Flotation
The issuing of a company's shares on the stock market for the first time is known as flotation.

Forex
Market shorthand for 'foreign exchange' or the currency market. The forex market is huge. An estimated $1.25 trillion in marks, krone, pounds, yen, lire, etc., change hands every day over an electronic bazaar that connects trading rooms across the world. Fluctuations in the forex market can affect how multinational companies perform in overseas markets and how appealing domestic markets are for foreign investors. Around Europe and Asia, foreign exchange rates are a component of evening news programmes. Americans, whose currency is the reserve currency almost everywhere, don't seem to care as much.

Front-end load
A load paid when you first invest.

FT 30
Little-quoted index, aping the Dow Jones, predating the FTSE 100 but now largely superseded by it.

FTSE 100
The index including the 100 largest companies on the LSE.

FTSE 250
The index including the 250 largest public companies on the LSE.

FTSE All Share Index
A combination of the FTSE 100, the FTSE 250 and the FTSE SmallCap.

FTSE SmallCap
This index covers around 500 small UK companies valued at between £40m and £250m.

Fungible
The same as and interchangeable with.

Funny Money
A catch-all phrase for new, innovative or unusual forms of securities.

Futures
Instruments providing the holder the right to buy a fixed commodity for a fixed price on an agreed date in the future.

Gilt-edged securities
UK government bonds or loan stocks.

Golden handcuffs
Financial inducements arranged to tie employees to their jobs.

Golden handshake
Lump-sum payment to sacked or redundant employees. Usually associated with senior management and directors.

Golden parachute
Financial agreements designed to ensure substantial payouts to directors and/or senior management in case their company is taken over.

Hang Seng Index
The leading share price index of the Hong Kong Stock Exchange.

Hedge fund
Usually international funds run by aggressive go-getting managers and subscribed to by rich individuals looking to beat the markets by heavy betting in areas such as currencies. Sometimes, but not always, for the purposes of hedging.

Independent financial adviser
Living off their commission IFAs are not employed by the companies whose products they sell.

Inland Revenue
Government department responsible for assessing and collecting tax.

Insolvency
A company becomes insolvent either when its liabilities outweigh its assets, or when it no longer has the cash to pay its bills.

Internet Service Provider (ISP)
As the name implies, Internet Service Providers (ISPs) furnish consumers and corporations with access to the Internet. Some larger ISPs are folding into telephone companies.

Internet telephony

Internet telephony refers to the blending technologies of telephone service and data networking. Its proponents say the Internet, which carries data messages in separate packets and reassembles them at the destination, has grown reliable enough to deliver voice conversations with little delay or 'latency'. When it works, Internet telephony can be cheaper than conventional phone systems.

Intrinsic value

Value of a company based on an underlying perception or calculation of corporate value. Intrinsic value includes such hidden assets as brand-name recognition, management expertise or hard assets carried on the balance sheet at a cost significantly below their market value. The stock price may be compared to this intrinsic value, and the investor may perceive an undervalued company despite full valuation on traditional ratios.

Investment bank

Commonly the US term to describe banks equivalent to UK merchant banks. The main business of these banks is the issuing and underwriting, buying and selling of securities, and the provision of corporate advice. In recent years established British merchant banks have been bought up by larger groups and are often now know as investment banks.

Investment trust

A close-ended investment fund listed as a company on the Stock Exchange.

Invisible earnings
A nation's overseas earnings from dividends.

IPO
Initial Public Offering – the first time a company sells its stock on the public market. After an IPO, shareholders, stock analysts and fund managers are allowed to ask questions like, 'Why does the boss spend £500 a week on Tipp-Ex?'

ISEQ
The major Irish stock market index.

January effect
US term. At the end of the year, investors start worrying about taxes. To that end, they may sell some stocks that they've seen a loss on – not because they don't like them any more, but because they can take these losses out of their annual bill from Uncle Sam. This selling will knock stocks down a bit towards the end of the year – particularly SmallCaps, since they're not as liquid. In January, investors will be in there buying back their lost darlings, giving stocks a boost. That's the theory, anyway. But it hasn't happened in years because, many say, once our efficient markets recognised the phenomenon it got priced in.

Junk bond
A high-risk bond which is rated by credit-rating agencies below treble-B – a level below which investments are considered to be risky.

Kerb market

An unofficial securities or commodities market often active in parallel with an official market with trades taking place by direct telephone. Kerb markets are usually most active after the official markets have closed.

LAN

A Local Area Network. A technology that connects computers across a short distance; for example, within a building.

Launder

To clean up money obtained through illegal means (theft, drugs, etc.) by running it through a process that makes it appear to have different origins.

Leasing

Users of a piece of equipment make regular payments for its use rather than buying it from the outset. In the past leasing offered various tax opportunities, but these have recently diminished.

Level load

An annual load that is usually lowered gradually based on the number of years you keep your money in the fund.

Limit up, limit down

Some securities/futures markets limit the amount by which a price can rise or fall in a single day. If that price reaches the top of its limit it is described as 'limit up', and if it reaches the bottom it has reached 'limit down'.

Load

Also called a sales charge, this is a fee imposed on mutual fund buyers that is generally divided between the fund family and the financial adviser who sells the fund, such as a broker. Loads can be as high as 8 per cent but usually range from 2 to 5 per cent. While TheStreet.co.uk is loath to give a thumbs-up to load funds, investors should realise that a hefty expense ratio (1.4 per cent is average, though it varies by fund objective) can be a lot more damaging if you're a long-term holder, as that bites into your returns every year. Most loads, in contrast, are a one-time charge.

Lloyd's

Major London insurance markets consisting of members who deposit substantial sums of collateral, and 'names' who pledge their assets to Lloyd's and in return receive an income.

London International Financial Futures and Options Exchange (LIFFE)

Pronounced 'life', Europe's largest futures market (and the world's third largest after the Chicago Board of Trade and the Chicago Mercantile Exchange). The market offers futures in various instruments including long-dated gilt-edged stocks, various government bonds, short-term sterling, euro interest rates, individual shares and the FTSE index.

London Metal Exchange (LME)
One of London's two major commodities exchanges (the other being the London Commodity Exchange which sells soft commodities), this is the centre of world trading for non-ferrous metals, and trades in copper, lead, zinc, nickel, tin and aluminium.

London Stock Exchange (LSE)
The UK's largest stock exchange is the world's third biggest (after the NYSE and the Tokyo Stock Exchange).

M&A
Mergers and acquisitions.

Management fee
This is a fee that a fund pays to its investment adviser for managing its portfolio. It is usually 0.5 per cent–1 per cent of the fund's total assets annually, and is included in the overall expense ratio.

Margin
A term used to describe the practice of clients only being required to put down a deposit on what they buy – a margin – which must be topped up if it is eroded by unfavourable price movements. Margins are common in the futures market.

Margin call
Notice that the margin needs topping up. If an investor does not meet a margin call they will be closed out.

Market capitalization
Overall measure of the total value of a company arrived at by multiplying the number of shares issued by the current share price.

Momentum
Refers to a company's technical price momentum or fundamental earnings momentum. Companies with strong momentum have prices and earnings that are going up, while companies with weak momentum have prices and earnings that are going down, or going nowhere. Importantly, all momentum is measured at the margin, so a company with high momentum must accelerate to maintain its place, while a company with weak momentum can merely stabilise to get out of the doghouse.

Money market instrument
A type of short-term investment traded on the money markets which can quickly and simply be turned into cash.

Monopolies & Mergers Commission (MMC)
The body that investigates proposed takeovers and makes a recommendation to the government as to whether the takeover in question will seriously diminish competition.

Moratorium
If a business is unable to repay a loan or debt, the debtor can agree to postpone immediate repayment in the hope that this may be the best way of getting the money back in the long run. This is called granting a moratorium.

Mortgage
A loan to buy a home. Usually the buyer uses the property as security against the loan.

Mutual company
A mutual company has no shares but is owned by either policy-holders or members (e.g. building societies, friendly societies and co-operatives).

Mutual fund
US version of a unit trust.

Naked writer
The creator (writer) of an option who does not own the share against which the options are matched.

Nasdaq
The National Association of Securities Dealers Automated Quotation system, now known as the Nasdaq Stock Market, lists more than 5,540 domestic and foreign companies. The market is entirely computer-based and has no trading floor, which led Nasdaq to design a big wall of ever-shifting monitors called MarketSite as a backdrop for TV reporters and school groups. The Nasdaq was originally almost entirely a small-capitalization market but now includes some of America's largest companies, such as Intel and Microsoft.

The measure most often used to track the value of the Nasdaq is the Nasdaq Composite Index – words almost invariably preceded in news reports by some variation on 'tech-heavy' (TheStreet.com's personal favourite is 'tech-tumescent'). That's because high-technology companies like Intel, Microsoft, Dell and Oracle account for the lion's share of the index's price activity. The Nasdaq 100, an index of the largest Nasdaq companies, also gets considerable attention.

Negative equity
When an asset is worth less than the purchase price.

Negative surprise
When a company fails to meet earnings estimates.

Negative yield curve
If short-term interest rates are higher than long-term ones then when rates for deposits and securities are plotted on a graph the line starts high and curves downwards. This is a negative yield curve – sometimes described as an inverse yield curve.

Net asset value
The value obtained when a fund takes all its assets (including cash), subtracts out any liabilities (i.e. any financial obligations like bank overdrafts or transfer agent and trustees' fees) and then divides by the total number of shares outstanding. It's like a company's stock price, and it's tracked in most newspapers and on TheStreet.co.uk.

Net fund flows
Tracked by several different companies, fund flows represent the amount of new money coming into mutual funds less the amount of money 'redeemed' by investors. Though a decidedly inexact

science, fund flow tracking has become a cottage industry, as market watchers use the figures to measure public sentiment towards the market and liquidity.

New York Stock Exchange (NYSE)
The NYSE traces its roots back to 1792, when twenty-four brokers and merchants gathered on Wall Street and agreed to trade securities on a common commission basis. Trading was done under a button-wood tree. It's a different scene now. The largest open–call stock exchange in the world, the NYSE is where the country's biggest companies (with a few notable Nasdaq exceptions) are traded. While by some lights the kind of electronic trading done on the Nasdaq seems sure to overshadow the NYSE's floor trading, it certainly hasn't happened yet.

No-load
Funds that do not charge a load. Note: funds can impose a sales charge of up to 1 per cent and still be considered no-load.

Non-voting shares
A class of ordinary share issued to ensure that the founders can continue to control a company without holding 51 per cent of the ordinary shares.

Occupational pension scheme
Contribute to your firm's pension scheme and get a maximum of 40/60ths of your final salary. Few, very few, get this much, though. Your occupational pension may well not be enough for your retirement.

Off balance sheet items
An umbrella term for several items, usually liabilities, which do not appear on a company's balance sheet.

Old Lady of Threadneedle Street
The Bank of England.

Open Ended Investment Company (OEIC)
A relatively recent investment vehicle which is basically a more flexible unit trust (a unit trust/investment trust hybrid).

Option
A contract which guarantees the right – but does not compel – to buy or sell an agreed number of shares at an agreed price at an agreed date.

Park (of shares)
The allotting of shares to a third party when one company wants to disguise its shareholding in another (probably to illegally avoid disclosure rules).

Penny stocks
Those shares quoted at prices of just a few pence. Traditionally these used to be the subject of much speculation, centring either on the company becoming insolvent or turning around and experiencing a major price rise. However, today few low-priced stocks are priced quite so low in order to avoid such speculation.

Physical market
A market in which a deal actually leads to the physical delivery of a commodity (thus excluding futures trades, which are closed out by other futures contracts).

Preference shares
Preference shareholders have a higher claim on assets than ordinary shareholders (but rank after creditors) if a company goes into liquidation.

Price-sensitive information
Information which is likely to lead to movement in a share price.

Public limited company (plc)
A public company is one in which partial ownership is publicly held in the form of shares.

Ramping
The practice of talking up – over-promoting – a share for the sole purpose of jacking its price up.

Reinvested dividends
Fund investors have the option of receiving pay-outs for any dividends generated by the securities in funds they own, or reinvesting the income represented by the dividends in the form of purchases of new shares in the fund. Most reinvest by checking a little box when they buy the fund.

Remote access
End users can 'access' a computer network, or the Internet itself, from a remote location. Often they dial into the network through a modem attached to a phone system.

Retail Price Index (RPI)
A means of measuring inflation based upon the price of a selection of family goods.

Reverse takeover
The process of a smaller company taking over a larger one, or when the company being bought will become the dominant part of the new company.

Roll up
The practice of a borrower adding the interest to the outstanding capital of a loan instead of making regular interest payments.

Router
A special computer that connects different networks. One router forwards a message to another router and so forth, until the message reaches its destination. While a switch relays signals through one network, the router works across two or more networks.

Russell 2000
A US index set by Frank Russell & Co., the Russell 2000 measures the bottom 2,000 of the 3,000 companies with the biggest market capitalisations (there's also a Russell 1000, for the top 1,000, and a Russell 3000, for the whole top 3,000, but nobody pays much

attention to them). The most common measure for SmallCaps, the Russell gets rebalanced every year on the last trading day in June. The rebalancing creates all kinds of fun in the market, as Russell-tracking funds, as well as some SmallCap funds that shadow the index to some extent, drop the stocks exiting the index and load up on those entering it.

S&P 500

A US index of the 500 largest US publicly traded companies, as determined by Standard & Poor's. Considered by many to be the best indicator of the US stock market's general direction and health, the S&P 500's profile has been raised recently by the many portfolio-manager-beating index funds that track it. There is also an S&P 400, which tracks mid-cap companies, and an S&P 600, which tracks SmallCaps, but these don't get much attention. Unlike the Dow, the S&P indices are weighted by a company's market capitalisation.

S&P 500 futures

S&P 500 futures contracts give buyers the right to a basket of the stocks in the S&P 500 on expiration date. Priced at 250 times the index, they're used mostly by institutional investors. A lot of stock trading is based on what is deemed 'fair value' for the S&P 500 futures. Trading in the S&P 500 futures goes on in Chicago for a half-hour past the New York close. Even after the Chicago close, the futures continue to trade, albeit thinly, in after-hours Globex trading. If, in the morning, the futures are trading much higher than the cash S&P 500, institutions will sell the futures and buy the underlying stocks, giving stocks a boost at the open. If, on the other hand, the futures aren't trading much higher than the S&P 500's close, stocks can go down.

Secondary issue
When shares offered for sale are already listed and the further shares offered come from the existing owners.

Secondary market
The primary market is the one in which new securities are sold to investors, and the secondary market is where those securities are resold and bought among investors. Most major stock markets actually include both functions.

Securities
Umbrella term for shares, bonds and options.

Security & Exchange Commission (SEC)
US agency responsible for ensuring an open and free stock market. All US stock markets and listed companies must abide by SEC rules and regulations.

Securities & Futures Authority (SFA)
The organisation that regulates UK stockbrokers.

Securities & Investments Board (SIB)
Now part of the new Financial Services Authority.

Serious Fraud Office
The government department that handles and investigates major frauds.

SERPS
State Earnings Related Pension Scheme.

Share
A security in the form of part-ownership of a company.

Share classes
A load fund will often offer several share classes, each with a different load and expense-ratio combination. The idea is to give investors a choice of whether they want to get smacked with a load right away or put off the inevitable.

Shell company
An often small and almost always inactive company, with few assets and little income, usually with a stock market quotation. Often used as ready-made stock market vehicles by entrepreneurs who buy them up and use them to run their own businesses.

Short selling
Short selling is pretty much the reverse of investing. Instead of buying a stock with the object of selling it at a higher price, you borrow a stock (through your broker) and immediately sell it. If and when the stock falls to your objective, you then buy it and return the shares to the stock loan department of the brokerage firm, and on to their rightful owner. But be warned: while there's

no limit to shorting a stock – other than the limits on your own ability to tolerate a loss – there's always the possibility that the owners of the stock could ask that they be returned immediately. When they're orchestrated *en masse*, these so-called 'buy-ins' are considered a short squeeze and cause the stock's price to rise rapidly. The risk can be somewhat tempered by including a loss limit or stop-buy order, which would cause your broker to automatically sell the stock if it reaches a certain level. You can also use options-related hedging techniques, but first you had better understand options and their risks.

Sinking fund
A financial reserve within a company's accounts which includes a sum to cover the eventual repayment of an existing debt.

Soft commissions
Commissions for financial services paid in kind rather than in cash.

Soft loan
An umbrella term used to describe loans made on terms better than those available to the normal commercial market.

Split (share split)
If the price of a stock becomes too high (heavy) the company may decide to split the share.

Spread
A term with two meanings: either the range between the price at which someone is prepared to sell and the price at which they are prepared to bid; or the margin a borrower pays above a benchmark interest rate.

Stamp duty
A tax payable on buying ordinary shares.

Switch
Device that breaks a data message into packets, intersperses them with packets from other messages, then sends that stream of signals across a network (either a LAN or a WAN). Each packet contains a header that specifies the packet's final destination, which is another computer on the network. This process of 'packet switching' allows computers to share network access and use bandwidth more efficiently.

Tax haven
A country or principality with low tax rates where a company can register or where an individual can reside in order to minimise their tax burden.

Tax shelter
A framework within which assets can be held in order to minimise tax liability.

Total return
Return on investment including price appreciation with reinvested dividends or income over a specific period of time.

Tracker funds
Funds designed to ape the performance of an index.

Transfer agent
Usually a bank. They do all the paperwork for a fund, keeping track of all the fund-owners' records.

Treasury
The UK government's finance department.

Triple-A-rated
In rating systems designed to indicate the trustworthiness of a borrower, triple-A rated borrowers are the safest.

Triple-witching
Also called triple expiration, triple-witching refers to the quarterly expiration of index futures, index future options and certain stock options on the third Friday of March, June, September and December. This can cause some pretty big swings in the stock market. For instance, if a lot of people think that the next futures contract looks expensive, they may decide not to 'roll' their contracts and instead buy the underlying stocks. That will add some buying pressure to the market and, if there's not much else moving the market that day, drive stocks higher. Nowadays, many futures and options players unwind positions ahead of triple-witching Friday, so the effect has been dampened in recent years.

Turnover ratio

This ratio shows the number of times a year that a fund's holdings are turned over. If a fund has $100 million in assets and sells stocks accounting for $40 million, the turnover ratio is 40 per cent. High turnover often, but not always, leads to big tax bills.

Unit trust

The pooling of money to form a collective investment fund which may invest in stocks, bonds or other fixed-interest instruments.

Venture capital

Venture capital money is offered to new and growing businesses where the capital is partly given in return for shares (equity) in the business.

Volume

The number of shares traded in a given stock or in an index. The New York Stock Exchange trades about 500 million shares a day, the Nasdaq about 650 million and the little old American Stock Exchange about 30 million. There's some dispute about the Nasdaq's high volume figures, which count trades by market makers as well as by customers.

WAN

Wide Area Network. A network technology covering a large geographical distance that interconnects LANs.

Wasting asset
An asset with a finite lifespan the value of which decreases as its remaining life gets shorter.

Winding up
A process of shutting down a business, realising its assets and distributing them.

Withholding tax
A process of preventing people from not paying tax by deducting it at source (often on interest, dividends, etc.).

Write
In options terms, a verb that means sell.

Write down, write off
When an asset no longer has the value shown in company accounts it needs to be written down. When it no longer has any value at all it must be written off.

Written-down value
The value in the books after write-downs.

Yield
Income generated by a fund's investments.

Zero coupon
A type of fixed-income bond which misleadingly pays no interest at all during its life; return comes solely from its redemption price.

Index

Figures in bold indicate the Glossary definition.